CLIFFS

Graduate Record Examination

General Test

PREPARATION GUIDE

by

William A. Covino, Ph.D.
Bernard V. Zandy, M.A.
David A. Kay, M.S.

Consulting Author
Howard Horwitz, M.A.

Consultants
Ramona Knowles, M.A.
Merritt L. Weisinger, J.D.

Cliffs Notes
INCORPORATED
LINCOLN, NEBRASKA   68501

ACKNOWLEDGMENTS

We would like to thank Michele Spence of Cliffs Notes for final editing and careful attention to the production process and Dr. Albert Upton for the use of excerpts from his outstanding book Design for Thinking.

We would also like to thank our typist, Lynne Turner, for exceptional work in preparing the manuscript.

CONTENTS

PART III: PRACTICE-REVIEW-ANALYZE-PRACTICE
Two Full-Length Practice Tests

PREFACE

YOUR GRE SCORES MAKE THE DIFFERENCE! And better scores result from thorough preparation. Therefore, your study time must be used most effectively. You need the most comprehensive test preparation guide that you can realistically complete in a reasonable time. It must be thorough, direct, precise, and easy to use, giving you all the information you need to do your best on the GRE.

In keeping with the fine tradition of Cliffs Notes, this guide was developed by leading experts in the field of test preparation as part of a series to specifically meet these standards. The testing strategies, techniques, and materials have been researched, tested, and evaluated, and are presently used at GRE preparation programs at many leading colleges and universities. This guide features the PATTERNED PLAN OF ATTACK for each section and focuses on six major areas:

1. The Ability Tested
2. The Basic Skills Necessary
3. Understanding Directions
4. Analysis of Directions
5. Suggested Approaches With Samples
6. Practice-Review-Analyze-Practice

These major areas include important mathematical symbols, terminology, and formulas, and a helpful list of prefixes, suffixes, and roots. Two complete practice exams follow with answers and *in-depth* explanations.

This guide was written to give you the edge in doing your best by maximizing your effort in the minimum amount of time. If you take the time to follow the Study Guide Checklist in this book, you will get the best preparation possible.

STUDY GUIDE CHECKLIST

_____ 1. Read the GRE Information Bulletin.

_____ 2. Become familiar with the Test Format, page 3.

_____ 3. Familiarize yourself with the answers to Questions Commonly Asked about the GRE, page 5.

_____ 4. Learn the techniques of a Successful Overall Approach, page 8.

_____ 5. Carefully read Part II, Analysis of Exam Areas, beginning on page 11.

_____ 6. Review math Symbols, Terminology, Formulas, and General Information, page 46.

_____ 7. Strictly observing time allotments, take Practice Test 1, section-by-section (review answers after each section), page 63.

_____ 8. Check your answers and analyze your results, page 114.

_____ 9. Fill out the Tally Sheet for Problems Missed to pinpoint your mistakes, page 119.

_____10. While referring to each item of Practice Test 1, study ALL the Answers and Explanations that begin on page 123.

_____11. Review as necessary Basic Skills, Symbols, Terminology, Formulas, and General Information given in Part II of this book.

_____12. Strictly observing time allotments, take Practice Test 2, page 163.

_____13. Check your answers and analyze your results, page 214.

_____14. Fill out the Tally Sheet for Problems Missed to pinpoint your mistakes, page 219.

_____15. While referring to each item of Practice Test 2, study ALL the Answers and Explanations that begin on page 223.

_____16. Again, selectively review materials as needed.

_____17. Carefully reread Part II, Analysis of Exam Areas, beginning on page 11.

_____18. Go over "FINAL PREPARATION" on page 260.

Part I: Introduction

FORMAT OF A RECENT GRE GENERAL TEST

Section I	Verbal Ability	35–40 Questions
30 Minutes	Sentence Completion	6–8 Questions
	Analogies	8–10 Questions
	Reading Comprehension (2 passages)	10–12 Questions
	Antonyms	10–12 Questions
Section II	**Verbal Ability**	**35–40 Questions**
30 Minutes	Sentence Completion	6–8 Questions
	Analogies	8–10 Questions
	Reading Comprehension (2 passages)	10–12 Questions
	Antonyms	10–12 Questions
Section III	**Quantitative Ability**	**Approximately 30 Questions**
30 Minutes	Quantitative Comparison	15 Questions
	Math Ability (with graphs)	15 Questions
Section IV	**Quantitative Ability**	**Approximately 30 Questions**
30 Minutes	Quantitative Comparison	15 Questions
	Math Ability (with graphs)	15 Questions
Section V	**Analytical Ability**	**Approximately 25 Questions**
30 Minutes	Analytical Reasoning	22 Questions
	Logical Reasoning	3 Questions
Section VI	**Analytical Ability**	**Approximately 25 Questions**
30 Minutes	Analytical Reasoning	19 Questions
	Logical Reasoning	6 Questions
Section VII **30 Minutes**	**Either Verbal, Quantitative, Analytical, or Experimental**	**Approximately** **30 Questions**

NOTE: The order in which the sections appear and the number of questions in each section may vary because there are several forms of the new GRE. The actual test will contain a seventh section of experimental questions; this section may appear at any point in the test.

GENERAL DESCRIPTION

The GRE General Test is used along with other information about your college achievements in order to assess your potential for success in graduate school. The test lasts approximately three hours and consists entirely of multiple-choice questions.

The verbal section tests your reading comprehension and the breadth of your vocabulary. The quantitative section presents problems in arithmetic, algebra, and geometry. The analytical section tests your ability to read closely and reason logically from given information. All questions have the same point value.

QUESTIONS COMMONLY ASKED ABOUT THE GRE

Q: WHO ADMINISTERS THE GRE?
A: The GRE is administered by Educational Testing Service (ETS) which is located in Princeton, New Jersey. If you wish any information not covered in this book, write to ETS at Box 1502, Berkeley, California 94701, or at Box 955, Princeton, New Jersey 08540.

Q: CAN I TAKE THE GRE MORE THAN ONCE?
A: Yes. But be aware that your scores from each testing will appear on your score report. Therefore, even when you take the test for "practice," the results can have a real impact on your record.

Q: WHAT MATERIALS MAY I BRING TO THE GRE?
A: Bring your registration form, positive identification, a watch, three or four sharpened Number 2 pencils, and a good eraser. You may not bring scratch paper, calculators, or books. You may do your figuring in the space provided in the test booklet.

Q: IF NECESSARY, MAY I CANCEL MY SCORE?
A: Yes. You may cancel your score on the day of the test by telling the test center supervisor, or you may write or telegraph ETS; your cancelation request must reach ETS within four days of the test date. Your GRE score report will note that you have canceled a score.

Q: SHOULD I GUESS ON THE GRE?
A: YES! There is no penalty for guessing on the new GRE. Before taking a wild guess, remember that eliminating one or more of the choices increases your chances of choosing the right answer.

Q: HOW SHOULD I PREPARE FOR THE GRE?
A: Understanding and practicing test-taking strategies will help a great deal, especially on the verbal and analytical sections. Subject-matter review is particularly useful for the math section. Both subject matter and strategies are fully covered in this book.

Q: WHEN IS THE GRE ADMINISTERED?
A: The GRE is administered nationwide six times during the school year, in October, December, January, February, April, and June, on Saturdays. The General Test begins at 8:30 A.M. and the Advanced Tests begin at 1:30 P.M. There are special summer administrations, given in limited locations, in July, August, and September.

Q: Where is the GRE administered?
A: The GRE is administered at hundreds of schools and colleges in and out of the United States. A list of testing centers is included in the GRE information bulletin published by ETS. The testing or placement office at your college or university should have information about local administrations.

Q: How and when should I register?
A: A registration packet, complete with return envelope, is attached to the GRE information bulletin published by ETS. Mailing in the forms provided, plus the appropriate fees, completes the registration process. You should register about six weeks prior to the exam date.

Q: Is walk-in registration provided?
A: Yes, on a limited basis. If you are unable to meet regular registration deadlines, you may attempt to register on the day of the test (an additional fee is required). You will be admitted only if space remains after preregistered students have been seated.

Q: What is the difference between the General Test and the Advanced Test?
A: Your general scholastic ability is measured by the General Test; the questions on this section presume a broad, general college background. The Advanced Test deals with specific subject matter corresponding to your specific graduate study; the questions measure your undergraduate knowledge of the discipline you wish to pursue in graduate school.

Q: What subjects are covered by the Advanced Tests?
A: You may take an Advanced Test in any one of the following areas: Biology, Chemistry, Computer Science, Economics, Education, Engineering, French, Geography, Geology, German, History, Literature in English, Mathematics, Music, Philosophy, Physics, Political Science, Psychology, Sociology, and Spanish. Subscores are reported for the tests in Biology, Engineering, French, Geography, Geology, History, Music, Psychology, and Spanish.

Q: Should I prepare differently for the Advanced Test than for the General Test?
A: The test-taking strategies which help on the General Test will also help on the Advanced Test, because it too consists entirely of multiple-choice questions. A short sample Advanced Test is sent to Advanced Test registrants by ETS; its questions are the most reliable indication of the level and range of questions you can expect. A general review of the material covered by the courses in your undergraduate major will be helpful insofar as it refreshes your memory of key facts, concepts, and personalities.

Constructing multiple-choice questions of your own, based on what you have learned, is an ideal way to prepare.

Q: WHAT IS THE DIFFERENCE BETWEEN THE "OLD" GRE AND THE "NEW" GRE?

A: Until October of 1981, the GRE consisted of five sections: Verbal Ability (50 minutes, 80 questions), Quantitative Ability (Quantitative Comparison-Math Ability, 50 minutes, 55 questions), Analytical Ability (Analysis of Explanations, 25 minutes, 40 questions), Analytical Ability (Logical Diagrams-Analytical Reasoning, 25 minutes, 30 questions), and a Verbal, Math, Analytical, or Experimental section (25 minutes). The "new" GRE is composed of seven sections, each 30 minutes in length: two sections of Verbal Ability (35–40 questions each), two sections of Math Ability (30 questions each), two sections of Analytical Ability (Analytical Reasoning-Logical Reasoning, 25 questions each), and one section that is experimental. The "new" GRE has eliminated Analysis of Explanations and Logical Diagrams. The score on the "new" test does equate with the score on the "old" test.

Q: HOW WILL COLLEGES USE MY SCORE ON THE NEW ANALYTICAL SECTION?

A: The use of this section varies from college to college. Many colleges still discount the analytical score and emphasize the verbal and quantitative scores, simply because the analytical section is so new. For some schools, the analytical score is considered quite seriously; for others it is used to substitute for possible weaknesses in your verbal or quantitative scores. Consult the graduate school to which you are applying to find out precisely how they consider your analytical score.

TAKING THE GRE: A SUCCESSFUL OVERALL APPROACH

Many who take the GRE don't get the score that they are entitled to because they spend too much time dwelling on hard questions, leaving insufficient time to answer the easy questions they can get right. Don't let this happen to you. Use the following system to mark your answer sheet:

1. Answer easy questions immediately.
2. Place a "+" next to any problem that seems solvable but is too time-consuming.
3. Place a "−" next to any problem that seems impossible. Act quickly; don't waste time deciding whether a problem is a "+" or a "−."

After working all the problems you can do immediately, go back and work your "+" problems. If you finish them, try your "−" problems (sometimes when you come back to a problem that seemed impossible you will suddenly realize how to solve it).

Your answer sheet should look something like this after you finish working your easy questions:

   1. Ⓐ ● Ⓒ Ⓓ Ⓔ
+2. Ⓐ Ⓑ Ⓒ Ⓓ Ⓔ
   3. Ⓐ Ⓑ ● Ⓓ Ⓔ
−4. Ⓐ Ⓑ Ⓒ Ⓓ Ⓔ
+5. Ⓐ Ⓑ Ⓒ Ⓓ Ⓔ

Since there is now *no penalty for guessing,* be sure to fill in an answer for each question. *Make sure you erase your "+" and "−" marks before your exam is over.* The scoring machine may count extraneous marks as wrong answers.

By using this overall approach, you are bound to achieve your best possible score.

Part II: Analysis of Exam Areas

This section is designed to introduce you to each GRE area by carefully reviewing the

1. Ability Tested
2. Basic Skills Necessary
3. Directions
4. Analysis of Directions
5. Suggested Approach with Sample Questions

This section features the PATTERNED PLAN OF ATTACK for each subject area and emphasizes important test-taking techniques and strategies and how to apply them to a variety of problem types. It also includes valuable symbols, terminology, formulas, basic math information, and a compact list of prefixes, suffixes, and roots to assist you in the verbal section.

INTRODUCTION TO VERBAL ABILITY

There are two Verbal Ability sections on the GRE, each 30 minutes in length. The two sections contain a total of about 80 questions (35–40 questions each). Each Verbal Ability section consists of four types of questions: antonyms, analogies, sentence completion, and reading comprehension. The total of the two sections is scaled from 200 to 800, with an average score of about 490.

A CAREFUL ANALYSIS OF EACH TYPE OF VERBAL ABILITY QUESTION FOLLOWS.

ANTONYMS

Ability Tested

The Antonym section tests your vocabulary—your ability to understand the meanings of words and to distinguish between fine shades of meaning.

Basic Skills Necessary

This section requires a strong college- or graduate-level vocabulary. A strong vocabulary cannot be developed instantly: it grows over a long period of time spent reading widely and learning new words. Knowing the meanings of prefixes, suffixes, and roots will help you to derive word meanings on the test.

Directions

Each word in CAPITAL LETTERS is followed by five words or phrases. The correct choice is the word or phrase whose meaning is most nearly *opposite* to the meaning of the word in capitals. You may be required to distinguish fine shades of meaning. Look at all choices before marking your answer.

Analysis

1. Although your choice may not be a "perfect" opposite, it must be the *most nearly opposite* of the five choices provided.
2. You should consider all the choices, keeping in mind that in most cases *three* of the five choices can be quickly eliminated as not at all opposite to the original word.

11

Suggested Approach with Samples

1. The prefix, root, and (sometimes) suffix of the original word may help you locate its opposite. *Sample:*

PROFUSION
(A) deficiency   (C) proliferation   (E) maximum
(B) certainty   (D) largeness

The prefix *pro-* has several meanings, and all of them have "positive" connotations; here it means "forward." Of the five choices, the prefix most opposite to the meaning of *pro-* is *de-*. The connotations of *de-* are usually "negative"; most often, it means "away from," "off," or "down."

Profusion means "abundance," and *deficiency* refers to "being inadequate or incomplete." Given these definitions, we see that these two terms are the most nearly opposite of those given. However, even without your knowing the definitions, the prefixes, in this case, provide strong clues.

2. Without considering the parts of the original word, you may be able to detect whether it is "positive" or "negative" in meaning. If the original word is positive, your choice must be negative, and vice versa. *Sample:*

GHASTLY
(A) stupendous   (C) lovely   (E) standard
(B) infectious   (D) acceptable

Ghastly is a strongly negative word. Although *acceptable* is a positive word, and therefore opposite to *ghastly, lovely* is a better choice. *Lovely* is more strongly positive than *acceptable* and therefore suits the strongly negative meaning of *ghastly*.

3. Working from the answer choices and looking for a single choice that "stands out" can be a useful strategy. *Sample:*

DILAPIDATED
(A) ruined   (C) renovated   (E) hasty
(B) unconscionable   (D) bizarre

Assessing the choices for "positive" or "negative" meaning, notice that only *renovated* is not clearly a negative word; thus, it "stands out" among the other choices. In this case, *renovated* (made good as new) is the opposite of *dilapidated,* which means "falling apart."

4. Don't choose an antonym that is too broad or too limited to be an opposite. *Sample.*

GARRULOUS
(A) edited   (C) censored   (E) unyielding
(B) speechless   (D) narrow minded

Garrulous means "talking much." Although (A), (C), (D), and (E) are all partial opposites because they contain the idea of restricting language, only (B) specifically refers to speech.

5. Try using the given word in a short, clear sentence; try to think of how you've heard the word used before. You may discover a context for it that will help you make a choice. *Sample:*

PATHOLOGICAL
(A) unsteady	(C) predictable	(E) selective
(B) cured	(D) stubborn	

Sentence: "One of my friends is a pathological liar." Since *pathological* here refers to a negative characteristic, the correct choice is positive, (B).

A PATTERNED PLAN OF ATTACK

Antonyms

Read the word, remembering you are looking for the most nearly opposite.

↓

If the word is unfamiliar to you, try to put it into a sentence, or break the word up using knowledge of prefixes, roots, and suffixes for assistance, or check for a positive or negative connotation associated with the word.

↓

Remember, if the word has a positive connotation, its antonym is *negative,* and vice versa.

↓

Your answer should not be too broad or too limited to be an opposite.

ANALOGIES

Ability Tested

The Analogy section tests your ability to understand logical relationships between pairs of words. Your vocabulary—your ability to understand the meanings of words—is also tested.

Basic Skills Necessary

The basic skills necessary for this section are, once again, a strong college- or graduate-level vocabulary and the ability to distinguish similarities and differences between words or ideas.

Directions

In each following sample, you are given a related pair of words or phrases. Select the lettered pair that *best* expresses a relationship similar to that in the original pair of words.

Analysis

It is important that you focus on understanding the *relationship* between the original pair, because this is really what you are trying to parallel.

Notice that you are to select the BEST answer or most similar relationship; therefore, the correct answer may not be directly parallel. The use of the word "best" also implies that there may be more than one good answer.

Categories of Relationship

1. Opposites and Synonyms

   Although a pair of analogies may not be *exact* opposites or *exact* synonyms, a number of pairs may have a roughly opposite or synonymous relationship.

   ERASE : RECORD :: RELINQUISH : ACQUIRE
   PRESENT : INTRODUCE :: SUCCEED : ACCOMPLISH

2. Action/Activity

   Relationship between action and its meaning:
   YAWN : FATIGUE :: SOB : SORROW

Relationship between action and its performer:
ORATORY : CANDIDATE :: SOLILOQUY : ACTOR

Relationship between action and its object:
HATE : VILLAINY :: WORSHIP : DEITY

Relationship between action and its recipient:
DRAMA : AUDIENCE :: WRITING : READER

3. Characteristic/Condition

Relationship between a characteristic and a related action:
OPPRESSED : LIBERATION :: MELANCHOLY : CHEER

Relationship between a characteristic and a related person:
CRAFTSMANSHIP : ARTISAN :: STATESMANSHIP : GOV-
ERNOR

Relationship between a characteristic and a related result:
DISSATISFACTION : COMPLAINT :: CURIOSITY : QUESTION-
ING

4. Effect

Relationship between an effect and its cause:
VERDICT : DELIBERATION :: DEFICIT : OVERSPENDING

Relationship between an effect and its object:
OXIDATION : PAINT :: PHOTOSYNTHESIS : PLANT

5. Time and Space

Relationship between specific and general:
SONNET : LITERATURE :: FOOTBALL : SPORT

Relationship between larger and smaller:
SKYLIGHT : PORTHOLE :: TOME : PAMPHLET

Relationship between younger and older:
SAPLING : TREE :: NEW STAR : NOVA

Relationship between container and contained:
PHOTOGRAPH : IMAGES :: NOVEL : CHAPTERS

Relationship between part and whole:
DIGIT : RATIO :: SYLLABLE : CLAUSE

Relationship between concrete and abstract:
STORY : HEIGHT :: DEGREE : TEMPERATURE

NOTE: Many of these relationships can be presented in a "negative" rather than "positive" sequence. For instance, instead of a pair of words denoting an effect and its cause, you might encounter the *negation* of this relationship, an effect coupled with something that *cannot* be its cause: HAPPINESS : INJURY :: PEACEFULNESS : STRESS. "Happiness is not the effect of injury in the same way as peacefulness is not the effect of stress." The relationship here may be represented as EFFECT : (−) CAUSE, using the minus sign to indicate the negative element in the pair.

Suggested Approach with Samples

1. To determine the relationship between the original pair of words, try to construct a sentence with words that link the pair. *Sample:*

ORATORY : COMMUNICATION : :
(A) key : ignition
(B) concept : paragraph
(C) dancing : recreation
(D) stalling : conversation
(E) cursing : crime

In this case, you might say to yourself, "oratory is a specific kind of communication" and thus recognize that the relationship here is between specific and general.

2. Narrow your choice to a pair of words that demonstrates most precisely the same relationship as the original pair. Test the precision of the relationship by applying the sentence, "A is to B in the same way as C is to D." In the example above, you would say to yourself, "Oratory is a specific kind of communication in the same way as . . . (A) a key is a specific kind of ignition?, (B) a concept is a specific kind of paragraph?, (C) dancing is a specific kind of recreation?, (D) stalling is a specific kind of conversation?, (E) cursing is a specific kind of crime?" After following this procedure, the best choices, those that demonstrate the relationship of the original pair, are (C) and (E).

To make your final choice, decide which pair of words expresses a "specific to general" relationship that is either *necessary* or *typical*. For instance, cursing is not *necessarily or typically* a specific kind of crime; however, dancing is *necessarily* and *typically* a specific kind of recreation. Therefore, (C) is the best choice.

3. Often you will need to consider not only the *primary* relationship between the original words, but also a secondary relationship. *Sample:*

PERJURY : TRUTH : :
(A) attorney : client
(B) treason : loyalty
(C) courage : cowardice
(D) sorcery : witchcraft
(E) patience : indecision

"Perjury is the opposite of truth." This sentence tells us that the primary relationship between the original words is one of opposites. Beyond this primary relationship, there are secondary relationships to consider. First, notice that *perjury* is an *unlawful* act. Second, notice that, considering more specifically the relationship of *perjury* to *truth*, we may conclude that *perjury* is a *violation* of *truth*. Scanning the choices, you see that *treason* is the opposite of *loyalty* and that *courage* is the opposite of *cowardice*. However, only choice (B) presents a relationship in which the first term is an *unlawful* act and in which the first term is a *violation* of the second. Thus, taking the secondary relationships of the original pair fully into account, you should conclude that (B) is the best choice.

To sum up this effective approach to solving analogies: (1) Determine the relationship between the original pair of words by using them in a sentence. (2) Narrow your choices to pairs that typically or necessarily express a similar relationship. (3) Choose the pair that expresses the original relationship most precisely by taking into account the secondary relationship(s) between the words in the original pair.

A PATTERNED PLAN OF ATTACK

Analogies

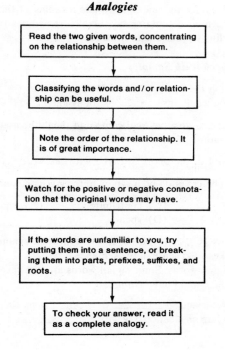

SENTENCE COMPLETION

Ability Tested

This section tests your ability to complete sentences with a word or words that retain the meaning of the sentence, and are structurally and stylistically correct.

Basic Skills Necessary

Good reading comprehension skills help in this section, as does a good college- or graduate-level vocabulary.

Directions

Each blank in the following sentences indicates that something has been omitted. Considering the lettered words beneath the sentence, choose the word or set of words that best fits the whole sentence.

Analysis

Note that you must choose the *best* word or words. In cases where several choices *might* fit, prefer the one that fits the meaning of the sentence most precisely. If the sentence contains two blanks, remember that *both* of the words corresponding to your choice must fit.

Suggested Approach With Samples

1. *After* reading the sentence and *before* looking at the answer choices, think of words you would insert and look for synonyms to them. *Sample:*

Money _____ to a political campaign should be used for political purposes and nothing else.

How would you fill in the blank? Maybe with the word *given* or *donated*?

Now look at the choices and find a synonym for *given* or *donated:*

(A) used   (C) contributed   (E) channeled
(B) forwarded   (D) spent

The best choice is (C), *contributed;* it is the nearest synonym to *given* or *donated* and makes good sense in the sentence.

2. Look for signal words. Some signal words are "however," "although," "on the other hand," and "but." *Sample:*

Most candidates spend _____ they can raise on their campaigns, but others wind up on election day with a _____ .

(A) so . . . bankroll

(B) time . . . vacation

(C) everything . . . surplus

(D) every cent . . . deficit

(E) nothing . . . war chest

But signals that the first half of the sentence *contrasts* with the second half. The fact that most candidates spend *everything* (and end up with nothing) contrasts with those who end up with a *surplus.* (C) is the correct answer.

3. Watch for contrasts between positive and negative words. Look for words like "not," "never," and "no." *Sample:*

A virtuous person will not shout _____ in public; he will respect the _____ of other people.

The first blank is obviously a negative word, something a good person would *not* do; the second blank is a positive word, something that a good person *would* do. *Here are the choices:*

(A) obscenities . . . feelings

(B) loudly . . . comfort

(C) anywhere . . . presence

(D) blessings . . . cynicism

(E) insults . . . threat

(B) is neutral-positive; (C) is neutral-neutral; (D) is positive-negative; (E) is negative-negative. Only (A) offers a negative-positive pair of words; (A) is the best choice.

4. Sometimes it is more efficient to work from the second blank first. *Sample:*

The merger will eliminate _____ and provide more _____ cross-training of staff.

(A) profit . . . and more

(B) paperwork . . . or less

(C) duplication . . . effective

(D) bosses . . . wasteful

(E) competitors . . . aggressive

The second blank is something that is "provided." Chances are that something provided is a positive word, and *effective* seems like a good choice. Reading choice (C) into the sentence, we find that it makes good sense and is stylistically or structurally correct.

5. What "sounds wrong" should be eliminated. *Sample:*

High school students should not be _____ as being immature or naive.

(A) helped

(B) shoved

(C) directed

(D) categorized

(E) taught

The only word that sounds right with "as" is *categorized;* (D) is the best choice.

A PATTERNED PLAN OF ATTACK

Sentence Completion

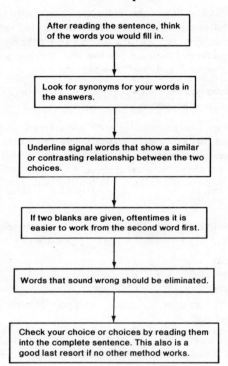

After reading the sentence, think of the words you would fill in.

↓

Look for synonyms for your words in the answers.

↓

Underline signal words that show a similar or contrasting relationship between the two choices.

↓

If two blanks are given, oftentimes it is easier to work from the second word first.

↓

Words that sound wrong should be eliminated.

↓

Check your choice or choices by reading them into the complete sentence. This also is a good last resort if no other method works.

READING COMPREHENSION

Ability Tested

This section tests your ability to understand, interpret, and analyze reading passages on a variety of topics.

Basic Skills Necessary

Students who have read widely and know how to read and mark a passage actively and efficiently tend to do well on this section.

Directions

Each passage in this group is followed by questions based on its content. After reading a passage, choose the best answer to each question and blacken the corresponding space on the answer sheet. Answer all questions following a passage on the basis of what is *stated* or *implied* in that passage. You may refer back to the passage.

Analysis

1. Answer all the questions for one passage before moving on to the next one. If you don't know the answer, take an educated guess or skip it.
2. Use only the information given or implied in a passage. Do not consider outside information, even if it seems more accurate than the given information.

Suggested Approach With Short Sample Passage

1. Skim the questions first, marking words which give you a clue about what to look for when you read the passage.
2. Skim the passage, reading only the first sentence of each paragraph.
3. Read the passage, marking main points, important conclusions, names, definitions, places, and numbers. Make only a few marks per paragraph.

Short Sample Passage

St. Augustine was a contemporary of Jerome. After an early life of pleasure, he became interested in a philosophical religion called Manichaeism, a derivative of a Persian religion, in which the forces of good constantly struggle with those of evil. Augustine was eventually converted to Christianity by St. Ambrose of Milan. His *Confessions* was an autobiography that served as an inspiration to countless thousands who believed that virtue would ultimately win.

Sample Questions With Explanations

1. St. Augustine's conversion to Christianity was probably influenced by
   - (A) his confessional leanings
   - (B) his contemporaries
   - (C) the inadequacy of a Persian religion to address Western moral problems
   - (D) his earlier interest in the dilemma of retaining virtue
   - (E) the ravages of a life of pleasure

Having skimmed this question, you should have marked the portion of the passage which mentions Augustine's conversion and paid attention to the events (influences) leading to it. (A) requires speculating beyond the facts in the paragraph; there is also no evidence in the passage to support (C) or (E). (B) is too vague and general to be the best answer. (D) points toward Augustine's earlier interest in Manichaeism, and the last sentence suggests that Augustine's interest in retaining virtue continued through his Christian doctrine. Well supported as it is, (D) is the best answer.

2. From the information in the passage, we must conclude that Augustine was a
   - (A) fair-weather optimist
   - (B) cockeyed optimist
   - (C) hardworking optimist
   - (D) failed optimist
   - (E) glib optimist

Skimming *this* question is not very helpful; it does not point specifically to any information in the passage. Questions of this sort usually assess your overall understanding of the meaning, style, tone, or point of view of the passage. In this case, you should recognize that Augustine is a serious person; therefore, more lighthearted terms like "fair-weather" (A), "cock-eyed" (B), and "glib" (E) are probably inappropriate. (D) contradicts Augustine's success as an "inspiration to countless thousands." (C) corresponds with his ongoing, hopeful struggle to retain virtue in the world; it is the best answer.

3. Judging from the reaction of thousands to Augustine's *Confessions*, we may conclude that much of his world at that time was in a state of
   - (A) opulence
   - (B) misery
   - (C) heresy
   - (D) reformation
   - (E) sanctification

Having skimmed this question, you should have marked the last sentence of the passage as the place to look for the answer. That Augustine's readers were inspired implies that they *required inspiration*, that they were in some sort of uninspiring, or *negative* situation. (A) and (E) must therefore be eliminated because they are positive terms. (D) is not necessarily a negative term, and so is probably not the best answer. (C), although a negative term, does not describe a state of being which thirsts for inspiration. (B) does, and (B) therefore is the best choice.

A PATTERNED PLAN OF ATTACK

Reading Comprehension

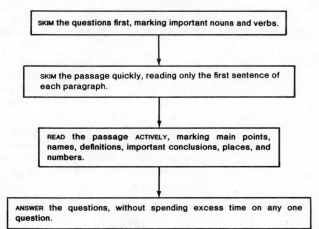

COMMON PREFIXES, SUFFIXES, AND ROOTS

The following list should help you to arrive at definitions of unfamiliar words on the Verbal Section of the GRE. These prefixes, suffixes, and roots apply to thousands of words.

Prefixes

Prefix	Meaning	Example
1. pre-	before	precede
2. de-	away, from	deter
3. inter-	between	interstate
4. ob-	against	objection
5. in-	into	instruct
6. mono-	alone, one	monolith
7. epi-	upon	epilogue
8. mis-	wrong	mistake
9. sub-	under	submarine
10. trans-	across, beyond	transcend
11. over-	above	overbearing
12. ad-	to, toward	advance
13. non-	not	nonentity
14. com-	together, with	composite
15. re-	back, again	regress
16. ex-	out of	expel
17. in-	not	insufficient
18. pro-	forward	propel
19. anti-	against	antidote
20. omni-	all, everywhere	omniscient
21. equi-	equal, equally	equivalent
22. homo-	same, equal, like	homogenized
23. semi-	half, partly	semicircle
24. un-	not	unneeded
25. bi-	two	bicycle
26. poly-	many	polymorphous
27. retro-	backward	retrograde
28. mal-	bad	malfunction
29. hyper-	over, too much	hyperactive
30. hypo-	under, too little	hypodermic

Suffixes

Suffix	Meaning	Example
1. -able, -ible	able to	usable
2. -er, -or	one who does	competitor
3. -ism	the practice of	rationalism
4. -ist	one who is occupied with	feminist
5. -less	without, lacking	meaningless
6. -ship	the art or skill of	statesmanship
7. -fy	to make	dignify
8. -ness	the quality of	aggressiveness
9. -tude	the state of	rectitude
10. -logue	a particular kind of speaking or writing	prologue

Roots

Root	Meaning	Example
1. arch	to rule	monarch
2. belli	war, warlike	belligerent
3. bene	good	benevolent
4. chron	time	chronology
5. dic	to say	indicative
6. fac	to make, to do	artifact
7. graph	writing	telegraph
8. mort	to die	mortal
9. port	to carry	deport
10. vid, vis	to see	invisible

INTRODUCTION TO QUANTITATIVE ABILITY

There are two Quantitative Ability sections on the GRE, each 30 minutes in length. The two sections contain a total of about 60 questions (30 questions each). Each Quantitative Ability section consists of two basic types of questions: Quantitative Comparison and regular Math Ability multiple–choice questions. The total of the two sections generates a scaled score that ranges from 200 to 800, with an average score of about 550.

A CAREFUL ANALYSIS OF EACH TYPE OF QUANTITATIVE ABILITY QUESTION FOLLOWS.

QUANTITATIVE COMPARISON

Ability Tested

Quantitative Comparison tests your ability to use mathematical insight, approximation, simple calculation, or common sense to quickly compare two given quantities.

Basic Skills Necessary

This section requires twelfth-grade competence in high school arithmetic, algebra, and intuitive geometry. Skills in approximating, comparing, and evaluating are also necessary. No advanced mathematics is necessary.

Directions

In this section you will be given two quantities, one in column A and one in column B. You are to determine a relationship between the two quantities and mark

(A) if the quantity in column A is greater than the quantity in column B.
(B) if the quantity in column B is greater than the quantity in column A.
(C) if the two quantities are equal.
(D) if the comparison cannot be determined from the information given.

Analysis

The purpose here is to make a comparison; therefore, exact answers are not always necessary. (Remember that you can tell whether you are taller than someone in many cases without knowing that person's height. Comparisons such as this can be made with only partial information—just enough to compare.) (D) is not a possible answer if there are *values* in each column, because you can always compare values.

If you get different relationships, depending on the values you choose for variables, then the answer is always (D). Notice that there are only four possible choices here. *Never* mark (E) on your answer sheet for Quantitative Comparison.

Note that you can add, subtract, multiply, and divide both columns by the same value and the relationship between them will not change. EXCEPTION— You should not multiply or divide each column by negative numbers because then the relationship reverses. Squaring both columns is permissible, as long as each side is positive.

Suggested Approach With Sample Problems

1. This section emphasizes shortcuts, insight, and quick techniques. Long and/or involved mathematical computation is unnecessary and is contrary to the purpose of this section. *Sample:*

Column A	Column B
$21 \times 43 \times 56$	$44 \times 21 \times 57$

Canceling (or dividing) 21 from each side leaves

43×56	44×57

The rest of this problem should be done by inspection, because it is obvious that column B is greater than column A without doing any multiplication. You could have attained the correct answer by actually multiplying out each column, but you would then not have enough time to finish the section. The correct answer is (B).

2. The use of partial comparisons can be valuable in giving you insight into finding a comparison. If you cannot simply make a complete comparison, look at each column part by part. *Sample:*

Column A	Column B
$\dfrac{1}{57} - \dfrac{1}{65}$	$\dfrac{1}{58} - \dfrac{1}{63}$

Since finding a common denominator would be too time-consuming, you should first compare the first fraction in each column (partial comparison). Notice that $1/57$ is greater than $1/58$. Now compare the second fractions and notice that $1/65$ is less than $1/63$. Using some common sense and insight, if you start with a larger number and a smaller number, it must be greater than starting with a smaller number and subtracting a larger number, as pointed out below.

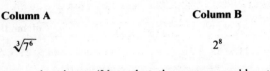

The correct answer is (A).

3. Always keep the columns in perspective before starting any calculations. Take a good look at the value in each column before starting to work on one column. *Sample:*

Column A	Column B
$\sqrt[3]{7^6}$	2^8

After looking at each column (Note that the answer could not be (D) because there are values in each column), compute the value on the left. Since you are taking a cube root, simply divide the power of 7 by 3 leaving 7^2, or 49. There is no need to take 2 out to the 8th power, just do as little as necessary: $2^2 = 4$, $2^3 = 8$, $2^4 = 16$, $2^5 = 32$. STOP. It is evident that 2^8 is much greater than 49; the correct answer is (B). Approximating can also be valuable while remembering to keep the columns in perspective.

4. If a problem involves variables (without an equation), substitute in the numbers 0, 1, and −1. Then try ½, and 2 if necessary. Using 0, 1, and −1 will often tip off the answer. *Sample:*

Column A	Column B
a + b	ab

Substituting 0 for a and 0 for b gives

0 + 0	0(0)

Therefore   0   =   0

Using these values for a and b gives the answer (C). But anytime you multiply two numbers, it is not the same as when you add them, so try some other values.

Substituting 1 for a and −1 for b gives

	1 + (−1)	1(−1)
Therefore	0	−1
	>	

and the answer is now (A).

Anytime you get more than one comparison (different relationships), depending on the values chosen, the correct answer must be (D) (the relationship cannot be determined). Notice that if you had substituted the values a = 4, b = 5; or a = 6, b = 7; or a = 7, b = 9; and so on, you would repeatedly have gotten the answer (B) and might have chosen the incorrect answer.

5. Oftentimes simplifying one or both columns can make an answer evident. *Sample:*

Column A	**Column B**
	a, b, c, all greater than 0	
a(b + c)	ab + ac

Using the distributive property on column A to simplify, gives ab and ac; therefore, the columns are equal.

6. Sometimes you can solve for a column directly, in one step, without solving and substituting. If you have to solve an equation or equations to give the columns values, take a second and see if there is a very simple way to get an answer before going through all of the steps. *Sample:*

Column A	**Column B**
	4x + 2 = 10	
2x + 1	4

Hopefully, you would spot that the easiest way to solve for 2x + 1 is directly by dividing 4x + 2 = 10, by 2, leaving 2x + 1 = 5.

Therefore

5	>	4

Solving for x first in the equation, and then substituting, would also have worked, but would have been more time-consuming. The correct answer is (A).

7. Marking diagrams can be very helpful for giving insight into a problem. Remember that figures and diagrams are meant for positional information only. Just because something "looks" larger, is not enough reason to choose an answer. *Sample:*

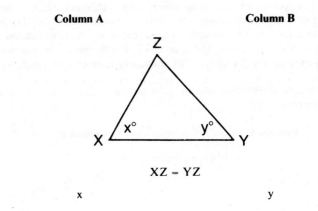

Column A   **Column B**

$$XZ = YZ$$

x   y

Even though x appears larger, this is not enough. Mark in the diagrams as shown.

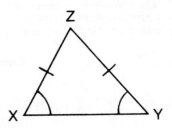

Notice that you should mark things of equal measure with the same markings, and since angles opposite equal sides in a triangle are equal, x = y. The correct answer is (C).

8. If you are given information that is unfamiliar to you and difficult to work with, change the number slightly (but remember what you've changed) to something easier to work with. *Sample:*

Column A   **Column B**

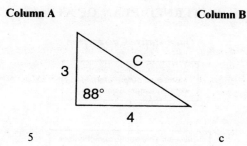

5   c

Since the 88° shown in the figure is unfamiliar to work with, change it to 90° for now, so that you may use the Pythagorean theorem to solve for c.

$$a^2 + b^2 = c^2$$

Solving for c as follows

$$(3)^2 + (4)^2 = c^2$$
$$9 + 16 = c^2$$
$$25 = c^2$$

Therefore

$$5 = c$$

But since you used 90° instead of 88°, you should realize that the side opposite the 88° will be slightly smaller or less than 5. The correct answer is then (A), $5 > c$. (Some students may have noticed the 3:4:5 triangle relationship and have not needed the Pythagorean theorem.)

A PATTERNED PLAN OF ATTACK

Quantitative Comparison

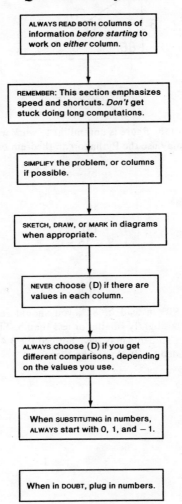

ALWAYS READ BOTH columns of information *before starting* to work on *either* column.

REMEMBER: This section emphasizes speed and shortcuts. *Don't* get stuck doing long computations.

SIMPLIFY the problem, or columns if possible.

SKETCH, DRAW, or MARK in diagrams when appropriate.

NEVER choose (D) if there are values in each column.

ALWAYS choose (D) if you get different comparisons, depending on the values you use.

When SUBSTITUTING in numbers, ALWAYS start with 0, 1, and − 1.

When in DOUBT, plug in numbers.

MATH ABILITY

Ability Tested

The Math Ability section tests your ability to solve mathematical problems involving arithmetic, algebra, geometry, and word problems by using problem-solving insight, logic, and application of basic skills.

Basic Skills Necessary

The basic skills necessary to do well on this section include high school algebra and intuitive geometry—no formal trigonometry or calculus is necessary. Skills in arithmetic and basic algebra, along with some logical insight into problem-solving situations, are also necessary.

Directions

Solve each problem in this section by using the information given and your own mathematical calculations. Then select the *one* correct answer of the five choices given. Use the available space on the page for scratchwork.

Note: Some problems may be accompanied by figures or diagrams. These figures are drawn as accurately as possible *except* when it is stated in a specific problem that the figure is not drawn to scale. The figure is meant to provide information useful in solving the problem or problems.

Unless otherwise stated or indicated, all figures lie in a plane.

All numbers used are real numbers.

Analysis

All scratchwork is to be done in the test booklet; get used to doing this because no scratch paper is allowed into the testing area.

You are looking for the *one* correct answer; therefore although other answers may be close, there is never more than one right answer.

Suggested Approach With Samples

1. Take advantage of being allowed to mark on the test booklet by always underlining or circling what you are looking for. This will ensure that you are answering the right question. *Sample:*

If $x + 6 = 9$, then $3x + 1 =$
(A) 3   (B) 9   (C) 10   (D) 34   (E) 46

You should first circle or underline $3x + 1$, because this is what you are solving for. Solving for x leaves $x = 3$ and then substituting into $3x + 1$ gives $3(3) + 1$, or 10. The most common mistake is to solve for x, which is 3, and *mistakenly choose* (A) as your answer. But remember, you are solving for 3x + 1, not just x. You should also notice that most of the other choices would all be possible answers if you made common or simple mistakes. The correct answer is (C). *Make sure that you are answering the right question.*

2. Substituting numbers for variables can often be an aid to understanding a problem. Remember to substitute simple numbers, since *you* have to do the work. *Sample:*

If $x > 1$, which of the following decreases as x decreases?

$$\text{I. } x + x^2$$
$$\text{II. } 2x^2 - x$$
$$\text{III. } \frac{1}{x + 1}$$

(A) I   (B) II   (C) III   (D) I and II   (E) II and III

This problem is most easily solved by taking each situation and substituting simple numbers. However, in the first situation, I, $x + x^2$, you should recognize that this expression will decrease as x decreases. Trying $x = 2$ gives $2 + (2)^2$ which equals 6. Now trying $x = 3$ gives $3 + (3)^2 = 12$. Notice that choices (B), (C), and (E) are already eliminated because they do not contain I. You should also realize that now you only need to try the values in II; since III is not paired with I as a possible choice, III cannot be one of the answers. Trying $x = 2$ in the expression $2x^2 - x$, gives $2(2)^2 - 2$, or $2(4) - 2$, which leaves 6. Now trying $x = 3$ gives $2(3)^2 - 3$, or $2(9) - 3 = 18 - 3 = 15$. This expression also decreases as x decreases. Therefore the correct answer is (D). Once again notice that III was not even attempted, because it was not one of the possible choices.

3. Sometimes you will immediately recognize the proper formula or method to solve a problem. If this is not the situation, try a reasonable approach and then work from the answers. *Sample:*

Barney can mow the lawn in 5 hours and Fred can mow the lawn in 4 hours. How long will it take them to mow the lawn together?

(A) 5 hours   (C) 4 hours   (E) 1 hour
(B) 4½ hours   (D) 2⅖ hours

Suppose that you are unfamiliar with the type of equation for this problem. Try the "reasonable" method. Since Fred can mow the lawn in 4 hours by himself, it will take less than 4 hours if Barney helps him. Therefore choices (A), (B), and (C) are ridiculous. Taking this method a little further, suppose that Barney could also mow the lawn in 4 hours. Then together it would take Barney and Fred 2 hours. But since Barney is a little slower than this, the total time should be a little more than 2 hours. The correct answer is (D), $2\frac{2}{9}$ hours.

Using the equation for this problem would give the following calculations:

$$\frac{1}{5} + \frac{1}{4} = \frac{1}{x}$$

In 1 hour, Barney could do $\frac{1}{5}$ of the job and in 1 hour Fred could do $\frac{1}{4}$ of the job; unknown $1/x$ is that part of the job they could do together in one hour. Now solving, you calculate as follows:

$$\frac{4}{20} + \frac{5}{20} = \frac{1}{x}$$

$$\frac{9}{20} = \frac{1}{x}$$

Cross multiplying gives $9x = 20$
Therefore, $x = \frac{20}{9}$, or $2\frac{2}{9}$.

4. "Pulling" information out of the word problem structure can often give you a better look at what you are working with and therefore you gain additional insight into the problem. *Sample:*

If a mixture is $\frac{3}{7}$ alcohol by volume and $\frac{4}{7}$ water by volume, what is the ratio of the volume of alcohol to the volume of water in this mixture?

(A) $\frac{3}{7}$ (B) $\frac{4}{7}$ (C) $\frac{3}{4}$ (D) $\frac{4}{3}$ (E) $\frac{7}{4}$

The first bit of information that should be pulled out should be what you are looking for: "ratio of the volume of alcohol to the volume of water." Rewrite it as A:W and then into its working form: A/W. Next, you should pull out the volumes of each; $A = \frac{3}{7}$ and $W = \frac{4}{7}$. Now the answer can be easily figured by inspection or substitution: using $(\frac{3}{7})/(\frac{4}{7})$, invert the bottom fraction and multiply to get $\frac{3}{7} \times \frac{7}{4} = \frac{3}{4}$. The ratio of the volume of alcohol to the volume of water is 3 to 4. The correct answer is (C). When pulling out information, actually write out the numbers and/or letters to the side of the problem, putting them into some helpful form and eliminating some of the wording.

5. Sketching diagrams or simple pictures can also be very helpful in problem solving because the diagram may tip off either a simple solution or a method for solving the problem. *Sample:*

What is the maximum number of pieces of birthday cake of size 4″ by 4″ that can be cut from a cake 20″ by 20″?

(A) 5   (B) 10   (C) 16   (D) 20   (E) 25

Sketching the cake and marking in as follows makes this a fairly simple problem.

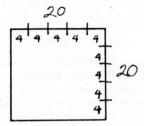

Notice that 5 pieces of cake will fit along each side, therefore 5 × 5 = 25. The correct answer is (E). Finding the total area of the cake and dividing it by the area of one of the 4 × 4 pieces would have also given you the correct answer, but beware of this method because it may *not* work if the pieces do not fit evenly into the original area.

6. Marking in diagrams as you read them can save you valuable time. Marking can also give you insight into how to solve a problem because you will have the complete picture clearly in front of you. *Sample:*

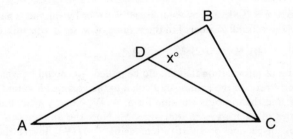

In the triangle above, CD is an angle bisector, angle ACD is 30° and angle ABC is a right angle. Find the measurement of angle x in degrees.

(A) 30°   (B) 45°   (C) 60°   (D) 75°   (E) 80°

You should have read the problem and marked as follows:

In the triangle above, CD is an angle bisector (STOP AND MARK IN THE DRAWING), angle ACD is 30° (STOP AND MARK IN THE DRAWING), and angle ABC is a right angle (STOP AND MARK IN THE DRAWING). Find the measurement of angle x in degrees (STOP AND MARK IN OR CIRCLE WHAT YOU ARE LOOKING FOR IN THE DRAWING).

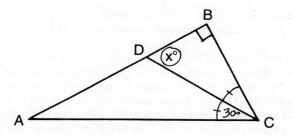

Now with the drawing marked in, it is evident that, since angle ACD is 30°, then angle BCD is also 30° because they are formed by an angle bisector (divides an angle into two equal parts). Since angle ABC is 90° (right angle) and BCD is 30°, then angle x is 60°, because there are 180° in a triangle, 180 − (90 + 30) = 60. The correct answer is (C). ALWAYS MARK IN DIAGRAMS AS YOU READ DESCRIPTIONS AND INFORMATION ABOUT THEM. THIS INCLUDES WHAT YOU ARE LOOKING FOR.

7. If it appears that extensive calculations are going to be necessary to solve a problem, check to see how far apart the choices are, and then approximate. The reason for checking the answers first is to give you a guide for how freely you can approximate. *Sample:*

The value for $\dfrac{.889 \times 55}{9.97}$ to the nearest tenth is

(A) 49.1   (C) 4.9   (E) .5
(B) 7.7   (D) 4.63

Before starting any computations, take a glance at the answers to see how far apart they are. Notice that the only close answers are (C) and (D), except (D) is not possible, since it is to the nearest hundredth, not tenth. Now, making some quick approximations, .889 = 1 and 9.97 = 10, leaves the problem in this form

$$\frac{1 \times 55}{10} = \frac{55}{10} = 5.5$$

The closest answer is (C), therefore it is the correct answer. Notice that choices (A) and (E) were not reasonable.

8. In some instances, it will be easier to work from the answers. Do not disregard this method, because it will at least eliminate some of the choices and could give you the correct answer. *Sample:*

Find the counting number that is less than 15 and when divided by 3 has a remainder of 1 and divided by 4 has a remainder of 2.

(A) 5   (B) 8   (C) 10   (D) 12   (E) 13

By working from the answers, you eliminate wasting time on other numbers from 1 to 14. Choices (B) and (D) can be immediately eliminated because they are divisible by 4, leaving no remainder. Choices (A) and (E) can also be eliminated because they leave a remainder of 1 when divided by 4. Therefore the correct answer is (C); 10 leaves a remainder of 1 when divided by 3 and a remainder of 2 when divided by 4.

A PATTERNED PLAN OF ATTACK

Math Ability

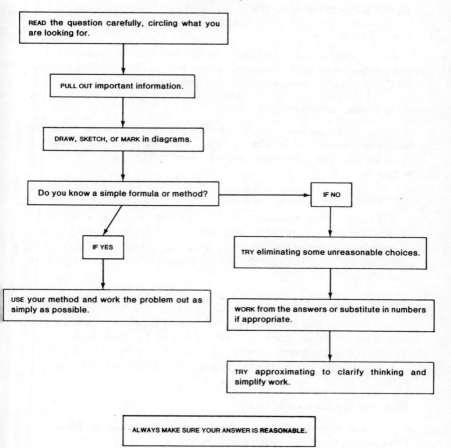

READ the question carefully, circling what you are looking for.

PULL OUT important information.

DRAW, SKETCH, or MARK in diagrams.

Do you know a simple formula or method?

IF NO

IF YES

USE your method and work the problem out as simply as possible.

TRY eliminating some unreasonable choices.

WORK from the answers or substitute in numbers if appropriate.

TRY approximating to clarify thinking and simplify work.

ALWAYS MAKE SURE YOUR ANSWER IS **REASONABLE**.

GRAPHS AND CHARTS

Graphs and charts are included in the Quantitative Comparison and/or Math Ability sections of the GRE.

Ability Tested

You will need to understand and to derive information from charts, tables, and graphs. Many of the problems require brief calculations based on the data, so your mathematical ability is also tested.

Basic Skills Necessary

The mathematics associated with graphs and charts does not go beyond high-school level. Your familiarity with a wide range of charts and graph types will help you feel comfortable with these problems and read the data accurately.

Directions

You are given data represented in chart or graph form. Following each set of data are questions based on that data. Select the *best* answer to each question by referring to the appropriate chart or graph and mark your choice on the answer sheet. Use only the given or implied information to determine your answer.

Analysis

1. Remember that you are looking for the *best* answer, not necessarily the perfect answer. Often, graph questions ask you for an *approximate* answer; if this happens, don't forget to round off numbers to make your work easier.
2. Use only the information given; never "read into" the information on a graph.

Suggested Approach with Samples

Here are some helpful strategies for extracting accurate information followed by some sample graph questions.
1. Skim the questions and quickly examine the whole graph before starting to work problems; this sort of prereading will tell you what to look for.
2. Use your answer sheet as a straightedge in order to align points on the graph with their corresponding number values.
3. Sometimes the answer to a question is available in supplementary information given with a graph (headings, scale factors, legends, etc.); be sure to read this information.
4. Look for the obvious: dramatic trends, high points, low points, etc.— obvious information often leads directly to an answer.

Graph and Chart Questions

Questions 1–3 refer to the graph.

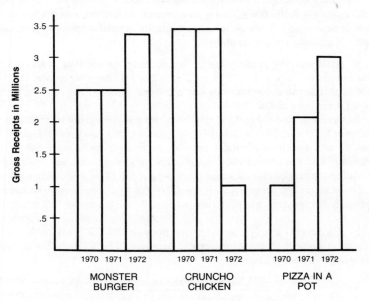

Gross Receipts of Several Fast-Food Restaurants
1970-1972

1. The 1970–72 gross receipts for Monster Burger exceeded those of Pizza In A Pot by approximately how much?

   (A) 0.2 million   (C) 8.2 million   (E) 17 million
   (B) 2 million   (D) 8.4 million

2. From 1971 to 1972, the percent increase in receipts for Pizza In A Pot exceeded the percent increase of Monster Burger by approximately how much?

   (A) 0%   (B) 2%   (C) 10%   (D) 15%   (E) 43%

3. The 1972 decline in Cruncho Chicken's receipts may be attributed to
   (A) an increase in the popularity of burgers
   (B) an increase in the popularity of pizza
   (C) a decrease in the demand for chicken
   (D) a predictable slump attributable to the deceleration of the Vietnamese War
   (E) it cannot be determined from the information given

Answers and Explanations

This is a bar graph. Typically, this type of graph has a number scale along one edge and individual categories along another edge. Here we have multiple bars representing each fast-food category; each single bar stands for the receipts from a single year.

You may be tempted to write out the numbers as you do your arithmetic (3.5 million = 3,500,000). This is unnecessary, as it often is on graphs which use large numbers. Since *all* measurements are in millions, adding zeros does not add precision to the numbers.

1. (B) Referring to the Monster Burger bars, we see that gross receipts are as follows: 1970 = 2.5, 1971 = 2.5, 1972 = 3.4 (use your answer sheet as a straightedge to determine this last number). Totaling the receipts for all three years, we get 8.4.

Referring to the Pizza In A Pot bars, we see that gross receipts are as follows: 1970 = 1, 1971 = 2.1, 1972 = 3 (once again, use your straightedge, but do not designate numbers beyond the nearest tenth since the graph numbers and the answer choices prescribe no greater accuracy than this). Totaling the receipts for all three years, we get 6.1.

So Monster Burger exceeds Pizza In A Pot by 2.3 million. The answer which best approximates this figure is (B).

2. (C) Several graph and chart questions on the GRE may ask you to calculate percent increase or percent decrease. The formula for figuring either of these is the same:

$$\frac{\text{amount of the change}}{\text{``starting'' amount (follows the word } from)}$$

In this case, we may first calculate the percent increase for Monster Burger.

Gross receipts in 1971 = 2.5
Gross receipts in 1972 = 3.4
Amount of the change = .9

The 1971 amount is the "starting" or "from" amount.

$$\frac{\text{amount of the change}}{\text{``starting'' amount}} = \frac{.9}{2.5} = .36 = 36\%$$

Percent increase for Pizza In A Pot:

Gross receipts in 1971 = 2.1
Gross receipts in 1972 = 3
Amount of the change = .9

$$\frac{\text{amount of the change}}{\text{``starting'' amount}} = \frac{.9}{2.1} = .428 \approx 43\%$$

So, Pizza In A Pot exceeds Monster Burger by 7% (43% − 36%). The answer which best approximates this figure is (C).

3. (E) Never use information that you know is not given. In this case, the multiple factors which could cause a decline in receipts are not represented by the graph. All choices except (E) require you to speculate beyond the information given.

Questions 4–6 refer to the graph.

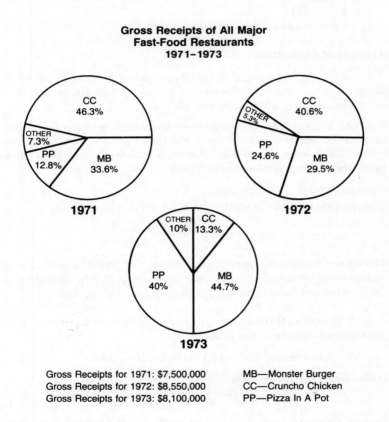

**Gross Receipts of All Major
Fast-Food Restaurants
1971–1973**

Gross Receipts for 1971: $7,500,000   MB—Monster Burger
Gross Receipts for 1972: $8,550,000   CC—Cruncho Chicken
Gross Receipts for 1973: $8,100,000   PP—Pizza In A Pot

4. The gross receipts for 1971 are approximately what percentage of the gross receipts for all three years?
   (A) 30%   (D) 46.7%
   (B) 46.3%   (E) 50%
   (C) it cannot be determined from the information given

5. Over all three years, the average percentage of gross receipts for Cruncho Chicken exceeds the average percentage of gross receipts for Pizza In A Pot by approximately how much?
   (A) 53%   (B) 30%   (C) 23%   (D) 8%   (E) 4%

6. The gross receipts earned by other restaurants in 1973 amounts to *precisely* how much?
   (A) $453,150
   (B) $547,500
   (C) $810,000
   (D) $1,810,650
   (E) a precise amount cannot be determined

Answers and Explanations

This is a circle graph, or pie chart. 100 percent is represented by the whole circle, and the various "slices" represent portions of that 100 percent. The larger the slice, the higher the percentage.

4. (A) You can solve this problem without referring to the graphs; the necessary information is available in the list of gross receipts below the graphs. Don't write out all the zeros when calculating with these large figures; brief figures are easier to work with.

Gross receipts for 1971 = 7.5 million.
Gross receipts for all three years = 7.5 + 8.6 + 8.1 = 24.2 million.

$$\frac{7.5}{24.2} = 31\%$$

The answer which best approximates 31% is 30% (A). Notice that even without doing the calculations, you may approximate 30% by realizing that the gross receipts for any one year are about one-third of the total.

5. (D) To calculate the average percentage for Cruncho Chicken, add the percentages for each year and divide by 3.

$$46.3 + 40.6 + 13.3 = 100.2 \div 3 = 33.4\%$$

Do the same for Pizza In A Pot.

$$12.8 + 24.6 + 40 = 77.4 \div 3 = 25.8\%$$

Cruncho Chicken exceeds Pizza In A Pot by 33.4 − 25.8 = 7.6. (D), 8%, best approximates this figure.

6. (C) In 1973, other restaurants earned precisely 10%. 10% of $8,100,000 = $810,000, (C).

A PATTERNED PLAN OF ATTACK

Graphs and Charts

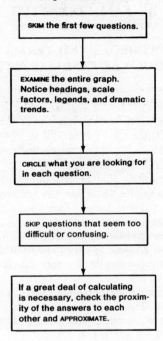

SKIM the first few questions.

EXAMINE the entire graph. Notice headings, scale factors, legends, and dramatic trends.

CIRCLE what you are looking for in each question.

SKIP questions that seem too difficult or confusing.

If a great deal of calculating is necessary, check the proximity of the answers to each other and APPROXIMATE.

IMPORTANT SYMBOLS, TERMINOLOGY, FORMULAS, AND GENERAL MATHEMATICAL INFORMATION THAT YOU SHOULD BE FAMILIAR WITH

COMMON MATH SYMBOLS AND TERMS THAT YOU SHOULD BE FAMILIAR WITH

Symbol References:

$=$ is equal to	$\geq$ is greater than or equal to
$\neq$ is not equal to	$\leq$ is less than or equal to
$>$ is greater than	$\parallel$ is parallel to
$<$ is less than	$\perp$ is perpendicular to

Natural numbers—the counting numbers: 1, 2, 3, . . .

Whole numbers—the counting numbers beginning with zero: 0, 1, 2, 3, . . .

Integers—positive and negative whole numbers and zero: . . . $-3, -2, -1, 0, 1, 2, \ldots$

Odd numbers—numbers not divisible by 2: 1, 3, 5, 7, . . .

Even numbers—numbers divisible by 2: 0, 2, 4, 6, . . .

Prime number—number divisible by only 1 and itself: 2, 3, 5, 7, 11, 13, . . .

Composite number—number divisible by more than just 1 and itself: 4, 6, 8, 9, 10, 12, 14, 15, . . .

Squares—the result when numbers are multiplied by themselves, $(2 \cdot 2 = 4)$ $(3 \cdot 3 = 9)$: 1, 4, 9, 16, 25, 36, . . .

Cubes—the result when numbers are multiplied by themselves twice, $(2 \cdot 2 \cdot 2 = 8)$, $(3 \cdot 3 \cdot 3 = 27)$: 1, 8, 27, . . .

MATH FORMULAS THAT YOU SHOULD BE FAMILIAR WITH

Triangle	Perimeter $= s_1 + s_2 + s_3$
	Area $= \frac{1}{2}bh$
Square	Perimeter $= 4s$
	Area $= s \cdot s$, or s^2
Rectangle	Perimeter $= 2(b + h)$, or $2b + 2h$
	Area $= bh$, or lw
Parallelogram	Perimeter $= 2(l + w)$, or $2l + 2w$
	Area $= bh$
Trapezoid	Perimeter $= b_1 + b_2 + s_1 + s_2$
	Area $= \frac{1}{2}h(b_1 + b_2)$, or $h\left(\dfrac{b_1 + b_2}{2}\right)$

Circle	Circumference $= 2\pi r$, or πd
	Area $= \pi r^2$

Pythagorean theorem (for right triangles) $a^2 + b^2 = c^2$

The sum of the squares of the legs of a right triangle equals the square of the hypotenuse.

Cube	Volume $= s \cdot s \cdot s = s^3$
	Surface area $= s \cdot s \cdot 6$
Rectangular Prism	Volume $= l \cdot w \cdot h$
	Surface area $= 2(lw) + 2(lh) + 2(wh)$

IMPORTANT EQUIVALENTS THAT CAN SAVE YOU TIME

Memorizing the following can eliminate unnecessary computations:

$\frac{1}{100} = .01 = 1\%$

$\frac{1}{10} = .1 = 10\%$

$\frac{1}{5} = \frac{2}{10} = .2 = .20 = 20\%$

$\frac{3}{10} = .3 = .30 = 30\%$

$\frac{2}{5} = \frac{4}{10} = .4 = .40 = 40\%$

$\frac{1}{2} = \frac{5}{10} = .5 = .50 = 50\%$

$\frac{3}{5} = \frac{6}{10} = .6 = .60 = 60\%$

$\frac{7}{10} = .7 = .70 = 70\%$

$\frac{4}{5} = \frac{8}{10} = .8 = .80 = 80\%$

$\frac{9}{10} = .9 = .90 = 90\%$

$\frac{1}{4} = \frac{25}{100} = .25 = 25\%$

$\frac{3}{4} = \frac{75}{100} = .75 = 75\%$

$\frac{1}{3} = .33\frac{1}{3} = 33\frac{1}{3}\%$

$\frac{2}{3} = .66\frac{2}{3} = 66\frac{2}{3}\%$

$\frac{1}{8} = .125 = .12\frac{1}{2} = 12\frac{1}{2}\%$

$\frac{3}{8} = .375 = .37\frac{1}{2} = 37\frac{1}{2}\%$

$\frac{5}{8} = .625 = .62\frac{1}{2} = 62\frac{1}{2}\%$

$\frac{7}{8} = .875 = .87\frac{1}{2} = 87\frac{1}{2}\%$

$\frac{1}{6} = .16\frac{2}{3} = 16\frac{2}{3}\%$

$\frac{5}{6} = .83\frac{1}{3} = 83\frac{1}{3}\%$

$1 = 1.00 = 100\%$

$2 = 2.00 = 200\%$

$3\frac{1}{2} = 3.5 = 3.50 = 350\%$

MEASURES

Customary System, or English System

Length
   12 inches (in) = 1 foot (ft)
   3 feet = 1 yard (yd)
   36 inches = 1 yard
   1760 yards = 1 mile (mi)
   5280 feet = 1 mile

Area
144 square inches (sq in) = 1 square foot (sq ft)
9 square feet = 1 square yard (sq yd)

Weight
16 ounces (oz) = 1 pound (lb)
2000 pounds = 1 ton (T)

Capacity
2 cups = 1 pint (pt)
2 pints = 1 quart (qt)
4 quarts = 1 gallon (gal)
4 pecks = 1 bushel

Time
365 days = 1 year
52 weeks = 1 year
10 years = 1 decade
100 years = 1 century

Metric System, or The International System of Units
(SI, *Le Système International d'Unités*)

Length—meter
Kilometer (km) = 1000 meters (m)
Hectometer (hm) = 100 meters
Dekameter (dam) = 10 meters

Meter
10 decimeters (dm) = 1 meter
100 centimeters (cm) = 1 meter
1000 millimeters (mm) = 1 meter

Volume—liter
Common measures
1000 milliliters (ml, or mL) = 1 liter (l, or L)
1000 liters = 1 kiloliter (kl, or kL)

Mass—gram
Common measures
1000 milligrams (mg) = 1 gram (g)
1000 grams = 1 kilogram (kg)
1000 kilograms = 1 metric ton (t)

WORDS AND PHRASES THAT CAN BE HELPFUL IN SOLVING PROBLEMS

Words that signal an operation:

ADDITION

- Sum
- Total
- Plus
- Increase
- More than
- Greater than

MULTIPLICATION

- Of
- Product
- Times
- At (Sometimes)
- Total (Sometimes)

SUBTRACTION

- Difference
- Less
- Decreased
- Reduced
- Fewer
- Have left

DIVISION

- Quotient
- Divisor
- Dividend
- Ratio
- Parts

GEOMETRY TERMS AND BASIC INFORMATION

Angles

Vertical angles—Formed by two intersecting lines, across from each other, always equal

Adjacent angles—Next to each other, share a common side and vertex

Right angle—Measures 90 degrees

Obtuse angle—Greater than 90 degrees

Acute angle—Less than 90 degrees

Straight angle, or line—Measures 180 degrees

Angle bisector—Divides an angle into two equal angles

Supplementary angles—Two angles whose total is 180 degrees

Complementary angles—Two angles whose total is 90 degrees

Lines

Two points determine a line

Parallel lines—Never meet

Perpendicular lines—Meet at right angles

Polygons

Polygon—A many-sided (more than two sides) closed figure
Regular polygon—A polygon with all sides and all angles equal
Triangle—Three-sided polygon; the interior angles total 180 degrees
    Equilateral triangle—All sides equal
    Isosceles triangle—Two sides equal
    Scalene triangle—All sides of different lengths
    Right triangle—A triangle containing a right angle
In a triangle—Angles opposite equal sides are equal
In a triangle—The longest side is across from the largest angle, and the shortest side is across from the smallest angle
In a triangle—The sum of any two sides of a triangle is larger than the third side
In a triangle—An exterior angle is equal to the sum of the remote two angles
Median of a triangle—A line segment that connects the vertex and the midpoint of the opposite side
Quadrilateral—Four-sided polygon; the interior angles total 360 degrees
    Parallelogram—A quadrilateral with opposite sides parallel
      Rectangle—A parallelogram with all right angles
      Rhombus—A parallelogram with equal sides
      Square—A parallelogram with equal sides and all right angles
    Trapezoid—A quadrilateral with two parallel sides
Pentagon—A five-sided polygon
Hexagon—A six-sided polygon
Octagon—An eight-sided polygon

Circles

Radius of a circle—A line segment from the center of the circle to the circle itself
Diameter of a circle—A line segment that starts and ends on the circle and goes through the center
Chord—A line segment that starts and ends on the circle
Arc—A part of the circle
Circle—Composed of 360°

INTRODUCTION TO ANALYTICAL ABILITY

There are two Analytical Ability sections on the GRE, each 30 minutes in length. The two sections contain a total of about 50 questions (25 questions each). The Analytical Ability sections consist of two basic types of questions: Analytical Reasoning and Logical Reasoning. The total of the two sections is scaled from 200 to 800, with an average score of about 500.

Ability Tested

You will need to draw reasonable conclusions from complex statements or situations.

Basic Skills Necessary

No knowledge of formal logic is required. Familiarity with constructing logical and spatial relationships from a given situation is valuable.

Directions and Sample Questions

No standard set of directions characterizes Analytical Ability. However, here are some common question types to consider.

The general directions are: The following questions or group of questions are based on a passage or set of statements. Choose the best answer for each question and blacken the corresponding space on your answer sheet. It may be helpful to draw rough diagrams or simple charts in attempting to answer these questions.

Logical Reasoning From a Statement or Argument

United States dependence on foreign oil has tended to overshadow the beneficial effects of gasoline-powered machines on our society. More than ever before, the American automobile allows us to enjoy the many pleasures this country offers.

1. This argument would be weakened by pointing out that

   I. smog generated by automobiles is not a pleasure
  II. at the turn of the century, Americans rarely ventured far from home
 III. inflation helped by rising oil prices has made many automobiles virtually unaffordable

    (A) I and III   (D) I and II
    (B) II and III   (E) I, II, and III
    (C) II only

2. The argument above is based upon which of the following assumptions?

I. Many American pleasures cannot be walked to.
II. The automobile is the most significant gasoline-powered machine.
III. U.S. dependence upon foreign oil is beneficial.

(A) I only
(B) II only
(C) III only
(D) I and II
(E) I and III

For this problem type, skim the questions before reading the passage, in order to see which aspects of the passage you should focus on. Then read the passage *actively,* underlining two or three important words or phrases. Answer the questions using only the information expressed or implied in the passage.

Answers and Explanations

1. (A), I and III. This problem combines roman numeral choices and letter choices; it's a kind of *multiple-multiple choice.* Work from the numeral choices, asking yourself whether each is *true* or *false.* Statement I is true—it would weaken the argument for pleasure. Eliminate (C) and (B) because they do not contain I. II is false—it would *not* weaken the argument for driving as a modern pleasure. Eliminate (D) and (E) because both contain II. III is true—it would weaken the argument for automobiles as a source of pleasure. Choose (A), the only remaining possibility.

2. (D), I and II. I is true (eliminate (B) and (C) because neither contains I). II is true (eliminate (A) and (E)). Choose (D) because it's the only choice left. Notice that by working from the roman numerals in this way, you did not need to spend time considering III.

Analytical Reasoning

Seven people are seated in the front row of a theater. There is a woman at either end. A man is seated in the middle of the group. No man is seated next to another man. The man in the middle is flanked by women. So are two other men.

Using this information, answer the following questions.

1. There are how many women seated in the row?
(A) 2   (B) 4   (C) 6   (D) 2 or 4   (E) 4 or 6

2. The man in the middle has other men
   - (A) to his right
   - (B) to his left
   - (C) to his right and to his left
   - (D) at either end
   - (E) nowhere in the row

3. *Without violating the given information,* wishing to change seats with a man, a woman must
   - (A) be initially seated at either end
   - (B) remain where she is
   - (C) switch with the man in the middle
   - (D) ask another woman to also switch her seat
   - (E) add more people to the row

Answers and Explanations

For this type of question, *draw* diagrams or make charts to gather information for your answers. Even a partial chart will help more than no chart at all. For this problem, we first number seven spaces.

1	2	3	4	5	6	7

Then place a woman at either end.

1	2	3	4	5	6	7
W						W

Then place a man in the middle.

1	2	3	4	5	6	7
W			M			W

Then flank the middle man with women.

1	2	3	4	5	6	7
W		W	M	W		W

Then add two more men who are also flanked by women.

1	2	3	4	5	6	7
W	M	W	M	W	M	W

Notice that no man is seated next to another man. The chart is complete. Now you may answer the questions as follows:

1. (B) Simply refer to your chart.
2. (C) Simply refer to your chart.
3. (B) Every choice except (B) violates the original information.

Some Analytical Reasoning problems are variations of the types illustrated thus far. These variations occur in the Practice Tests in this book and are fully explained in the Answers section. *Review them carefully*.

A PATTERNED PLAN OF ATTACK

Analytical Ability

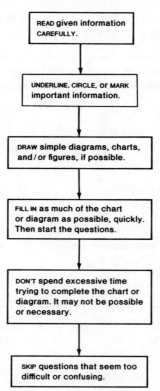

Part III: Practice-Review-Analyze-Practice

Two Full-Length Practice Tests

This section contains two full-length practice simulation GREs. The practice tests are followed by complete answers, explanations, and analysis techniques. The format, levels of difficulty, question structure, and number of questions are similar to those on the actual GRE. The actual GRE is copyrighted and may not be duplicated and these questions are not taken directly from the actual tests.

When taking these exams, try to simulate the test conditions by following the time allotments carefully. Remember the total testing time for each practice test is approximately 3½ hours and each section is 30 minutes.

Part III. Erie Union Review and Analysis

PRACTICE TEST 1

Section I: Verbal Ability—30 Minutes; 39 Questions
Section II: Verbal Ability—30 Minutes; 38 Questions
Section III: Quantitative Ability—30 Minutes; 30 Questions
Section IV: Quantitative Ability—30 Minutes; 30 Questions
Section V: Analytical Ability—30 Minutes; 25 Questions
Section VI: Analytical Ability—30 Minutes; 25 Questions
Section VII: Quantitative Ability—30 Minutes; 30 Questions

ANSWER SHEET FOR PRACTICE TEST 1
(Remove This Sheet and Use It to Mark Your Answers)

SECTION I

1 Ⓐ Ⓑ Ⓒ Ⓓ Ⓔ	31 Ⓐ Ⓑ Ⓒ Ⓓ Ⓔ
2 Ⓐ Ⓑ Ⓒ Ⓓ Ⓔ	32 Ⓐ Ⓑ Ⓒ Ⓓ Ⓔ
3 Ⓐ Ⓑ Ⓒ Ⓓ Ⓔ	33 Ⓐ Ⓑ Ⓒ Ⓓ Ⓔ
4 Ⓐ Ⓑ Ⓒ Ⓓ Ⓔ	34 Ⓐ Ⓑ Ⓒ Ⓓ Ⓔ
5 Ⓐ Ⓑ Ⓒ Ⓓ Ⓔ	35 Ⓐ Ⓑ Ⓒ Ⓓ Ⓔ
6 Ⓐ Ⓑ Ⓒ Ⓓ Ⓔ	36 Ⓐ Ⓑ Ⓒ Ⓓ Ⓔ
7 Ⓐ Ⓑ Ⓒ Ⓓ Ⓔ	37 Ⓐ Ⓑ Ⓒ Ⓓ Ⓔ
8 Ⓐ Ⓑ Ⓒ Ⓓ Ⓔ	38 Ⓐ Ⓑ Ⓒ Ⓓ Ⓔ
9 Ⓐ Ⓑ Ⓒ Ⓓ Ⓔ	39 Ⓐ Ⓑ Ⓒ Ⓓ Ⓔ
10 Ⓐ Ⓑ Ⓒ Ⓓ Ⓔ	
11 Ⓐ Ⓑ Ⓒ Ⓓ Ⓔ	
12 Ⓐ Ⓑ Ⓒ Ⓓ Ⓔ	
13 Ⓐ Ⓑ Ⓒ Ⓓ Ⓔ	
14 Ⓐ Ⓑ Ⓒ Ⓓ Ⓔ	
15 Ⓐ Ⓑ Ⓒ Ⓓ Ⓔ	
16 Ⓐ Ⓑ Ⓒ Ⓓ Ⓔ	
17 Ⓐ Ⓑ Ⓒ Ⓓ Ⓔ	
18 Ⓐ Ⓑ Ⓒ Ⓓ Ⓔ	
19 Ⓐ Ⓑ Ⓒ Ⓓ Ⓔ	
20 Ⓐ Ⓑ Ⓒ Ⓓ Ⓔ	
21 Ⓐ Ⓑ Ⓒ Ⓓ Ⓔ	
22 Ⓐ Ⓑ Ⓒ Ⓓ Ⓔ	
23 Ⓐ Ⓑ Ⓒ Ⓓ Ⓔ	
24 Ⓐ Ⓑ Ⓒ Ⓓ Ⓔ	
25 Ⓐ Ⓑ Ⓒ Ⓓ Ⓔ	
26 Ⓐ Ⓑ Ⓒ Ⓓ Ⓔ	
27 Ⓐ Ⓑ Ⓒ Ⓓ Ⓔ	
28 Ⓐ Ⓑ Ⓒ Ⓓ Ⓔ	
29 Ⓐ Ⓑ Ⓒ Ⓓ Ⓔ	
30 Ⓐ Ⓑ Ⓒ Ⓓ Ⓔ	

SECTION II

1 Ⓐ Ⓑ Ⓒ Ⓓ Ⓔ	31 Ⓐ Ⓑ Ⓒ Ⓓ Ⓔ
2 Ⓐ Ⓑ Ⓒ Ⓓ Ⓔ	32 Ⓐ Ⓑ Ⓒ Ⓓ Ⓔ
3 Ⓐ Ⓑ Ⓒ Ⓓ Ⓔ	33 Ⓐ Ⓑ Ⓒ Ⓓ Ⓔ
4 Ⓐ Ⓑ Ⓒ Ⓓ Ⓔ	34 Ⓐ Ⓑ Ⓒ Ⓓ Ⓔ
5 Ⓐ Ⓑ Ⓒ Ⓓ Ⓔ	35 Ⓐ Ⓑ Ⓒ Ⓓ Ⓔ
6 Ⓐ Ⓑ Ⓒ Ⓓ Ⓔ	36 Ⓐ Ⓑ Ⓒ Ⓓ Ⓔ
7 Ⓐ Ⓑ Ⓒ Ⓓ Ⓔ	37 Ⓐ Ⓑ Ⓒ Ⓓ Ⓔ
8 Ⓐ Ⓑ Ⓒ Ⓓ Ⓔ	38 Ⓐ Ⓑ Ⓒ Ⓓ Ⓔ
9 Ⓐ Ⓑ Ⓒ Ⓓ Ⓔ	
10 Ⓐ Ⓑ Ⓒ Ⓓ Ⓔ	
11 Ⓐ Ⓑ Ⓒ Ⓓ Ⓔ	
12 Ⓐ Ⓑ Ⓒ Ⓓ Ⓔ	
13 Ⓐ Ⓑ Ⓒ Ⓓ Ⓔ	
14 Ⓐ Ⓑ Ⓒ Ⓓ Ⓔ	
15 Ⓐ Ⓑ Ⓒ Ⓓ Ⓔ	
16 Ⓐ Ⓑ Ⓒ Ⓓ Ⓔ	
17 Ⓐ Ⓑ Ⓒ Ⓓ Ⓔ	
18 Ⓐ Ⓑ Ⓒ Ⓓ Ⓔ	
19 Ⓐ Ⓑ Ⓒ Ⓓ Ⓔ	
20 Ⓐ Ⓑ Ⓒ Ⓓ Ⓔ	
21 Ⓐ Ⓑ Ⓒ Ⓓ Ⓔ	
22 Ⓐ Ⓑ Ⓒ Ⓓ Ⓔ	
23 Ⓐ Ⓑ Ⓒ Ⓓ Ⓔ	
24 Ⓐ Ⓑ Ⓒ Ⓓ Ⓔ	
25 Ⓐ Ⓑ Ⓒ Ⓓ Ⓔ	
26 Ⓐ Ⓑ Ⓒ Ⓓ Ⓔ	
27 Ⓐ Ⓑ Ⓒ Ⓓ Ⓔ	
28 Ⓐ Ⓑ Ⓒ Ⓓ Ⓔ	
29 Ⓐ Ⓑ Ⓒ Ⓓ Ⓔ	
30 Ⓐ Ⓑ Ⓒ Ⓓ Ⓔ	

ANSWER SHEET FOR PRACTICE TEST 1
(Remove This Sheet and Use It to Mark Your Answers)

SECTION III

1 Ⓐ Ⓑ Ⓒ Ⓓ Ⓔ
2 Ⓐ Ⓑ Ⓒ Ⓓ Ⓔ
3 Ⓐ Ⓑ Ⓒ Ⓓ Ⓔ
4 Ⓐ Ⓑ Ⓒ Ⓓ Ⓔ
5 Ⓐ Ⓑ Ⓒ Ⓓ Ⓔ

6 Ⓐ Ⓑ Ⓒ Ⓓ Ⓔ
7 Ⓐ Ⓑ Ⓒ Ⓓ Ⓔ
8 Ⓐ Ⓑ Ⓒ Ⓓ Ⓔ
9 Ⓐ Ⓑ Ⓒ Ⓓ Ⓔ
10 Ⓐ Ⓑ Ⓒ Ⓓ Ⓔ

11 Ⓐ Ⓑ Ⓒ Ⓓ Ⓔ
12 Ⓐ Ⓑ Ⓒ Ⓓ Ⓔ
13 Ⓐ Ⓑ Ⓒ Ⓓ Ⓔ
14 Ⓐ Ⓑ Ⓒ Ⓓ Ⓔ
15 Ⓐ Ⓑ Ⓒ Ⓓ Ⓔ

16 Ⓐ Ⓑ Ⓒ Ⓓ Ⓔ
17 Ⓐ Ⓑ Ⓒ Ⓓ Ⓔ
18 Ⓐ Ⓑ Ⓒ Ⓓ Ⓔ
19 Ⓐ Ⓑ Ⓒ Ⓓ Ⓔ
20 Ⓐ Ⓑ Ⓒ Ⓓ Ⓔ

21 Ⓐ Ⓑ Ⓒ Ⓓ Ⓔ
22 Ⓐ Ⓑ Ⓒ Ⓓ Ⓔ
23 Ⓐ Ⓑ Ⓒ Ⓓ Ⓔ
24 Ⓐ Ⓑ Ⓒ Ⓓ Ⓔ
25 Ⓐ Ⓑ Ⓒ Ⓓ Ⓔ

26 Ⓐ Ⓑ Ⓒ Ⓓ Ⓔ
27 Ⓐ Ⓑ Ⓒ Ⓓ Ⓔ
28 Ⓐ Ⓑ Ⓒ Ⓓ Ⓔ
29 Ⓐ Ⓑ Ⓒ Ⓓ Ⓔ
30 Ⓐ Ⓑ Ⓒ Ⓓ Ⓔ

SECTION IV

1 Ⓐ Ⓑ Ⓒ Ⓓ Ⓔ
2 Ⓐ Ⓑ Ⓒ Ⓓ Ⓔ
3 Ⓐ Ⓑ Ⓒ Ⓓ Ⓔ
4 Ⓐ Ⓑ Ⓒ Ⓓ Ⓔ
5 Ⓐ Ⓑ Ⓒ Ⓓ Ⓔ

6 Ⓐ Ⓑ Ⓒ Ⓓ Ⓔ
7 Ⓐ Ⓑ Ⓒ Ⓓ Ⓔ
8 Ⓐ Ⓑ Ⓒ Ⓓ Ⓔ
9 Ⓐ Ⓑ Ⓒ Ⓓ Ⓔ
10 Ⓐ Ⓑ Ⓒ Ⓓ Ⓔ

11 Ⓐ Ⓑ Ⓒ Ⓓ Ⓔ
12 Ⓐ Ⓑ Ⓒ Ⓓ Ⓔ
13 Ⓐ Ⓑ Ⓒ Ⓓ Ⓔ
14 Ⓐ Ⓑ Ⓒ Ⓓ Ⓔ
15 Ⓐ Ⓑ Ⓒ Ⓓ Ⓔ

16 Ⓐ Ⓑ Ⓒ Ⓓ Ⓔ
17 Ⓐ Ⓑ Ⓒ Ⓓ Ⓔ
18 Ⓐ Ⓑ Ⓒ Ⓓ Ⓔ
19 Ⓐ Ⓑ Ⓒ Ⓓ Ⓔ
20 Ⓐ Ⓑ Ⓒ Ⓓ Ⓔ

21 Ⓐ Ⓑ Ⓒ Ⓓ Ⓔ
22 Ⓐ Ⓑ Ⓒ Ⓓ Ⓔ
23 Ⓐ Ⓑ Ⓒ Ⓓ Ⓔ
24 Ⓐ Ⓑ Ⓒ Ⓓ Ⓔ
25 Ⓐ Ⓑ Ⓒ Ⓓ Ⓔ

26 Ⓐ Ⓑ Ⓒ Ⓓ Ⓔ
27 Ⓐ Ⓑ Ⓒ Ⓓ Ⓔ
28 Ⓐ Ⓑ Ⓒ Ⓓ Ⓔ
29 Ⓐ Ⓑ Ⓒ Ⓓ Ⓔ
30 Ⓐ Ⓑ Ⓒ Ⓓ Ⓔ

SECTION V

1 Ⓐ Ⓑ Ⓒ Ⓓ Ⓔ
2 Ⓐ Ⓑ Ⓒ Ⓓ Ⓔ
3 Ⓐ Ⓑ Ⓒ Ⓓ Ⓔ
4 Ⓐ Ⓑ Ⓒ Ⓓ Ⓔ
5 Ⓐ Ⓑ Ⓒ Ⓓ Ⓔ

6 Ⓐ Ⓑ Ⓒ Ⓓ Ⓔ
7 Ⓐ Ⓑ Ⓒ Ⓓ Ⓔ
8 Ⓐ Ⓑ Ⓒ Ⓓ Ⓔ
9 Ⓐ Ⓑ Ⓒ Ⓓ Ⓔ
10 Ⓐ Ⓑ Ⓒ Ⓓ Ⓔ

11 Ⓐ Ⓑ Ⓒ Ⓓ Ⓔ
12 Ⓐ Ⓑ Ⓒ Ⓓ Ⓔ
13 Ⓐ Ⓑ Ⓒ Ⓓ Ⓔ
14 Ⓐ Ⓑ Ⓒ Ⓓ Ⓔ
15 Ⓐ Ⓑ Ⓒ Ⓓ Ⓔ

16 Ⓐ Ⓑ Ⓒ Ⓓ Ⓔ
17 Ⓐ Ⓑ Ⓒ Ⓓ Ⓔ
18 Ⓐ Ⓑ Ⓒ Ⓓ Ⓔ
19 Ⓐ Ⓑ Ⓒ Ⓓ Ⓔ
20 Ⓐ Ⓑ Ⓒ Ⓓ Ⓔ

21 Ⓐ Ⓑ Ⓒ Ⓓ Ⓔ
22 Ⓐ Ⓑ Ⓒ Ⓓ Ⓔ
23 Ⓐ Ⓑ Ⓒ Ⓓ Ⓔ
24 Ⓐ Ⓑ Ⓒ Ⓓ Ⓔ
25 Ⓐ Ⓑ Ⓒ Ⓓ Ⓔ

ANSWER SHEET FOR PRACTICE TEST 1
(Remove This Sheet and Use It to Mark Your Answers)

SECTION VI   SECTION VII

SECTION VI	SECTION VII
1 Ⓐ Ⓑ Ⓒ Ⓓ Ⓔ	1 Ⓐ Ⓑ Ⓒ Ⓓ Ⓔ
2 Ⓐ Ⓑ Ⓒ Ⓓ Ⓔ	2 Ⓐ Ⓑ Ⓒ Ⓓ Ⓔ
3 Ⓐ Ⓑ Ⓒ Ⓓ Ⓔ	3 Ⓐ Ⓑ Ⓒ Ⓓ Ⓔ
4 Ⓐ Ⓑ Ⓒ Ⓓ Ⓔ	4 Ⓐ Ⓑ Ⓒ Ⓓ Ⓔ
5 Ⓐ Ⓑ Ⓒ Ⓓ Ⓔ	5 Ⓐ Ⓑ Ⓒ Ⓓ Ⓔ
6 Ⓐ Ⓑ Ⓒ Ⓓ Ⓔ	6 Ⓐ Ⓑ Ⓒ Ⓓ Ⓔ
7 Ⓐ Ⓑ Ⓒ Ⓓ Ⓔ	7 Ⓐ Ⓑ Ⓒ Ⓓ Ⓔ
8 Ⓐ Ⓑ Ⓒ Ⓓ Ⓔ	8 Ⓐ Ⓑ Ⓒ Ⓓ Ⓔ
9 Ⓐ Ⓑ Ⓒ Ⓓ Ⓔ	9 Ⓐ Ⓑ Ⓒ Ⓓ Ⓔ
10 Ⓐ Ⓑ Ⓒ Ⓓ Ⓔ	10 Ⓐ Ⓑ Ⓒ Ⓓ Ⓔ
11 Ⓐ Ⓑ Ⓒ Ⓓ Ⓔ	11 Ⓐ Ⓑ Ⓒ Ⓓ Ⓔ
12 Ⓐ Ⓑ Ⓒ Ⓓ Ⓔ	12 Ⓐ Ⓑ Ⓒ Ⓓ Ⓔ
13 Ⓐ Ⓑ Ⓒ Ⓓ Ⓔ	13 Ⓐ Ⓑ Ⓒ Ⓓ Ⓔ
14 Ⓐ Ⓑ Ⓒ Ⓓ Ⓔ	14 Ⓐ Ⓑ Ⓒ Ⓓ Ⓔ
15 Ⓐ Ⓑ Ⓒ Ⓓ Ⓔ	15 Ⓐ Ⓑ Ⓒ Ⓓ Ⓔ
16 Ⓐ Ⓑ Ⓒ Ⓓ Ⓔ	16 Ⓐ Ⓑ Ⓒ Ⓓ Ⓔ
17 Ⓐ Ⓑ Ⓒ Ⓓ Ⓔ	17 Ⓐ Ⓑ Ⓒ Ⓓ Ⓔ
18 Ⓐ Ⓑ Ⓒ Ⓓ Ⓔ	18 Ⓐ Ⓑ Ⓒ Ⓓ Ⓔ
19 Ⓐ Ⓑ Ⓒ Ⓓ Ⓔ	19 Ⓐ Ⓑ Ⓒ Ⓓ Ⓔ
20 Ⓐ Ⓑ Ⓒ Ⓓ Ⓔ	20 Ⓐ Ⓑ Ⓒ Ⓓ Ⓔ
21 Ⓐ Ⓑ Ⓒ Ⓓ Ⓔ	21 Ⓐ Ⓑ Ⓒ Ⓓ Ⓔ
22 Ⓐ Ⓑ Ⓒ Ⓓ Ⓔ	22 Ⓐ Ⓑ Ⓒ Ⓓ Ⓔ
23 Ⓐ Ⓑ Ⓒ Ⓓ Ⓔ	23 Ⓐ Ⓑ Ⓒ Ⓓ Ⓔ
24 Ⓐ Ⓑ Ⓒ Ⓓ Ⓔ	24 Ⓐ Ⓑ Ⓒ Ⓓ Ⓔ
25 Ⓐ Ⓑ Ⓒ Ⓓ Ⓔ	25 Ⓐ Ⓑ Ⓒ Ⓓ Ⓔ
	26 Ⓐ Ⓑ Ⓒ Ⓓ Ⓔ
	27 Ⓐ Ⓑ Ⓒ Ⓓ Ⓔ
	28 Ⓐ Ⓑ Ⓒ Ⓓ Ⓔ
	29 Ⓐ Ⓑ Ⓒ Ⓓ Ⓔ
	30 Ⓐ Ⓑ Ⓒ Ⓓ Ⓔ

SECTION I: VERBAL ABILITY

Time: 30 Minutes
39 Questions

In this section, choose the best answer for each question and blacken the corresponding space on the answer sheet.

Sentence Completion

DIRECTIONS

Each blank in the following sentences indicates that something has been omitted. Considering the lettered words beneath the sentence, choose the word or set of words that best fits the whole sentence.

1. Although the thirteen-year-old boys grew _____under the teacher's new discipline policy, the girls seemed _____by it.
   - (A) anxious . . . hostile
   - (B) argumentative . . . frustrated
   - (C) restive . . . unperturbed
   - (D) remorseful . . . ingenuous
   - (E) taciturn . . . reticent

2. The New Testament was not only written in the Greek language, but ideas derived from Greek philosophy were _____ in many parts of it.
   - (A) altered
   - (B) criticized
   - (C) incorporated
   - (D) nullified
   - (E) translated

3. President Eisenhower was widely_____for refusing to _____ the excesses of the loathed Senator McCarthy.
   - (A) applauded . . . implement
   - (B) accused . . . prevent
   - (C) criticized . . . curb
   - (D) condemned . . . promote
   - (E) supported . . . ostracize

4. During the *Pax Romana* the _____ of material prosperity in the ancient world was reached.
   - (A) simplification
   - (B) stratification
   - (C) majority
   - (D) depth
   - (E) pinnacle

5. Society and civilization have reached very much the same point that was reached eighteen centuries earlier; it is strongly _____ that the only real difference may be that they have held off using nuclear weapons for a slightly longer time, _____ the lesson of the past to some extent.
   - (A) asserted . . . clouding
   - (B) believed . . . knocking
   - (C) intended . . . enhancing
   - (D) implied . . . heeding
   - (E) expounded . . . juxtaposing

6. *Rite of Passage* is a good novel by any standards; _____, it should rank high on any list of science fiction.
   - (A) consistently
   - (B) invariably
   - (C) lingeringly
   - (D) consequently
   - (E) fortunately

7. Because of great _____, large numbers, and an advanced division of labor, a number of scholars see a growth of _____ relationships and consequent impersonality.
   - (A) homogeneity . . . lasting
   - (B) societies . . . sexual
   - (C) heterogeneity . . . segmental
   - (D) masses . . . unwieldy
   - (E) leaders . . . powerful

8. When finishing an essay, do not end with a(n) _____ for not having said anything, or with a(n) _____ statement about the unfairly small time period.
   - (A) fluorish . . . unwarranted
   - (B) ellipsis . . . analogical
   - (C) apology . . . indignant
   - (D) smirk . . . silly
   - (E) pretense . . . political

Analogies

DIRECTIONS

In each question below, you are given a related pair of words or phrases. Select the lettered pair that *best* expresses a relationship similar to that in the original pair of words.

9. NAP : FABRIC : :
   - (A) flannel : shirt
   - (B) rough : sandpaper
   - (C) fur : dog
   - (D) smooth : satin
   - (E) yardage : cloth

10. AMBIGUOUS : CLEAR : :
    (A) many : few
    (B) singular : plural
    (C) synthetic : real
    (D) ambivalent : dexterity
    (E) indefinite : definite

11. COHERENCE : DISINTEGRATE : :
    (A) loyalty : betray
    (B) unity : harmony
    (C) brotherhood : fraternity
    (D) partnership : dissolve
    (E) similarity : differ

12. BESTIAL : BRUTISH : :
    (A) monster : gorilla
    (B) frivolous : trivial
    (C) heavy : heavier
    (D) smile : smirk
    (E) mediate : reconcile

13. SYMPATHETIC : OBDURATE : :
    (A) bathos : sentiment
    (B) verve : energy
    (C) impassioned : frigid
    (D) poignant : acute
    (E) torpor : insouciance

14. PHOTOSYNTHESIS : OXYGEN : :
    (A) camera : photograph
    (B) combustion : heat
    (C) heat : boiling
    (D) plant : light
    (E) inhalation : air

15. NOSTALGIA : MEMORY : :
    (A) antipathy : emotions
    (B) lethargy : ennui
    (C) past : present
    (D) music : prom
    (E) violins : romance

16. ANARCHY : OLIGARCHY : :
    (A) mob : meeting
    (B) violent : nonviolent
    (C) guided : misguided
    (D) disorder : order
    (E) hierarchy : monarchy

17. BANTER : PERSIFLAGE : :
    (A) similarity : analogy
    (B) ambiguity : anticlimax
    (C) simile : euphemism
    (D) talk : poetry
    (E) cliché : epigram

Reading Comprehension

DIRECTIONS

Questions follow each of the passages below. Using only the stated or implied information in each passage, answer the questions.

Today the study of language in our schools is somewhat confused. It is the most traditional of scholastic subjects being taught in a time when many of our traditions no longer fit our needs. You to whom these pages are addressed speak English and are therefore in a worse case than any other literate people.

People pondering the origin of language for the first time usually arrive at the conclusion that it developed gradually as a system of conventionalized grunts, hisses, and cries and must have been a very simple affair in the beginning. But when we observe the language behavior of what we regard as primitive cultures, we find it strikingly elaborate and complicated. Stefansson, the explorer, said that "in order to get along reasonably well an Eskimo must have at the tip of his tongue a vocabulary of more than 10,000 words, much larger than the active vocabulary of an average businessman who speaks English. Moreover these Eskimo words are far more highly inflected than those of any of the well-known European languages, for a single noun can be spoken or written in several hundred different forms, each having a precise meaning different from that of any other. The forms of the verbs are even more numerous. The Eskimo language is, therefore, one of the most difficult in the world to learn, with the result that almost no traders or explorers have even tried to learn it. Consequently there has grown up, in intercourse between Eskimos and whites, a jargon similar to the pidgin English used in China, with a vocabulary of from 300 to 600 uninflected words, most of them derived from Eskimo but some derived from English, Danish, Spanish, Hawaiian and other languages. It is this jargon which is usually referred to by travelers as 'the Eskimo language.' "[1] And Professor Thalbitzer of Copenhagen, who did take the trouble to learn Eskimo, seems to endorse the explorer's view when he writes: "The language is polysynthetic. The grammar is extremely rich in flexional forms, the conjugation of a common verb being served by about 350 suffixes, equivalent to personal pronouns and verb endings. For the declension of a noun there are 150 suffixes (for dual and plural, local cases, and possessive flexion). The demonstrative pronouns have a separate flexion. The derivative endings effective in the vocabulary and the construction of sentences or sentence-like words amount to at least 250. Notwithstanding all these constructive peculiarities, the grammatical and synthetic system is remarkably concise and, in its own way, logical."[2]

[1] *The Encyclopaedia Britannica,* Fourteenth Edition, Vol. 8, p. 709.
[2] Ibid., p. 707.

18. The size of the Eskimo language spoken by most whites is
    (A) spoken in England, Denmark, Spain, and Hawaii
    (B) less than the size of the language spoken by Eskimos
    (C) highly inflected
    (D) inestimable
    (E) irrelevant

19. Some of the evidence about language in the passage is taken from the observations of
    (A) linguists   (D) an explorer
    (B) Eskimos   (E) primitive cultures
    (C) businessmen

20. According to the passage, the language of primitive cultures was
    (A) nonexistent
    (B) only spoken by Eskimos
    (C) monosyllabic
    (D) simpleminded
    (E) elaborate and complicated

21. The author's overall point is that
    (A) primitive languages may be large, complex, and complicated
    (B) primitive languages may be large, complex, and logical
    (C) primitive languages may be large, old, and logical
    (D) primitive languages may be similar to pidgin English
    (E) primitive languages tell us little about the origin of language

Each method of counting bacteria has advantages and disadvantages; none is 100 percent accurate. Cell counts may be made with a counting chamber, a slide marked with a grid to facilitate counting of cells and to determine the volume of liquid in the area counted. Counts are made under a microscope and calculations made to determine the number of cells per ml of the original culture. Electronic cell counters can be used to count cells suspended in a liquid medium which passes through a hole small enough to allow the passage of only one bacterial cell at a time. The counter actually measures the rise in electric resistance of the liquid each time a cell passes through the hole. Smear counts are similar to cell counts: a known volume of culture is spread over a known area (1 cm^2) of a slide and then stained. Counts are made from several microscope fields, and calculations are made. In membrane filter counts a known volume of a culture is passed through a filter, which is then examined microscopically for cells. The advantage of cell counts, smear counts, and membrane filter counts is that they are quickly accomplished with little complicated equipment; however, both living and dead cells are counted.

The serial-dilution method involves the making of a series of dilutions, usually by a factor of 10, into a nutrient medium. The highest dilution producing growth gives a rough indication of the population of the original culture; for example, if the highest dilution to produce growth is the 1:100 dilution, the original culture had between 100 and 1,000 cells per ml.

Plate counts are made by making serial dilutions (usually in sterile tap water or an isotonic solution) of the original culture. Samples of known volume of the dilutions are transferred to petri dishes and mixed with nutrient agar. After a suitable incubation period the colonies on the plates with between 30 and 300 colonies are counted. Because each colony is assumed to have arisen from a single cell, calculations can be made to determine the original population size. Plate counts have the advantage of not including dead cells, and they can be used when the population is so low as to make other methods impractical, but they require more time than direct counts, and they detect only those organisms that can grow under the conditions of incubation; the development of one colony from more than one cell is also a source of error. In connection with this technique a modification of the membrane filter count can be used. After filtration, the filter is placed on a pad soaked in nutrient media and allowed to incubate; resulting colonies are counted and appropriate calculations made.

A colorimeter or spectrophotometer is used in turbidimetric methods; the instrument measures the amount of light transmitted by test tubes with and without cultures; the difference represents the light absorbed or scattered by the bacterial cells and gives an indication of their concentration.

The total cell volume in a sample can be determined by centrifuging the sample in a calibrated centrifuge tube. From the known volume of a single cell and the volume of the sample cells, the original population size can be calculated.

The dry weight of washed, dehydrated cells gives a reliable indication of population size. Chemical assays for the concentration of nitrogen or other cell constituents present in cells in fairly constant amounts are used to calculate population size. Because living cells produce chemical changes in their environments, these changes may reflect the number of cells present; changes in pH or in the concentration of a substrate or product may be measured.

In a typical growth curve there is no increase in number of viable cells in the lag phase, but the cells increase in size, imbibe water, and synthesize enzymes as they become adjusted to the new medium. This phase is long if the inoculum consists of dormant cells and/or cells that were previously cultivated on a different medium. Dormant cells have fewer ribosomes than actively growing ones, and some time is required for the formation of ribosomes on which enzymes are then synthesized.

In the logarithmic phase the growth rate is most rapid, and the length of the generation time is at its minimum. The growth rate is constant. This portion of the curve plots as a straight line on semilogarithmic paper. Cells are physiologically active; their characteristic biochemical abilities are most obvious at this time. Almost all cells in the culture are alive, and the population is more nearly uniform than in any other phase of the growth curve. As logarithmic growth proceeds, the food supply diminishes and waste products accumulate.

At the stationary phase the food supply has fallen to a limiting concentration and the waste products have reached an inhibiting concentration. There is no change in number of viable cells; the production of new cells is balanced by the deaths of other cells. The growth rate is zero, but the population size is at its highest level, called the maximum crop.

During the death phase the number of viable cells decreases as the number of deaths surpasses the number of new cells produced—slowly at first, then more rapidly. The number of viable cells decreases at a logarithmic rate. The length of the death phase varies with the species. It may be only a few days in the case of some gram-negative cocci, but for most species it lasts a few weeks or even months.

Cells can be maintained indefinitely in a logarithmic phase by continuously adding nutrients and removing toxic metabolic products and excess cells in a siphon overflow. The growth rate is controlled by the rate of introduction of fresh medium. Because the overflow contains cells as well as waste products, the population size remains constant.

22. One method of counting bacteria which does not suffer from a major disadvantage of a "cell count" is a
    (A) plate count
    (B) smear count
    (C) membrane filter count
    (D) serial-dilution count
    (E) down for the count

23. The lag phase is the time during which
    (A) some cells multiply faster than others which "lag" behind
    (B) cells nourish themselves, grow, and eventually reproduce
    (C) cell population is stable
    (D) actively growing cells contribute ribosomes to dormant ones
    (E) adjustment to the new environment is negligible

24. According to the passage, the typical result of incubation is
    (A) impractical
    (B) the precise population of the original culture
    (C) mutation of the nutrient agar
    (D) growth
    (E) 30 to 300 colonies

25. One of the characteristics of the logarithmic phase might be described as
   (A) physiological stasis
   (B) ennervation
   (C) mitosis
   (D) conspicuous consumption
   (E) the recycling of waste products

26. The passage allows us to conclude that a biologist in a hurry to do a bacterial count might choose to
   (A) seek out a spectrophotometer
   (B) estimate the total cell volume
   (C) perform a smear count
   (D) incubate
   (E) use a petri dish

27. During which phase is the population size described with a term commonly applied to agricultural production
   (A) stationary phase
   (B) lag phase
   (C) logarithmic phase
   (D) death phase
   (E) harvest phase

28. The author's primary purpose in this passage is to
   (A) argue for the development of a counting method that is 100% accurate
   (B) discuss the advantages and disadvantages of the various phases
   (C) show that new counting methods have surpassed more primitive ones
   (D) give instruction in the performance of cell counts
   (E) describe methods of counting bacteria and the several phases that cells pass through in a lifetime

Antonyms

DIRECTIONS

Each word in CAPITAL LETTERS is followed by five words or phrases. The correct choice is the word or phrase whose meaning is most nearly *opposite* to the meaning of the word in capitals. You may be required to distinguish fine shades of meaning. Look at all choices before marking your answer.

29. MITIGATED
   (A) repeated
   (B) aggravated
   (C) terminated
   (D) raised
   (E) risen

30. PROSELYTE
    (A) neophyte   (D) apostate
    (B) electrolyte   (E) renegade
    (C) delegate

31. CLOY
    (A) deny   (D) flay
    (B) clay   (E) glut
    (C) club

32. RESUSCITATE
    (A) succumb   (D) kill
    (B) crush   (E) succeed
    (C) flatten

33. RUSTICATED
    (A) deteriorated   (D) repatriated
    (B) urban   (E) emaciated
    (C) domesticated

34. PENURY
    (A) wealth   (D) impenetrability
    (B) penance   (E) second-to-last
    (C) pensiveness

35. LACONICALLY
    (A) compendiously   (D) lethargically
    (B) obtrusively   (E) creatively
    (C) verbosely

36. MORIBUND
    (A) spiritual   (D) progressive
    (B) eternal   (E) faded
    (C) extant

37. INEFFABLE
    (A) dictatable   (D) definable
    (B) separable   (E) ethereal
    (C) cogent

38. ELUTRIATE
    (A) emanate   (D) contaminate
    (B) purloin   (E) placate
    (C) tarnish

39. ESTHETICISM
    - (A) tastelessness
    - (B) formlessness
    - (C) pragmatism
    - (D) resolution
    - (E) enthusiasm

STOP. IF YOU FINISH BEFORE TIME IS CALLED, CHECK YOUR WORK ON THIS SECTION ONLY. DO NOT WORK ON ANY OTHER SECTION IN THE TEST.

SECTION II: VERBAL ABILITY

Time: 30 Minutes
38 Questions

In this section, choose the best answer for each question and blacken the corresponding space on the answer sheet.

Sentence Completion

DIRECTIONS

Each blank in the following sentences indicates that something has been omitted. Considering the lettered words beneath the sentence, choose the word or set of words that best fits the whole sentence.

1. The horrifying _____ of the fire was reported on all the news stations, and the arson squad worked later through the week to uncover the _____ of the tragedy.
   - (A) scene . . . rumble
   - (B) result . . . jeopardy
   - (C) aftermath . . . cause
   - (D) cost . . . liability
   - (E) origin . . . reality

2. Although the seemingly _____ nature of the task appeared basic and fundamental, further application of the principles seemed _____.
   - (A) facile . . . awkward
   - (B) complex . . . easy
   - (C) redundant . . . impossible
   - (D) parallel . . . obvious
   - (E) devious . . . ambiguous

3. Feeling restless and unhappy, he left the house to take a quiet stroll, hoping the tone of the day would not decline further into _____ and uncertainty.
   - (A) dissonance
   - (B) ardor
   - (C) perversity
   - (D) pretense
   - (E) reticence

4. If the patriotic legend revealed the hard _____ of Roman culture, the love story tended to show its _____ belly.
   - (A) facts . . . fictitious
   - (B) backbone . . . vulnerable
   - (D) times . . . easygoing
   - (D) stubbornness . . . abdominal
   - (E) paternalism . . . maternal

5. The reason for the existence and _____ of religion in most societies has concerned scholars from _____.
   - (A) worship . . . secularism
   - (B) essence . . . nonscholars
   - (C) prevalence . . . antiquity
   - (D) appearance . . . time to time
   - (E) docility . . . Catholicism

6. The population of a species at any given time is determined by the ratio of the biotic _____ to environmental resistance.
   - (A) jeopardy
   - (B) potential
   - (C) excitement
   - (D) lexicon
   - (E) annoyance

7. There has been a large amount of _____ and lack of _____ in the description of such categories as ethnic, and especially racial, groups.
   - (A) disagreement . . . consensus
   - (B) bias . . . prejudice
   - (C) agreement . . . harmony
   - (D) violence . . . lawfulness
   - (E) indoctrination . . . malaise

8. Brandon Smith's penetrating criticism of the new play, *Zoot Suit*, was as _____ as a surgeon's scalpel.
   - (A) truthful
   - (B) catty
   - (C) succinct
   - (D) trenchant
   - (E) verbose

9. The decline of _____ forms was hastened by the discovery of global trade routes, which soon produced basic _____ in the supply of money and price structure, thus dooming land as the basic element of wealth and preferment.
   - (A) feudal . . . alterations
   - (B) oligarchical . . . change
   - (C) democratic . . . remedies
   - (D) monarchical . . . alternatives
   - (E) barbaric . . . reductions

Analogies

DIRECTIONS

In each question below, you are given a related pair of words or phrases. Select the lettered pair that *best* expresses a relationship similar to that in the original pair of words.

10. COLOR : SPECTRUM : :
    - (A) flower : petal
    - (B) note : symphony
    - (C) cloud : sky
    - (D) choice : gamut
    - (E) red : pigment

11. POEM : METAPHOR : :
    - (A) garden : flower
    - (B) sonata : arpeggio
    - (C) boat : sail
    - (D) concert : musicians
    - (E) diva : opera

12. ANATHEMA : MALEDICTION : :
    - (A) calumny : disapprobation
    - (B) defamation : character
    - (C) cure : illness
    - (D) success : ambition
    - (E) personality : slander

13. SUPERCILIOUS : BEGGAR : :
    - (A) philanthropic : miser
    - (B) benevolent : policeman
    - (C) disdainful : misanthrope
    - (D) encouraging : guard
    - (E) superordinate : subject

14. MISOGYNIST : FEMINISM : :
    - (A) cynic : doubt
    - (B) bureaucrat : anarchy
    - (C) fatalist : suicide
    - (D) existentialist : existence
    - (E) type : belief

15. LOQUACIOUS : TACITURN : :
    - (A) forward : reticent
    - (B) opinionated : suave
    - (C) pompous : gullible
    - (D) erudite : complacent
    - (E) misanthropic : sour

16. MONOTHEISM : THEISM : :
    - (A) monologue : prologue
    - (B) unicycle : cycle
    - (C) banal : vain
    - (D) unison : unified
    - (E) monocle : glasses

17. PARSIMONIOUS : PROFLIGATE : :
    - (A) thrifty : wealthy
    - (B) conservative : liberal
    - (C) sanctimonious : sinful
    - (D) shortsighted : emotive
    - (E) precautionary : decisive

18. EXONERATE : OSTRACIZE : :
   (A) make amends : exclude
   (B) wash : smudge
   (C) praise : blame
   (D) forgive : ban
   (E) let in : take out

Reading Comprehension

DIRECTIONS

Questions follow each of the passages below. Using only the stated or implied information in each passage, answer the questions.

The Nellie, a cruising yawl, swung to her anchor without a flutter of the sails, and was at rest. The flood had made, the wind was nearly calm, and being bound down the river, the only thing for it was to come to and wait for the turn of the tide.

The sea-reach of the Thames stretched before us like the beginning of an interminable waterway. In the offing the sea and the sky were welded together without a joint, and in the luminous space the tanned sails of the barges drifting up with the tide seemed to stand still in red clusters of canvas sharply peaked, with gleams of varnished spirits. A haze rested on the low shores that ran out to sea in vanishing flatness. The air was dark above Gravesend, and farther back still seemed condensed into a mournful gloom, brooding motionless over the biggest, and the greatest, town on earth.

The Director of Companies was our captain and our host. We four affectionately watched his back as he stood in the bows looking to seaward. On the whole river there was nothing that looked half so nautical. He resembled a pilot, which to a seaman is trustworthiness personified. It was difficult to realize his work was not out there in the luminous estuary, but behind him, within the brooding gloom.

Between us there was, as I have already said somewhere, the bond of the sea. Besides holding our hearts together through long periods of separation, it had the effect of making us tolerant of each other's yarns—and even convictions. The Lawyer—the best of old fellows—had, because of his many years and many virtues, the only cushion on deck, and was lying on the only rug. The Accountant had brought out already a box of dominoes, and was toying architecturally with the bones. Marlow sat cross-legged right aft, leaning against the mizzen-mast. He had sunken cheeks, a yellow complexion, a straight back, an ascetic aspect, and, with his arms drooped, the palms of hands outwards, resembled an idol. The Director, satisfied the anchor had good hold, made his way aft and sat down amongst us. We exchanged a few words lazily. Afterwards there was silence on board the yacht. For some reason or other we did not begin that game of dominoes. We felt meditative, and fit for nothing but placid staring. The day was ending in a serenity of still and exquisite brilliance. The water shone pacifically; the sky, without a speck, was a benign immensity of unstained light; the very mist on the Essex marsh was like a gauzy and radiant fabric, hung from the wooded rises inland, and draping the low shores in diaphanous folds. Only the gloom to the west, brooding over the upper reaches, became more sombre every minute, as if angered by the approach of the sun.

And at last, in its curved and imperceptible fall, the sun sank low, and from glowing white changed to a dull red without rays and without heat, as if about to go out suddenly, stricken to death by the touch of that gloom brooding over a crowd of men.

19. The last paragraph describes
    (A) man's destruction of the sun
    (B) a sunrise
    (C) a change of seasons
    (D) a sunset
    (E) the death of a crowd of men

20. How many men are aboard the *Nellie?*
    (A) four   (D) cannot be determined
    (B) five   (E) more than five
    (C) three

21. In paragraph 4, "bones" is another word for
    (A) the architecture of the Accountant's hands
    (B) the skeletons which emerge at sunset
    (C) Marlow
    (D) the planks which make up the deck
    (E) dominoes

22. The author implies that each of the passengers is a former
    (A) seaman
    (B) storyteller
    (C) idol
    (D) pilot
    (E) personification of trustworthiness

23. The *Nellie* is
    (A) not moving
    (B) fluttering
    (C) stretching down the interminable waterway
    (D) becoming increasingly gloomy
    (E) a government vessel

24. The author of this passage is a (an)
    (A) pretentious narrator
    (B) omniscient narrator
    (C) unreliable narrator
    (D) first-person narrator
    (E) third-person narrator

Many people seem to think that science fiction is typified by the covers of some of the old pulp magazines; the Bug-Eyed Monster, embodying every trait and feature that most people find repulsive, is about to grab, and presumably ravish, a sweet, blonde, curvaceous, scantily-clad Earth girl. This is unfortunate because it demeans and degrades a worthwhile and even important literary endeavor. In contrast to this unwarranted stereotype, science fiction rarely empha-sizes sex, and when it does, it is more discreet than other contemporary fiction. Instead, the basic interest of science fiction lies in the relation between man and his technology and between man and the universe. Science fiction is a literature of change and a literature of the future, and while it would be foolish to claim that science fiction is a major literary genre at this time, the aspects of human life that it considers make it well worth reading and studying—for no other literary form does quite the same things.

The question is: what is science fiction? And the answer must be, unfortunately, that there have been few attempts to consider this question at any length or with much seriousness; it may well be that science fiction will resist any comprehensive definition of its character-istics. To say this, however, does not mean that there are no ways of defining it nor that various facets of its totality cannot be clarified. To begin, the following definition should be helpful: science fiction is a literary sub-genre which postulates a change (for human beings) from conditions as we know them and follows the implications of these changes to a conclusion. Although this definition will necessarily be modified and expanded, and probably changed, in the course of this exploration, it covers much of the basic groundwork and provides a point of departure.

The first point—that science fiction is a literary sub-genre—is a very important one, but one which is often overlooked or ignored in most discussions of science fiction. Specifically, science fiction is either a short story or a novel. There are only a few dramas which could be called science fiction, with Karel Capek's *RUR* (Rossum's Universal Robots) being the only one that is well known; the body of poetry that might be labeled science fiction is only slightly larger. To say that science fiction is a sub-genre of prose fiction is to say that it has all the basic characteristics and serves the same basic functions in much the same way as prose fiction in general—that is, it shares a great deal with all other novels and short stories.

Everything that can be said about prose fiction, in general applies to science fiction. Every piece of science fiction, whether short story or novel, must have a narrator, a story, a plot, a setting, characters, language, and theme. And like any prose, the themes of science fiction are concerned with interpreting man's nature and experience in relation to the world around him. Themes in science fiction are constructed and presented in exactly the same ways that themes are dealt with in any other kind of fiction. They are the result of a particular combination of narrator, story, plot, character, setting, and language. In short, the reasons for reading and enjoying science fiction, and the ways of studying and analyzing it, are basically the same as they would be for any other story or novel.

25. Science fiction is called a literary sub-genre because
    (A) it is not important enough to be a literary genre
    (B) it cannot be made into a dramatic presentation
    (C) it has its limits
    (D) it shares characteristics with other types of prose fiction
    (E) to call it a "genre" would subject it to literary jargon

26. Which of the following does not usually contribute to the theme in a piece of science fiction?
    (A) narrator   (D) setting
    (B) character   (E) rhyme
    (C) plot

27. The view of science fiction encouraged by pulp magazines, while wrong, is nevertheless
    (A) popular   (D) deranged
    (B) elegant   (E) accurate
    (C) fashionable

28. An appropriate title for this passage would be
    (A) On the Inaccuracies of Pulp Magazines
    (B) Man and the Universe
    (C) Toward a Definition of Science Fiction
    (D) A Type of Prose Fiction
    (E) Beyond the Bug-Eyed Monster

29. The author's definition suggests that all science fiction deals with
    (A) monsters
    (B) the same topics addressed by novels and short stories
    (C) the unfamiliar or unusual
    (D) Karel Capek's well-known postulate
    (E) the conflict between science and fiction

30. One implication of the final sentence in the passage is that
    (A) the reader should turn next to commentaries on general fiction
    (B) there is no reason for any reader not to like science fiction
    (C) all fiction consists of six basic elements
    (D) there are reasons for enjoying science fiction
    (E) those who can read and analyze fiction can also do so with science fiction

Antonyms

DIRECTIONS

Each word in CAPITAL LETTERS is followed by five words or phrases. The correct choice is the word or phrase whose meaning is most nearly *opposite* to the meaning of the word in capitals. You may be required to distinguish fine shades of meaning. Look at all choices before marking your answer.

31. LUXURIANT
    (A) profound
    (B) curious
    (C) small
    (D) miserly
    (E) peeling

32. TYRO
    (A) factotum
    (B) instigator
    (C) virtuoso
    (D) investigator
    (E) dilettante

33. UBIQUITOUS
    (A) hiding
    (B) localized
    (C) jailed
    (D) bilious
    (E) exhaustive

34. ABSTEMIOUS
    (A) punctual
    (B) vainglorious
    (C) gluttonous
    (D) finicky
    (E) disdainful

35. SOPORIFIC
    (A) exciting
    (B) terrific
    (C) specific
    (D) vapid
    (E) sophomoric

36. FACTOTUM
    (A) idol
    (B) amateur
    (C) specialist
    (D) tyro
    (E) investigator

37. VIRAGO
    (A) coquette
    (B) enchantress
    (C) amazon
    (D) Adonis
    (E) slave

38. MULCT
    (A) deprecate
    (B) award
    (C) send
    (D) impute
    (E) fertilize

STOP. IF YOU FINISH BEFORE TIME IS CALLED, CHECK YOUR WORK ON THIS SECTION ONLY. DO NOT WORK ON ANY OTHER SECTION IN THE TEST.

SECTION III: QUANTITATIVE ABILITY

Time: 30 Minutes
30 Questions

Quantitative Comparison

DIRECTIONS

In this section you will be given two quantities, one in column A and one in column B. You are to determine a relationship between the two quantities and mark
- (A) if the quantity in column A is greater than the quantity in column B
- (B) if the quantity in column B is greater than the quantity in column A
- (C) if the quantities are equal
- (D) if the comparison cannot be determined from the information that is given

Common Information:
  Information centered above both columns refers to one or both columns.
  All numbers used are real numbers.
  Figures are intended to provide useful positional information, but are not necessarily drawn to scale and should not be used to estimate sizes by measurement.
  Lines that appear straight can be assumed to be straight.

	Column A	Column B
1.	$3^2 + 4 \times 10^2 - 4^2$	$3^2 - 4 \times 10^2 - 4^2$

$$x^2 = 36$$

2.	6	x

x, y, z, are integers

3.	$z - x$	$x - y$

Column A	Column B

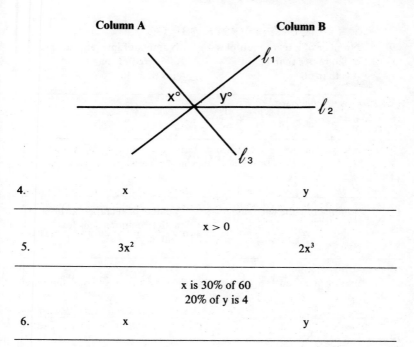

4.   x   y

$$x > 0$$

5. $3x^2$ $2x^3$

---

x is 30% of 60
20% of y is 4

6.   x   y

Questions 7–8 refer to the diagram.

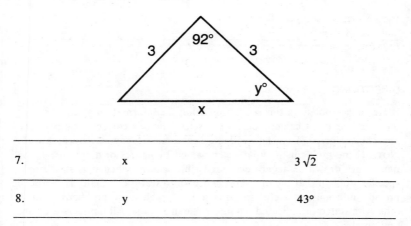

---

7.   x $3\sqrt{2}$

---

8.   y $43°$

	Column A	Column B
9.	Number of integer multiples of 8, greater than 8, but less than 50	Number of integer multiples of 6, greater than 6, but less than 40

10.	$1 + \dfrac{1}{2} + \dfrac{1}{4} + \dfrac{1}{16} + \dfrac{1}{32} + \dfrac{1}{64}$	2

$$0 < x + y < 2$$

11.	x	y

12.	Volume of cube with side 6	Volume of rectangular prism with two dimensions less than 6

	$x^2 + 2x + 1 = 0$	$y^2 - 2y + 1 = 0$
13.	x	y

14.	$8^{29} - 8^{28}$	8^{28}

$$x > y > 0$$

15.	$\sqrt{x} - \sqrt{y}$	$\sqrt{x - y}$

Math Ability

DIRECTIONS

Solve each problem in this section by using the information given and your own mathematical calculations. Then select the *one* correct answer of the five choices given. Use the available space on the page for scratchwork. NOTE: Some problems may be accompanied by figures or diagrams. These figures are drawn as accurately as possible, *except* when it is stated in a specific problem that the figure is not drawn to scale. The figure is meant to provide information useful in solving the problem or problems. Unless otherwise stated or indicated, all figures lie in a plane. All numbers used are real numbers.

16. Find .25% of 12
    (A) $\frac{3}{100}$ (B) $\frac{3}{10}$ (C) $\frac{1}{3}$ (D) 3   (E) 300

17. If $2/x = 4$ and if $2/y = 8$, then $x - y =$
    (A) $\frac{1}{8}$ (B) $\frac{1}{4}$ (C) $\frac{3}{4}$ (D) 4   (E) 24

18. Bob is older than Jane but he is younger than Jim. If Bob's age is b, Jane's age is c, and Jim's is d, then which of the following is true?
    (A) $c < b < d$ (B) $b < c < d$ (C) $b < d < c$
    (D) $c < d < b$ (E) $d < c < b$

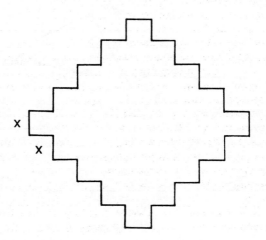

19. In the figure, all line segments meet at right angles and each segment has a length of x. What is the area of the figure in terms of x?
    (A) $25x$ (B) $36x$ (C) $36x^2$ (D) $41x^2$ (E) $41x^3$

20. A girl runs k miles in n hours. How many miles will she run in x hours at the same rate?
    (A) knx (B) $\frac{k}{n}$ (C) $\frac{kx}{n}$ (D) kx (E) $\frac{kn}{x}$

21. Find the total surface area in square meters of a rectangular solid whose length is 7 meters, width is 6 meters, and depth is 3 meters.
    (A) $32m^2$ (B) $81m^2$ (C) $126m^2$
    (D) $162m^2$ (E) $252m^2$

22. Which of the following is the smallest?
    (A) $\frac{1}{8}$ (B) $(.3)^2$ (C) $\frac{1}{3}$ (D) $\sqrt{.36}$ (E) $\frac{11}{100}$

Questions 23–24 refer to the graph.

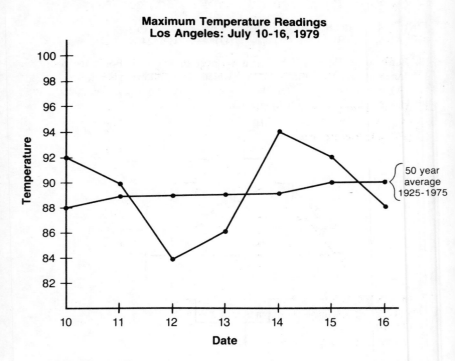

Maximum Temperature Readings
Los Angeles: July 10-16, 1979

50 year
average
1925-1975

23. Of the seven days shown, what percent of the days did the maximum
temperature exceed the average temperature?
(A) 3   (B) 4   (C) 43   (D) 57   (E) none of these

24. What was the percent increase in the maximum temperature from July
12 to July 14, 1979?
(A) 10   (B) 10.6   (C) 11.9   (D) cannot be determined
(E) none of these

25. A bus leaves Burbank at 9:00 A.M., traveling east at 50 miles per hour.
At 1:00 P.M. a plane leaves Burbank traveling east at 300 miles per hour.
At what time will the plane overtake the bus?
(A) 12:45 P.M.   (B) 1:10 P.M.   (C) 1:40 P.M.   (D) 1:48 P.M.
(E) 1:55 P.M.

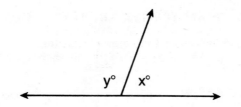

26. If in the figure x = ⅔y, then y =
    (A) 36   (B) 72   (C) 108   (D) 144
    (E) cannot be determined

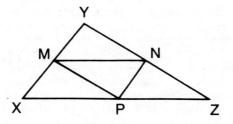

27. In △ XYZ, points M, N, and P are midpoints. If XY = 10, YZ = 15, and XZ = 17, what is the perimeter of △ MNP?
    (A) 10⅔   (B) 14   (C) 16   (D) 21
    (E) cannot be determined

28. If a and b are integers, which of the following conditions is sufficient

    $$\text{for } \frac{a^2 - b^2}{a - b} = a + b \text{ to be true?}$$

    (A) a > 0   (B) a < 0   (C) a > b   (D) b > 0
    (E) b < 0

29. What is the area of a square inscribed in a circle whose circumference is 16π?
    (A) 8   (B) 32   (C) 64   (D) 128   (E) 256

30. If the average of two numbers is y and one of the numbers is equal to z, then the other number is equal to

    (A) 2z − y   (B) $\frac{y + z}{2}$ (C) z − y   (D) 2y − z

    (E) cannot be determined

STOP. IF YOU FINISH BEFORE TIME IS CALLED, CHECK YOUR WORK ON THIS SECTION ONLY. DO NOT WORK ON ANY OTHER SECTION IN THE TEST.

SECTION IV: QUANTITATIVE ABILITY

Time: 30 Minutes
30 Questions

Quantitative Comparison

DIRECTIONS

In this section you will be given two quantities, one in column A and one in column B. You are to determine a relationship between the two quantities and mark

(A) if the quantity in column A is greater than the quantity in column B
(B) if the quantity in column B is greater than the quantity in column A
(C) if the quantities are equal
(D) if the comparison cannot be determined from the information that is given

Common Information:

Information centered above both columns refers to one or both columns.

All numbers used are real numbers.

Figures are intended to provide useful positional information, but are not necessarily drawn to scale and should not be used to estimate sizes by measurement.

Lines that appear straight can be assumed to be straight.

	Column A	Column B
1.	$\frac{1}{3} \times \frac{2}{5} \times \frac{1}{8}$	$.33 \times .4 \times .125$
2.	Area of rectangle with length 8	Area of rectangle with width 7
3.	35% of 50	50% of 35

$$a = 3b$$
$$b = -2$$

	Column A	Column B
4.	$\dfrac{a^2 + b}{ab}$	$\dfrac{a + b^2}{ab}$
5.	Number of ways to arrange four books on a shelf	12

Column A   Column B

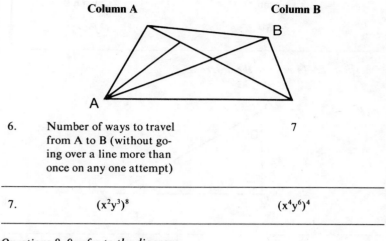

6. Number of ways to travel   7
    from A to B (without go-
    ing over a line more than
    once on any one attempt)

7. $(x^2y^3)^8$ $(x^4y^6)^4$

Questions 8–9 refer to the diagram.

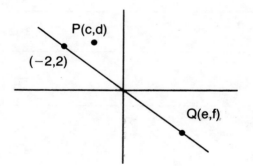

8.   c   d

9.   c + d   e + f

                        x > 0

10.   x(x + 2) + (x + 2)   (x + 1)(x + 3)

11. Number of seconds in two hours   Number of hours in 50 weeks

	Column A	Column B
12.	$\sqrt{3^{18}}$	$(\sqrt{27^3})^2$

Questions 13–14 refer to the diagram.

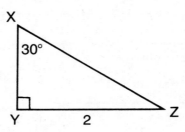

13.	XY	YZ

14.	XY	$3\sqrt{2}$

15.	$\dfrac{\sqrt{3}}{3}$	$\dfrac{1}{\sqrt{3}}$

Math Ability

DIRECTIONS

Solve each problem in this section by using the information given and your own mathematical calculations. Then select the *one* correct answer of the five choices given. Use the available space on the page for scratchwork. NOTE: Some problems may be accompanied by figures or diagrams. These figures are drawn as accurately as possible, *except* when it is stated in a specific problem that the figure is not drawn to scale. The figure is meant to provide information useful in solving the problem or problems. Unless otherwise stated or indicated, all figures lie in a plane. All numbers used are real numbers.

16. If $x = -2$, then $x^3 - x^2 - x - 1 =$
   (A) -15 (B) -11 (C) -3 (D) 0   (E) 13

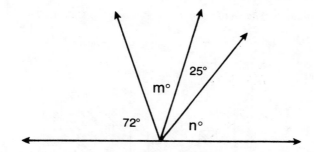

17. In the figure, what is the number of degrees in the sum of m + n?
    (A) 83   (B) 93   (C) 97   (D) 103
    (E) cannot be determined

18. If x is between 0 and 1, which of the following statements is (are) true?

    I. $x^2 > 1$ II. $x^2 > 0$ III. $x^2 > x$

    (A) I only   (B) II only   (C) III only   (D) I and II
    (E) II and III

19. If 15 students in a class average 80% on an English exam and 10 students average 90% on the same exam, what is the average in percent for all 25 students?
    (A) 86⅔%   (B) 85%   (C) 84%   (D) 83½%   (E) 83%

20. If a pipe can drain a tank in t hours, what part of the tank does it drain in 3 hours?
    (A) 3t   (B) t/3   (C) t + 3   (D) 3/t   (E) t − 3

21. If the volume and the total surface area of a cube are equal, how long must the edge of the cube be?
    (A) 2 units   (B) 3 units   (C) 4 units   (D) 5 units
    (E) 6 units

22. Which of the following is *never* true?

    I. The sum of 2 even integers is even.
    II. The product of 2 even integers is even.
    III. The sum of 2 odd integers is odd.
    IV. The sum of 3 odd integers is even.

    (A) I and II   (B) II and III   (C) III and IV
    (D) I and III   (E) II and IV

Questions 23–26 refer to the graph.

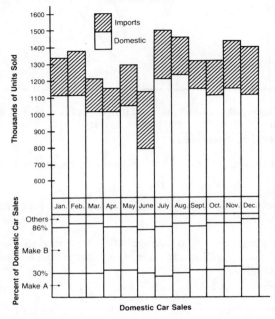

U.S. AUTO SALES—1978

23. Approximately how many cars of make B were sold in July?
    (A) 732,000   (B) 800,000   (C) 900,000   (D) 1,049,200
    (E) 1,290,000

24. During which month(s) did imports outsell domestics?
    (A) August   (B) June   (C) four months
    (D) no months   (E) none of these

25. What were the average monthly domestic sales (in millions) for the
    given year?
    (A) .6–1.8   (B) .8–1.0   (C) 1.0–1.2
    (D) 1.2–1.4   (E) 1.4–1.6

26. What is the approximate percent increase in total sales from June to
    December?
    (A) 10%   (B) 30%   (C) 60%   (D) 100%   (E) 150%

27. The base of an isosceles triangle exceeds each of the equal sides by 8 feet. If the perimeter is 89 feet, find the length of the base in feet.
    (A) 27   (B) 29⅔   (C) 35   (D) 54
    (E) cannot be determined

28. If two numbers have only the number 1 as a common divisor, then they are called "relatively prime." Which of the following are *not* relatively prime?

    I. 3   II. 4   III. 7   IV. 12

    (A) I and II, I and III
    (B) I and IV, II and IV
    (C) II and III, II and IV
    (D) II and IV, III and IV
    (E) I and II, I and IV

29. If $(a,b) \oplus (c,d) = (ac - bd, ad)$ then $(-2,3) \oplus (4,-1) =$
    (A) $(-5,2)$ (B) $(-5,-2)$ (C) $(-11,2)$ (D) $(-11,-2)$
    (E) $(-5,-3)$

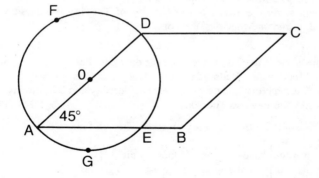

30. In the rhombus, BC = 6, AE ≈ 4, and angle DAE = 45°. AD is the diameter of the circle. If a man started at C and followed around the outer edge of this figure to D, F, A, G, E, B, and back to C, approximately how far did he travel?
    (A) $12 + 6\pi$ (B) $14 + (^{27}/_4)\pi$ (C) $14 + (^9/_2)\pi$
    (D) $14 + 6\pi$ (E) $12 + (^9/_2)\pi$

STOP. IF YOU FINISH BEFORE TIME IS CALLED, CHECK YOUR WORK ON THIS SECTION ONLY. DO NOT WORK ON ANY OTHER SECTION IN THE TEST.

SECTION V: ANALYTICAL ABILITY

Time: 30 Minutes
25 Questions

DIRECTIONS

The following questions or group of questions are based on a passage or set of statements. Choose the best answer for each question and blacken the corresponding space on your answer sheet. It may be helpful to draw rough diagrams or simple charts in attempting to answer these question types.

Questions 1–5

Liz, Jenni, Jolie, and Rick have an English final on Friday and they all would like to study together at least once before the test.
Liz can study only on Monday, Tuesday, and Wednesday nights, and Thursday afternoon and night.
Jenni can study only on Monday, Wednesday, and Thursday nights, and Tuesday afternoon and night.
Jolie can study only on Wednesday and Thursday nights, Tuesday afternoon, and Monday afternoon and night.
Rick can study the afternoons and nights of Tuesday, Wednesday, and Thursday, and on Monday afternoon.

1. If the group is to study twice, then the days could be
   (A) Monday and Wednesday   (D) Monday and Friday
   (B) Tuesday and Thursday   (E) Tuesday and Wednesday
   (C) Wednesday and Thursday

2. If three of them tried to study together when all four couldn't,
   (A) this would be possible twice
   (B) it would have to be on Wednesday night
   (C) Rick could not attend the three-person groups
   (D) this could be accomplished on Monday and Tuesday only
   (E) this would not be possible

3. If Liz decided to study every night,
   (A) she would never be able to study with Rick
   (B) she would never be able to study with Jolie
   (C) she would have at least two study partners each night
   (D) she would have to study alone on Monday night
   (E) she would study with only Jenni on Thursday night

94

4. If the test were moved up to Thursday morning, which of the following must be true?

   I. The complete group would not be able to study together.
   II. Liz could never study in the afternoon.
   III. Jolie and Jenni could study together three times.

   (A) I only
   (B) I and II only
   (C) I and III only
   (D) II and III only
   (E) I, II, and III

5. Dan wants to join the study group. If the larger study group is to be able to study all together then Dan will have to be available on
   (A) Wednesday night
   (B) Thursday afternoon
   (C) Tuesday night
   (D) Monday night
   (E) Wednesday afternoon

Questions 6–8

   It has been proven that the "lie detector" can be easily fooled. If the person is truly unaware that he is lying, when in fact he is, then the "lie detector" is worthless.

6. The author of this argument implies that
   (A) the lie detector is a useless device
   (B) a good liar can fool the device easily
   (C) a lie detector is often inaccurate
   (D) the lie detector is sometimes worthless
   (E) no one can fool the lie detector all of the time

7. This argument would be strengthened most by
   (A) demonstrating that one's awareness of truth or falsity is always undetectable
   (B) showing that the "truth" of any statement always relies on a subjective assessment
   (C) citing evidence that there are other means of measuring truth which are consistently less reliable than the lie detector
   (D) citing the number of cases in which the lie detector mistook falsehood for truth
   (E) claiming that ordinary, unbiased people are the best "lie detectors"

8. Without contradicting himself, the author might present which of the following arguments as a strong point in favor of the lie detector?
   (A) The methodology used by investigative critics of lie detectors is itself highly flawed.
   (B) Law-enforcement agencies have purchased too many detectors to abandon them now.
   (C) Circumstantial evidence might be more useful in a criminal case than is personal testimony.
   (D) The very threat of a lie-detector test has led a significant number of criminals to confess.
   (E) People are never "truly unaware" that they are lying.

Questions 9–13

Two women, Amy and Carla, and two men, Bernard and Doug, are doctors. One is a dentist, one a surgeon, one an optometrist, and one a general practitioner. They are seated around a square table with one person on each side.

1. Bernard is across from the dentist.
2. Doug is not across from the surgeon.
3. The optometrist is on Amy's left.
4. Carla is the general practitioner.
5. The surgeon and general practitioner are married to each other.
6. The general practitioner is not on Carla's left.
7. The general practitioner is across from the optometrist.

9. Which statement is repeated information?
   (A) 1   (B) 5   (C) 6   (D) 7   (E) none of these

10. Which of the following must be false?
    I. Bernard is the dentist.
    II. The surgeon and general practitioner are women.
    III. The dentist is across from the surgeon.

    (A) I   (B) II   (C) III   (D) I and II
    (E) II and III

11. Which of the following must be true?
    I. Two women sit next to each other.
    II. Two men sit across from each other.

    (A) I only   (D) either I or II, but not both
    (B) II only   (E) neither I nor II
    (C) both I and II

12. Which of the following must be true?

    I. Doug is the optometrist.
    II. The surgeon and general practitioner sit next to each other.

    (A) I only   (D) either I or II, but not both
    (B) II only   (E) neither I nor II
    (C) both I and II

13. Which of the following is true?

    (A) Doug is the general practitioner.
    (B) Bernard is the surgeon.
    (C) Carla is the dentist.
    (D) Amy is the optometrist.
    (E) none of the above

Questions 14–15

"The sum of behavior is to retain a man's dignity without intruding upon the liberty of others," stated Sir Francis Bacon. If this is the case, then not intruding upon another's liberty is impossible.

14. The conclusion strongly implied by the author's argument is that
    (A) retaining one's dignity is impossible without intruding upon another's liberty
    (B) retaining dignity never involves robbing others of liberty
    (C) dignity and liberty are mutually exclusive
    (D) there is always the possibility of a "dignified intrusion"
    (E) B. F. Skinner's *Beyond Freedom and Dignity* takes its cue from Bacon

15. The author's argument would be weakened if it was pointed out that

    I. Bacon's argument has been misinterpreted out of context
    II. neither liberty nor dignity can be discussed in absolute terms
    III. retaining dignity always involves a reduction of liberty

    (A) I, II, and III   (B) III only   (C) I only
    (D) II and III only   (E) I and II only

Questions 16–20

   The mythical countries of Bongo and Congo are exactly square shaped and lie next to each other in an east-west direction, though not necessarily in that order. Their common border spans the width of both countries. The capital city of one of the countries is "A." It lies due east from the other capital, "B."
"C" is the border city of Congo, on the Bongo boundary.
"D" is the harbor city of Bongo for ships coming from the west.
"E" is the easternmost city of Bongo.
"F" is 27 miles due west of Congo's capital city, in Congo.
The main highway, Bongo-Congo 1, goes from "B" eastward to the coastal city of "G."

16. Going east to west a traveler would encounter cities in which order?
    (A) G, A, E, C, F   (D) G, A, F, C, E
    (B) A, F, C, B, E   (E) C, B, E, F, A
    (C) D, B, E, C, F

17. When the sun rises, the first city to see it is
    (A) G   (B) F   (C) B   (D) E   (E) E

18. When the sun sets, the last city to see it is
    (A) G   (B) F   (C) B   (D) E   (E) E

19. Which of the following is (are) true?

    I. "B" is the capital city of Bongo.
    II. "A" is the capital city of Congo.
    III. "C" is the last Bongo city encountered on the way to Congo.

    (A) I   (D) I and II
    (B) II   (E) II and III
    (C) III

20. Which statement is true of city "E"?
    (A) It is the easternmost city of the easternmost country.
    (B) It is the westernmost city of the westernmost country.
    (C) It is the easternmost city of the westernmost country.
    (D) It is the westernmost city of the easternmost country.
    (E) It is due west of Bongo's capital city.

Questions 21–25

A small elevator starts at the 1st floor with 3 people and stops at the 5th floor with 5 people.
The elevator can accommodate only 5 people at any one time.
The elevator makes only 3 stops, including the destination.
On this trip, the elevator goes only up.
The elevator can hold only 1,000 pounds or it breaks.
3 people get on at the second floor.

21. Which of the following must be true?
   (A) At least 1 person gets off on the 2nd floor.
   (B) At least 2 persons get off on the 2nd floor.
   (C) No one gets off on the 3rd floor.
   (D) Only 1 person gets off on the 2nd floor.
   (E) At least 1 person gets on on the 3rd floor.

22. Which of the following must be true?
   (A) Only 1 person on the elevator weighed over 250 pounds.
   (B) 6 people could get on the elevator.
   (C) Each person getting on the elevator at the 1st stop weighed less than 150 pounds.
   (D) The average weight of the people at the 5th floor did not exceed 200 pounds.
   (E) none of the above

23. Which of the following must be false?

    I. The elevator stops at the 3rd floor.
   II. No one gets off at the 2nd floor.
  III. No one gets on at the 4th floor.

   (A) I only   (D) I and II
   (B) II only   (E) II and III
   (C) III only

24. If 2 people get off at the 2nd floor and 4 get on at the 3rd floor, what happened at the 4th floor?
   (A) 2 people get off.
   (B) 1 person gets off and 2 get on.
   (C) 3 people get off and 2 get on.
   (D) 5 people get off and 5 people get on.
   (E) The elevator doesn't stop.

25. If the elevator doesn't stop at the 2nd floor and no people get off at the 3rd or 4th floors, then which could be true?

    I. 1 person gets on at each, floor 3 and floor 4.
  II. 3 people get on at floors 3 and 4.

(A) I only
(B) II only
(C) I and II

(D) neither I nor II
(E) cannot be determined

STOP. IF YOU FINISH BEFORE TIME IS CALLED, CHECK YOUR WORK ON THIS SECTION ONLY. DO NOT WORK ON ANY OTHER SECTION IN THE TEST.

SECTION VI: ANALYTICAL ABILITY

Time: 30 Minutes
25 Questions

DIRECTIONS

The following questions or group of questions are based on a passage or set of statements. Choose the best answer for each question and blacken the corresponding space on your answer sheet. It may be helpful to draw rough diagrams or simple charts in attempting to answer these question types.

Questions 1–7

X, Y, and Z are 3 chemical elements.
If X reacts with X, the result is Y.
If X reacts with Z, the result is X.
If Y reacts with any element, the result is always Y.
If Z reacts with Z, the result is Z.
The order of the reaction makes no difference.

1. Which of the following must be true?

    I. If X reacts with any other element, the result is never X.
    II. If Z reacts with any element, the result is that element.
    III. If Y reacts with Y, the result is X.

  (A) I   (D) I and II
  (B) II   (E) II and III
  (C) III

2. If the result is Y, then

    I. Y had to be in the reaction
    II. Z had to be in the reaction

  (A) I   (D) both I and II
  (B) II   (E) neither I nor II
  (C) either I or II, but not both

3. If the result of X and Z reacts with the result of Y and Z, then the result is

  (A) X   (D) X or Z
  (B) Y   (E) cannot be determined
  (C) Z

4. Which of the following must be false?

   I. Whenever an element reacts with itself, the result is the original element.
   II. If the result is Z, then Z had to be in the reaction.

   (A) I   (D) both I and II
   (B) II   (E) neither I nor II
   (C) either I or II, but not both

5. If the result is X, then

   I. X had to be in the reaction
   II. Y could not be in the reaction
   III. Z had to be in the reaction

   (A) I   (D) II and III
   (B) I and II   (E) I, II, and III
   (C) I and III

6. If the result of X and X reacts with the result of Z and Z, then the result is

   (A) X   (D) X or Y
   (B) Y   (E) cannot be determined
   (C) Z

7. A new element W is introduced. When element W is added to any reaction, then the result is W, except when it reacts with Y, the result is Y. If the result of W and Z reacts with the result of W and Y, then the result is *not*

   (A) X   (D) X or Y
   (B) Y   (E) W, X, or Z
   (C) Z

Questions 8–9

   "All acts have consequences. Given this fact, we may wish to play it safe by never doing anything."

8. The speaker implies that
   (A) we may prefer to live safely
   (B) all acts have consequences
   (C) consequentiality is not safe
   (D) doing nothing has lesser consequences
   (E) not doing anything is not an act

9. What conclusion about consequences must we accept if we accept the writer's statement?
   (A) Consequences are significant only for active people.
   (B) All consequences are dangerous.
   (C) There are some acts that do not produce consequences.
   (D) Consequences have moral force.
   (E) Inaction has moral force.

Questions 10–15

   20 books are stacked evenly on 4 shelves, as follows:
   There are 3 types of books: science fiction, mystery, and biography.
   There are twice as many mysteries as science fictions.
   All 4 science fiction books are on shelf number 2.
   There is at least 1 mystery on each shelf.
   Shelves numbers 3 and 4 have equal numbers of mystery books.
   No shelf contains only 1 type of book.

10. Shelf number 3 has

   I. at least 1 mystery book
   II. no science fiction books

   (A) I   (D) either I or II, but not both
   (B) II   (E) neither I nor II
   (C) both I and II

11. Which of the following must be true?
   (A) No shelf has more than 2 mysteries.
   (B) No shelf has more than 2 biographies.
   (C) There is never only 1 mystery on a shelf.
   (D) There is never only 1 biography on a shelf.
   (E) There are always more mysteries than biographies on a given shelf.

12. If the books on shelves numbers 1 and 4 are put together, then

   I. they must contain equal numbers of mysteries and biographies
   II. they contain no science fiction
   III. they contain over half of the biographies

   (A) I   (D) I and II
   (B) II   (E) II and III
   (C) III

13. All of the following are true *except*
    (A) shelf number 2 contains no biographies
    (B) shelf number 3 contains no science fiction
    (C) shelf number 4 contains equal numbers of each book
    (D) shelf number 1 could contain mostly mysteries
    (E) shelf number 3 could contain 3 biographies

14. Shelf number 4 must have
    (A) 4 mysteries
    (B) 2 different types of books, in the ratio of 3 to 2
    (C) 2 different types of books, in the ratio of 4 to 1
    (D) all 3 different types of books, in the ratio of 2:2:1
    (E) cannot be determined

15. Shelf number 1 must have
    (A) 2 different types of books, in the ratio of 3 to 2
    (B) 2 different types of books, in the ratio of 4 to 1
    (C) 3 different types of books, in the ratio of 2:2:1
    (D) 4 mysteries
    (E) none of the above

16. All triangles are two-dimensional
    All squares are two-dimensional
    All triangles are squares

    This logic would be valid if
    (A) only squares are two-dimensional
    (B) only triangles are two-dimensional
    (C) some triangles are two-dimensional
    (D) some squares are two-dimensional
    (E) some squares are three-dimensional

Questions 17–18

   "We have nothing to fear but fear itself? Nonsense. Even the bravest of us may become terrified in the face of any number of gravely threatening situations."

17. To accept this author's argument, we must agree that becoming afraid is
    (A) an occasional trait of the fearless
    (B) fearful
    (C) a common and acceptable human quality
    (D) nonsense
    (E) allowable only in gravely threatening situations

18. The author's argument might be weakened by pointing out that
    (A) a less fearful attitude may minimize the threat of a situation
    (B) fear promotes more accurate responses to threatening situations
    (C) any blanket generalization is highly vulnerable to criticism
    (D) who we fear is more important than what we fear
    (E) brave people often admit that they have been afraid

Questions 19–25

Ten figures (six numbers: 1, 2, 3, 4, 5, 6 and four letters: A, B, C, D) are listed in a line on a piece of paper.
The numbers are not necessarily in order but the letters are in alphabetical order from left to right.
No two letters are next to each other.
The first two figures are 4 then 6, respectively.
D is between 1 and 3 and next to each of them.
2 is between B and C.

19. Which of the following must be false?

    I. C is between 1 and 2, and next to each.
    II. B is between 1 and A, and next to each.

    (A) I   (D) both I and II
    (B) II   (E) neither I nor II
    (C) either I or II, but not both

20. Which of the following must be true?

    I. A is next to 6, but not next to 3.
    II. 5 is next to A, but not next to C.

    (A) I   (D) both I and II
    (B) II   (E) neither I nor II
    (C) either I or II, but not both

21. If 3 is the last figure, then
    (A) B is next to 1
    (B) C is between 2 and 3, and next to each
    (C) A is between 4 and 6, and next to each
    (D) C is next to 1
    (E) D is next to 4

22. If the numbers next to B are added together, their total would be
    (A) 10   (B) 4   (C) 2   (D) 6   (E) 7

23. If someone wanted to add two more letters to the list, he or she
    (A) would have to put one letter between 4 and 6
    (B) would have to put one letter at the beginning
    (C) could not do so without breaking the rules
    (D) could do so only by rearranging the first four figures
    (E) would have to put both letters at the end

24. The letter that is most nearly in the center of the list is
    (A) A   (D) D
    (B) B   (E) cannot be determined
    (C) C

25. If you total the first two numbers in the list, they would be

    I. greater than the total of the last three numbers
    II. less than the total of the last three numbers
    III. twice the size of the third number

    (A) I   (D) I and II
    (B) II   (E) I and III
    (C) III

STOP. IF YOU FINISH BEFORE TIME IS CALLED, CHECK YOUR WORK ON THIS SECTION ONLY. DO NOT WORK ON ANY OTHER SECTION IN THE TEST.

SECTION VII: QUANTITATIVE ABILITY

Time: 30 Minutes
30 Questions

Quantitative Comparison

DIRECTIONS

In this section you will be given two quantities, one in column A and one in column B. You are to determine a relationship between the two quantities and mark.

   (A) if the quantity in column A is greater than the quantity in column B
   (B) if the quantity in column B is greater than the quantity in column A
   (C) if the quantities are equal
   (D) if the comparison cannot be determined from the information that is given

Common Information:

   Information centered above both columns refers to one or both columns.

   All numbers used are real numbers.

   Figures are intended to provide useful positional information, but are not necessarily drawn to scale and should not be used to estimate sizes by measurement.

   Lines that appear straight can be assumed to be straight.

	Column A	Column B
1.	Number of ones in 48	Number of tens in 68
2.	$\sqrt{48}$	7
3.	$x + 4$	$y - 3$
4.	40% of 60	60% of 40
5.	$.05 - .125$	$.1$

Column A   **Column B**

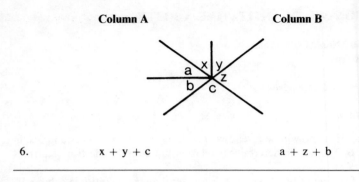

6.   x + y + c   a + z + b

Questions 7–8 refer to the diagram.

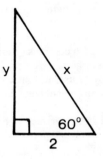

---

7.   x   y

---

8.   2 $\dfrac{x}{2}$

---

9.   5% $\dfrac{1}{20}$

Column A	Column B

Questions 10–12 refer to the diagram.

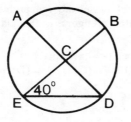

	Column A	Column B
10.	∠CED	½$\widehat{BD}$
11.	$\widehat{AB}$	$\widehat{AE}$
12.	∠BCD	∠CDE
13.	Number of diagonals in a hexagon	Number of sides of a hexagon

ABCD is a rhombus with
height 4 and area 20

14.	Length of side AB	Length of diagonal AC

T > x
y < m
x < y

15.	x + y	T + m

Math Ability

DIRECTIONS

Solve each problem in this section by using the information given and your own mathematical calculations. Then select the *one* correct answer of the five choices given. Use the available space on the page for scratchwork.

NOTE: Some problems may be accompanied by figures or diagrams. These figures are drawn as accurately as possible, *except* when it is stated in a specific problem that the figure is not drawn to scale. The figure is meant to provide information useful in solving the problem or problems. Unless otherwise stated or indicated, all figures lie in a plane. All numbers used are real numbers.

16. If $x - 4 = y$, what must $(y - x)^3$ equal?
    (A) -64 (B) -12 (C) 12 (D) 64
    (E) cannot be determined

Questions 17–21 refer to the graphs.

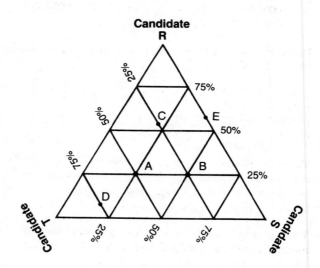

The above graph shows the distribution of votes among three candidates in five different cities in a statewide election.

The graph below shows the total votes cast for these three candidates in these five cities.

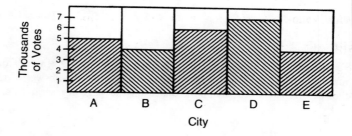

17. Which city cast the most votes for candidate R?
    (A) A   (B) B   (C) C   (D) D   (E) E

18. How many cities cast more votes for candidate S than candidate T?
    (A) 0   (B) 1   (C) 2   (D) 3   (E) 4

19. Which cities cast the same number of votes for candidate R?
    (A) A and B   (B) B and C   (C) C and D
    (D) cannot be determined   (E) all cities were different

20. About how many votes did candidate T receive total in the five cities?
    (A) 2000–4000   (B) 4000–6000   (C) 6000–8000
    (D) 8000–10,000   (E) 10,000–12,000

21. How many cities cast over two-thirds of their votes for one candidate?
    (A) 0   (B) 1   (C) 2   (D) 3   (E) 4

22. If $a/b = c/d$ and a, b, c, and d are positive integers, then which of the
    following is true?
    (A) $a/b = d/c$ (B) $ac = bd$ (C) $a + d = b + c$
    (D) $d/b = c/a$ (E) $a/d = c/b$

23. There are 36 students in a certain geometry class. If two-thirds of the
    students are boys and three-fourths of the boys are under six feet tall,
    how many boys in the class are under six feet tall?
    (A) 6   (B) 12   (C) 18   (D) 24   (E) 27

24. When a certain integer J is divided by 5, the remainder is 1. When
    integer J is divided by 3, then the remainder is 2. The value for J is
    (A) 6   (B) 11   (C) 12   (D) 16   (E) 21

25. A bag contains 20 gumballs. If there are 8 red, 7 white, and 5 green,
    what is the minimum number of gumballs one must pick from the bag to
    be assured of one of each color?
    (A) 16   (B) 9   (C) 8   (D) 6   (E) 3

26. If the ratio of x to y is ¾ and the ratio of y to z is ¹²⁄₁₃, then the ratio of x
    to z is
    (A) ³⁄₁₃   (B) ⁴⁄₁₃   (C) ⅓   (D) ⁹⁄₁₃   (E) ¹²⁄₁₃

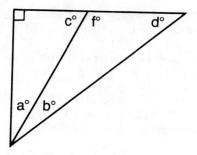

27. In the right triangle, c = 2a and d > 2b; therefore which of the following must be true?
    (A) c > b + d
    (B) angle a is greater than angle b
    (C) angle a equals angle b
    (D) angle b is greater than angle a
    (E) angle d equals twice angle a

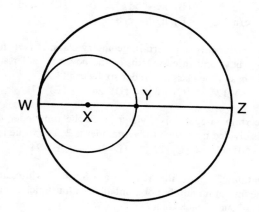

28. In the figure, X and Y are the centers of the two circles. If the area of the larger circle is 144π, what is the area of the smaller circle?
    (A) 72π   (B) 36π   (C) 24π   (D) 12π
    (E) cannot be determined

29. How much tea worth 93¢ per pound must be mixed with tea worth 75¢ per pound to produce 10 pounds worth 85¢ per pound?
    (A) 2⅔   (B) 3½   (C) 4⅘   (D) 5⁵⁄₉   (E) 9½

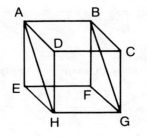

30. In the cube above, AH and BG are diagonals and the surface area of side ABFE is 16. What is the area of rectangle ABGH?

   (A) $4\sqrt{2}$ (B) $16\sqrt{2}$ (C) $16 + \sqrt{2}$ (D) 16   (E) $15\sqrt{3}$

STOP. IF YOU FINISH BEFORE TIME IS CALLED, CHECK YOUR WORK ON THIS SECTION ONLY. DO NOT WORK ON ANY OTHER SECTION IN THE TEST.

ANSWER KEY FOR PRACTICE TEST 1

Section I Verbal Ability	Section II Verbal Ability	Section III Quantitative Ability	Section IV Quantitative Ability
1. C	1. C	1. A	1. A
2. C	2. A	2. D	2. D
3. C	3. A	3. B	3. C
4. E	4. B	4. D	4. A
5. D	5. C	5. D	5. A
6. D	6. B	6. B	6. A
7. C	7. A	7. A	7. C
8. C	8. D	8. A	8. B
9. C	9. A	9. C	9. A
10. E	10. D	10. B	10. B
11. D	11. B	11. D	11. B
12. B	12. A	12. D	12. C
13. C	13. A	13. B	13. A
14. B	14. B	14. A	14. B
15. B	15. A	15. B	15. C
16. D	16. B	16. A	16. B
17. A	17. C	17. B	17. A
18. B	18. D	18. A	18. B
19. D	19. D	19. D	19. C
20. E	20. B	20. C	20. D
21. B	21. E	21. D	21. E
22. A	22. A	22. B	22. C
23. C	23. A	23. D	23. A
24. D	24. D	24. C	24. D
25. D	25. D	25. D	25. C
26. C	26. E	26. C	26. B
27. A	27. A	27. D	27. C
28. E	28. C	28. C	28. B
29. B	29. C	29. D	29. A
30. D	30. E	30. D	30. C
31. A	31. C		
32. D	32. C		
33. B	33. B		
34. A	34. C		
35. C	35. A		
36. B	36. C		
37. D	37. E		
38. D	38. B		
39. A			

ANSWER KEY FOR PRACTICE TEST 1

Section V Analytical Ability	Section VI Analytical Ability	Section VII Quantitative Ability
1. C	1. B	1. A
2. D	2. E	2. B
3. C	3. B	3. D
4. D	4. A	4. C
5. A	5. E	5. B
6. D	6. B	6. D
7. D	7. E	7. A
8. D	8. E	8. C
9. C	9. B	9. C
10. D	10. C	10. C
11. A	11. D	11. D
12. C	12. E	12. A
13. B	13. C	13. A
14. A	14. B	14. D
15. E	15. E	15. B
16. D	16. A	16. A
17. A	17. C	17. C
18. E	18. A	18. C
19. D	19. B	19. E
20. C	20. D	20. E
21. A	21. D	21. B
22. D	22. E	22. D
23. B	23. C	23. C
24. E	24. B	24. B
25. A	25. E	25. A
		26. D
		27. B
		28. B
		29. D
		30. B

HOW TO SCORE YOUR EXAM

1. Add the total number of correct responses for Sections I and II.
2. This total would be scaled to give a Verbal Ability score ranging from 200 to 800.
3. Repeat this process by adding the total correct responses for Sections III and IV.
4. This total would be scaled to give a Quantitative Ability score ranging from 200 to 800.
5. Repeat this process once again by adding the total correct responses for Sections V and VI.
6. This total would be scaled to give an Analytical Ability score ranging from 200 to 800.

NOTE: On this practice test we are assuming that Section VII is experimental and does not count on your score, although this is not always the case.

ANALYZING YOUR TEST RESULTS

The charts on the following pages should be used to carefully analyze your results and spot your strengths and weaknesses. The complete process of analyzing each subject area and each individual problem should be completed for each Practice Test. These results should then be reexamined for trends in types of errors (repeated errors) or poor results in specific subject areas. THIS REEXAMINATION AND ANALYSIS IS OF TREMENDOUS IMPORTANCE TO YOU IN ASSURING MAXIMUM TEST PREPARATION BENEFIT.

PRACTICE TEST 1: VERBAL ABILITY ANALYSIS SHEET

SECTION I

	Possible	Completed	Right	Wrong
Sentence Completion	8			
Analogies	9			
Reading Comprehension	10			
Antonyms	12			
SUBTOTALS	39			

SECTION II

	Possible	Completed	Right	Wrong
Sentence Completion	9			
Analogies	9			
Reading Comprehension	12			
Antonyms	8			
SUBTOTALS	38			
OVERALL VERBAL ABILITY TOTALS	77			

PRACTICE TEST 1: QUANTITATIVE ABILITY ANALYSIS SHEET

SECTION III

	Possible	Completed	Right	Wrong
Quantitative Comparison	15			
Math Ability	15			
SUBTOTALS	30			

SECTION IV

	Possible	Completed	Right	Wrong
Quantitative Comparison	15			
Math Ability	15			
SUBTOTALS	30			
OVERALL QUANTITATIVE ABILITY TOTALS	60			

SECTION VII

NOTE: For this practice test, do not include Section VII in your overall Quantitative Ability score.

	Possible	Completed	Right	Wrong
Quantitative Comparison	15			
Math Ability	15			
TOTALS	30			

PRACTICE TEST 1: ANALYTICAL ABILITY ANALYSIS SHEET

	Possible	Completed	Right	Wrong
Section V	25			
Section VI	25			
OVERALL ANALYTICAL ABILITY TOTALS	50			

WHY??????????????????????????????????

ANALYSIS: TALLY SHEET FOR PROBLEMS MISSED

One of the most important parts of test preparation is analyzing WHY! you missed a problem so that you can reduce the number of mistakes. Now that you have taken the practice test and corrected your answers, carefully tally your mistakes by marking them in the proper column.

REASON FOR MISTAKE

	Total Missed	Simple Mistake	Misread Problem	Lack of Knowledge
SECTION I: VERBAL ABILITY				
SECTION II: VERBAL ABILITY				
SUBTOTALS				
SECTION III: QUANTITATIVE ABILITY				
SECTION IV: QUANTITATIVE ABILITY				
SUBTOTALS				
SECTION V: ANALYTICAL ABILITY				
SECTION VI: ANALYTICAL ABILITY				
SUBTOTALS				
TOTAL VERBAL, QUANTITATIVE, AND ANALYTICAL				

Reviewing the above data should help you determine WHY you are missing certain problems. Now that you have pinpointed the type of error, take the next practice test focusing on avoiding your most common type.

COMPLETE ANSWERS AND EXPLANATIONS FOR
PRACTICE TEST 1

SECTION I: VERBAL ABILITY

Sentence Completion

1. (C) The answer here is *restive . . . unperturbed.* "Although" signals a contrast between the boys' behavior and the girls'. The correct pair of words then must be opposite in meaning. Choices (A), (B), and (E) are synonymous pairs and can be eliminated on that basis. Choice (D) is not a contrast—"remorseful" (sad) and "ingenuous" (naive) are not opposite in meaning. (C) is left as the only pair which satisfies the context and the contrast indicated by the rest of the sentence.

2. (C) The correct answer is *incorporated.* The signal words "not only written . . . but ideas derived" indicate that the ideas from Greek philosophy are considered as equally important, if not more so, in the latter part of the sentence as they were in the first half of the sentence. With crucial derivative ideas one would not "nullify," "criticize," or "alter" them.

3. (C) The answer is *criticized . . . curb.* The idiomatic expression in the second part of the sentence calls for a verb. "Excesses" are *curbed* not "implemented," "promoted," or "ostracized." Choice (B) is a possible completion, but "accused" is more idiomatically followed by "of" rather than "for," leaving (C) as the best choice.

4. (E) The signal word here is "reached"; the only choice which one can "reach" is *pinnacle.* If you had asked yourself, "What was reached?" this answer should have occurred to you.

5. (D) Working from the second blank first, notice that the blank applies to "lesson"; the society in the sentence is "obeying" the lesson, and a close synonym for "obeying" is *heeding.*

6. (D) The best choice is *consequently.* The semicolon is needed to connect the two clauses. The second part of the sentence positively extends the quality of the novel stated in the first part. The connecting word *consequently* provides the direction needed to extend the meaning of the first part of the sentence.

7. (C) So many key terms in this sentence suggest breaking apart— "division," "number," "impersonality." The choice which is most consistent with this theme of divisiveness is (C).

8. (C) A remark to explain not having written a substantial essay would be an *apology,* and a remark about unfairness would tend to be *indignant.*

Analogies

9. (C) *Nap* is to *fabric* in the same way as *fur* is to *dog*. The soft, fuzzy surface of *fabric* is analogous to *fur* on a *dog*.

10. (E) *Ambiguous* is to *clear* in the same way as *indefinite* is to *definite*. The relationship here is one of opposites. *Ambiguous* means "unclear or indefinite." *Clear* means "specific or definite." *Indefinite* is the opposite of *definite*.

11. (D) *Coherence* is to *disintegrate* in the same way as *partnership* is to *dissolve*. The relationship expressed here is one between a unity and the process of falling apart. *Coherence* (connectedness) and *disintegrate* (fall apart) are related in the same way as *partnership* and *dissolve*.

12. (B) *Bestial* is to *brutish* in the same way as *frivolous* is to *trivial*. The relationship here is one of synonymous words. In choice (D), "smirk" has a different connotation than "smile" and these words may be either nouns or verbs, but not adjectives. In choice (E), the words are verbs having similar but distinctly different meanings.

13. (C) *Sympathetic* is to *obdurate* in the same way as *impassioned* is to *frigid*. The relationship here is one of antonyms. Choices (A), (B), (D), and (E) are synonymous and can therefore be eliminated. Only (C) presents a pair of antonyms in *impassioned* (emotionally warm) and *frigid* (emotionally cool) similarly opposite as are *sympathetic* (with feeling) and *obdurate* (hardhearted).

14. (B) *Photosynthesis* is to *oxygen* in the same way *combustion* is to *heat*. The relationship here is one of the process to product. *Oxygen* is a product of *photosynthesis* in the same way that *heat* is a product of *combustion*.

15. (B) *Nostalgia* (a longing for something long ago or far away) is produced through *memory,* in the same way as *lethargy* (sluggishness, apathy) is often produced through *ennui* (boredom).

16. (D) *Anarchy* is to *oligarchy* in the same way as *disorder* is to *order*. The relationship here is one of opposites. *Anarchy* is a lack of government, while *oligarchy* is government by a select few. *Disorder* and *order* are opposites. (A) is close, but "mob" and "meetings" are not necessarily opposites.

17. (A) *Banter* (playful language) is a synonym for *persiflage* in the same way as *similarity* is a synonym for *analogy*.

Reading Comprehension

18. **(B)** Only answers **(B)**, **(D)**, and **(E)** could refer to *size*. **(B)** summarizes the information of the passage, which tells us that an Eskimo's vocabulary is over 10,000 words, whereas the conversation between Eskimos and whites is made up of 300 to 600 words—less than one-tenth of the real Eskimo vocabulary.

19. **(D)** "Stefansson, the explorer," makes an observation about the Eskimo language.

20. **(E)** This is directly stated in the passage.

21. **(B)** Choice **(E)** contradicts the passage's extensive concentration on primitive language. **(D)** contradicts the portion in which pidgin English is compared to a kind of Eskimo jargon different from native Eskimo. **(C)** and **(A)** each contain an unnecessary repetition: *primitive* and *old* are repetitious in **(C)**; *complex* and *complicated* are repetitious in **(A)**.

22. **(A)** According to the first paragraph, a disadvantage of cell counts, smear counts, and membrane filter counts is that "both living and dead cells are counted." This is not true of plate counts, which "have the advantage of not including dead cells" (paragraph 3).

23. **(C)** During the lag phase, "there is no increase in number of viable cells." **(B)** is partially true; it would be correct if not for the claim that cells reproduce.

24. **(D)** The third paragraph shows that incubation produces colonies, which means that there is population *growth*. Choice **(E)** describes only the range of colonies which are counted; it is too limited to be the best choice.

25. **(D)** During the logarithmic phase, "the food supply diminishes" (through consumption, of course), and "waste products accumulate" (conspicuous evidence of such consumption). **(A)** contradicts the passage, which speaks of the rapid growth rate during this phase.

26. **(C)** The smear count is one of the methods which is "quickly accomplished." The other choices are related to more time-consuming procedures.

27. **(A)** During the stationary phase, the highest level of population size is called the "maximum crop." "Crop" is, of course, commonly used as an agricultural term.

28. **(E)** The first six paragraphs describe various methods of counting bacteria, and the remainder of the passage describes each of the various cell "phases." **(A)** and **(D)** are incorrect because the author makes no attempts

to argue or persuade, and does not provide the detailed description that we might call instruction. (B) may be eliminated because the author presents advantages and disadvantages of bacterial counts, not of cell phases. (C) is incorrect because the distinction between "new" and "old" methods is not discussed.

Antonyms

29. (B) Something *mitigated* has become less severe or painful. Something *aggravated* has become worse. "Raised" merely indicates direction of movement, but not whether the movement is for better or worse.

30. (D) A *proselyte* is one who has been convinced to adopt a new religion, political party, or opinion. An *apostate* (*apo* = from; *sta* = stand) is one who forsakes his former system of beliefs. A "renegade" is a deserter from an army or tribe; since a "renegade" does not necessarily desert beliefs, the word is not a near opposite of *proselyte*.

31. (A) To *cloy* is to oversatisfy, or surfeit. Its opposite is *deny*.

32. (D) *Resuscitate* (*re* = again; *cit* = to put into motion) means to revive, bring back to life. Its opposite is *kill*. To "succumb" may mean to die, but could only be an opposite if *resuscitate* meant to live.

33. (B) To *rusticate* is to spend time in the country (*rus* = country); being *urban* means spending time in the city.

34. (A) *Penury* is abject poverty, the opposite of *wealth*.

35. (C) *Laconically* refers to a response which is very short. Its opposite is *verbosely*, which refers to using many words. "Compendiously" refers to saying much in few words.

36. (B) *Moribund* means dying, passing out of existence (*mori* = death). So the direct opposite is *eternal*, never-dying.

37. (D) *Ineffable* (*in* = not; *fab* = to speak) describes something which is inexpressible or indescribable. Its opposite is *definable*, which means capable of being described exactly. "Cogent" refers to something which is convincingly to the point.

38. (D) The correct answer is *contaminate*. *Elutriate* means to purify by washing. *Contaminate* would be the opposite.

39. (A) *Estheticism* is a strong liking for art, beauty, and good taste. Its opposite is *tastelessness*.

SECTION II: VERBAL ABILITY

Sentence Completion

1. (C) The correct choice is *aftermath . . . cause*. The best clue in this sentence comes from the second part of the sentence. The logical activity of an arson squad *after* a fire would be to "uncover" a *cause*. None of the other second word choices fit the context in this case. From this second word, then work back to the first.

2. (A) The correct answer is *facile . . . awkward*. There is a definitional clue in this sentence in the words "basic and fundamental." The first blank requires a word which is somewhat synonymous with these words. The signal word "although" sets up a contrast construction so that a word opposite in meaning to the first blank is required for the second. The only pair with a word that fits the first blank's definition and has a contrasting second term is (A).

3. (A) The correct choice is *dissonance*. The clue words are "tone" and "decline." The appropriate choice must be a term which is both negative and relates to "tone."

4. (B) *Backbone* corresponds with "belly," and *backbone* is to "belly" in the same way as "hard" is to *vulnerable*. These correspondences indicate (B).

5. (C) In this case, the second blank is easier to fill, by eliminating (A), (B), and (E) because they are neither idiomatically nor reasonably fitting. (C) is a better choice than (D) because "appearance" should precede "existence" to make logical sense (something appears before it exists), but *prevalence* is a state logically following existence.

6. (B) The best choice is *potential*. The clue words in this sentence are "ratio" and "resistance." The word "resistance" has a negative connotation. "Ratio" suggests that the answer will need to contrast with "resistance." The only positive words provided as choices are (B), *potential,* and (C), "excitement." "Excitement" does not provide the sentence with proper contextual meaning.

7. (A) These two blanks contrast each other; the first tells what there has been, the second what there has not been (what has been lacking). The two choices which offer contrasts are (A) and (D), and (D) may be eliminated because its terms are not appropriate to a "description."

8. (D) The correct answer is *trenchant*. This sentence's clue lies in the comparison. The answer must be similar to a "surgeon's scalpel." The

sharpness and keenness connoted by *trenchant* satisfy the context of the comparison.

9. (A) The key phrase here is "land as the basic element of wealth"; land equals wealth in a feudal society. Thus (A) is indicated.

Analogies

10. (D) *Color* is to *spectrum* in the same way *choice* is to *gamut*. Here the relationship is part-to-whole but specifically part to an entire range or series of things. In (A) "flower" and "petal" must be eliminated not only because of the whole-to-part instead of part-to-whole relationship but because "petal" is not one of a series or range of a whole as *choice* is to *gamut*. A "symphony" is certainly made up of "notes," but again the specific relationship of a part to a range is not present.

11. (B) *Poem* is to *metaphor* in the same way *sonata* is to *arpeggio*. The relationship here is one of artistic product and artistic tool or convention. The whole-to-part relationship of a *poem* which contains a *metaphor* is similar to a *sonata* which contains an *arpeggio*.

12. (A) *Anathema* is to *malediction* in the same way as *calumny* is to *disapprobation*. The relationship here is one of synonyms. An *anathema* (curse) is similar in meaning to *malediction* in the same way *calumny* (slander) is synonymous with *disapprobation* (strong disapproval).

13. (A) A *beggar* is not likely to be *supercilious* (disdainful, haughty) in the same way as a *miser* is not likely to be *philanthropic* (charitable).

14. (B) A *misogynist* (woman-hater) is never a supporter of *feminism*, in the same way as a *bureaucrat*, with his dependence upon being part of an organization, is never a supporter of *anarchy* (disorder, confusion).

15. (A) *Loquacious* (talkative) is to *taciturn* (silent, reserved) in the same way as *forward* is to *reticent* because both pairs refer to opposite types of social behavior.

16. (B) *Monotheism* is to *theism* in the same way as *unicycle* is to *cycle*. *Monotheism* means belief in one God as opposed to *theism*, which is a more general term referring to belief in God or gods. The relationship here is from a specific singular belief to a more general belief. *Unicycle* is a specific type of one-wheeled *cycle* as opposed to the more general group of *cycles*. (E) is close, but "glasses" have only two complete lenses and therefore the term is not as general.

17. (C) *Parsimonious* (stingy) is the opposite of *profligate* (wasteful) in the same way as *sanctimonious* (extremely pious) is the opposite of *sinful*.

18. (D) *Exonerate* is an opposite of *ostracize; exonerate* means *forgive* and *ostracize* means *ban,* so (D) is the best choice. This is an "opposites" analogy.

Reading Comprehension

19. (D) Although the paragraph compares the sunset to a death, it simply and explicitly states, "the sun sank low." If anything is responsible for this imagined "death," it is the "gloom" which surrounds the big town in the west.

20. (B) The five men are the Director of Companies (captain), the Lawyer, the Accountant, Marlow, and the narrator.

21. (E) "The bones" seems to refer to something just mentioned, and it is *dominoes* that were just mentioned.

22. (A) In paragraph 4 the author says, "Between us there was . . . the bond of the sea."

23. (A) The first sentence tells us that the *Nellie* "was at rest."

24. (D) The author is himself a part of the scene he describes (note the first sentence of paragraph 4); therefore, he is neither "omniscient" (detached and aware of *all* circumstances) nor a "third person" (that is, one not taking part in the scene). There is no evidence that the author is pretentious (A).

25. (D) This is stated in the last sentence of paragraph 3.

26. (E) Rhyme is characteristic of poetry, and paragraph 3 states that the body of science fiction poetry is quite small.

27. (A) The first sentence says that "many people" seem to define science fiction by pulp magazine standards. Something which is popular is something accepted by many people.

28. (C) The first paragraph leads up to the central question—"What is science fiction?" All of the passage is an attempt to answer that question. (A) and (D) are too specific; (B) is too general. (E) does not fit the tone of the passage.

29. (C) Paragraph 2 says that "science fiction . . . postulates a change (for human beings) from conditions as we know them"; in other words, science fiction treats the unknown, unfamiliar, unusual.

30. (E) The final sentence presents a general comparison between "any other story or novel" and science fiction, emphasizing their similarities, and

thus suggesting that the sub-genre of science fiction should be read as one reads fiction in general.

Antonyms

31. (C) *Luxuriant* (*luxus* = extravagance) means plentiful and is usually used to describe something which is abundant in growth. The opposite is *small*. "Miserly" is also opposite to plentiful, but since it refers to hoarding money, it is more nearly opposite to the idea of abundant wealth, not abundant growth.

32. (C) A *tyro* is a beginner at some particular profession, occupation, or art. The best opposite is (C) because it describes someone who is advanced and accomplished at a particular profession.

33. (B) Something *ubiquitous* is something found, or existing, everywhere (*ubique* = everywhere). (B) refers to one particular place, and is therefore more nearly opposite than (A) since "hiding" could refer to several locations.

34. (C) To be *abstemious* is to be moderate in the use of food or drink. (*ab* = from; *temetum* = strong drink). Clearly, the opposite is *gluttonous*.

35. (A) Something *soporific* induces sleep (*sopor* = sleep). The best opposite is *exciting,* (A). "Terrific," (B), is a fair choice, but not so associated with stimulation and wakefulness as (A).

36. (C) A *factotum* is a handyman, jack-of-all-trades (*facere* = do; *totum* = all). The most nearly opposite, then, is the term which opposes the *factotum's* broad talent with narrow talent: *specialist*.

37. (E) A *virago* is a scolding, nagging woman. The opposite to this overbearing sort would be someone extremely submissive, that is, a *slave*.

38. (B) *Mulct* means "to deprive of a possession unjustly." It is a negative word, so its opposite is a positive one; the only clearly positive choice is (B).

SECTION III: QUANTITATIVE ABILITY

Quantitative Comparison

1. **(A)** By inspection both sides are exactly the same, *except* in column A you are adding 4×10^2 and in column B you are subtracting 4×10^2. Therefore, column A is greater. Solving for values would give

$3^2 + 4 \times 10^2 - 4^2$	$3^2 - 4 \times 10^2 - 4^2$
$9 + 4 \times 100 - 16$	$9 - 4 \times 100 - 16$
$9 + 400 - 16$	$9 - 400 - 16$
$409 - 16$	$-391 - 16$
393 $\qquad >$	-407

2. **(D)** Solving $x^2 = 36$ gives $+6$ and -6. Therefore, x can be equal to 6 or less than 6, making no comparison possible.

3. **(B)** On the number line, if x, y, and z are integers, then by inspection $x = 1$, $y = -1$, and $z = 2$. Substituting these values into each column gives

$$2 - 1 \qquad \text{and} \qquad 1 - (-1)$$
$$\text{hence} \qquad 1 \qquad < \qquad 2$$

Therefore the correct answer is **(B)**.

4. **(D)** Since x and y are not vertical angles and no other information is given, no comparison can be made. The correct answer is **(D)**.

5. **(D)** Trying some small values is required here, keeping in mind that x must be greater than 0. Let $x = 1$ then

$3(1)^2$	$2(1)^3$
$3(1)$	$2(1)$
3 $\quad >$	2

In this case column A is greater. Now try another value for x. Let $x = 2$ then

$3(2)^2$	$2(2)^3$
$3(4)$	$2(8)$
12 $\quad <$	16

In this case column B is greater. Since there are different comparisons depending on the values chosen, the correct answer is **(D)**—cannot be determined.

6. (B) Solve the first problem as follows:

x is 30% of 60

Replacing "=" for "is" and "·" for "of" (30% = 3/10)
then x = (3/10) · 60
then x = 18

Solve the second problem as follows:

$$20\% \text{ of } y \text{ is } 4$$
$$(20\% = 1/5)$$
$$(1/5) \cdot y = 4$$
$$(1/5)y = 4$$

Multiplying by 5/1 gives (5/1) · (1/5)y = 4 · (5/1)
then y = 20

7. (A) If the top angle was 90°, then x would be $3\sqrt{2}$. This could be calculated using the Pythagorean theorem.

$$a^2 + b^2 = c^2$$
$$3^2 + 3^2 = x^2$$
$$9 + 9 = x^2$$
$$18 = x^2$$

Therefore $\sqrt{18} = x$

which simplified is $3\sqrt{2}$. But since the angle was originally larger than 90°, then the side across from 92° must be larger than $3\sqrt{2}$. The correct answer is (A).

8. (A) Since there are 180° in a triangle and 92° in one angle, that leaves 88° to be split equally between two angles. Thus angle y is 44°. (The degrees must be split equally because angles across from equal sides are equal). And the triangle has two equal sides (isosceles). The correct answer is (A).

9. (C) The integer multiples of 8 greater than 8 but less than 50 are 16, 24, 32, 40, and 48. Column A is therefore 5. The integer multiples of 6 greater than 6 but less than 40 are 12, 18, 24, 30, 36. Therefore, column B is also 5. The correct answer is (C).

10. (B) The easiest method is by inspection (and/or addition). Column A is approaching 2, but will not get here. Mathematically getting a common denominator and adding gives

$1 + \frac{1}{2} + \frac{1}{4} + \frac{1}{16} + \frac{1}{32} + \frac{1}{64}$, or

$1 + \frac{32}{64} + \frac{16}{64} + \frac{4}{64} + \frac{2}{64} + \frac{1}{64}$

$1 + \frac{55}{64}$

and $1\frac{55}{64} < 2$

11. **(D)** Substituting 0 for x and 1 for y fits the condition $0 < x + y < 2$ ($0 < 0 + 1 < 2$) and gives an answer of (B), column B is greater. Now substituting 1 for x and 0 for y, also fits the condition $0 < x + y < 2$ ($0 < 1 + 0 < 2$) but gives an answer of (A), column A is greater. Therefore the correct answer is (D). Since different values give different comparisons, no comparison can be made.

12. **(D)** Volume of cube with side 6 is $6 \times 6 \times 6 = 216$. Volume of rectangular prism with two dimensions less than 6 is not determinable because the third dimension is needed. Therefore no comparison can be made.

13. **(B)** Solve each equation as follows

	$x^2 + 2x + 1 = 0$	$y^2 - 2y + 1 = 0$
Factoring gives	$(x + 1)(x + 1) = 0$	$(y - 1)(y - 1) = 0$
then	$x + 1 = 0$	$y - 1 = 0$
leaves	$x = -1$	$y = 1$
Therefore		$x < y$

14. **(A)** To make this comparison it is necessary to factor column A.

$$8^{29} - 8^{28}$$
$$8^{28}(8^1 - 8^0)$$
$$8^{28}(8 - 1)$$
$$8^{28}(7) \qquad > \qquad 8^{28}$$

15. **(B)** Substitute $x = 9$ and $y = 4$ (note these are square numbers and they can make solving easier when dealing with square roots).

$\sqrt{x} - \sqrt{y}$	$\sqrt{x - y}$
$\sqrt{9} - \sqrt{4}$	$\sqrt{9 - 4}$
$3 - 2$	$\sqrt{5}$

then $1 \qquad\qquad < \qquad 2.23$

Now try two other numbers. You will find that column B will always be greater.

Math Ability

16. (A) $\dfrac{\text{percent}}{100} = \dfrac{\text{is number}}{\text{of number}}$

$\dfrac{.25}{100} = \dfrac{x}{12}$ (cross multiplying)

$100x = 3.00$

$\dfrac{100x}{100} = \dfrac{3.00}{100}$

$x = .03$, or $\dfrac{3}{100}$

17. (B) Solving the first equation for x as follows:

$\dfrac{2}{x} = 4$

$2 = 4x$

$\dfrac{2}{4} = x$

Therefore $\dfrac{1}{2} = x$

Now solving the second equation for y,

$\dfrac{2}{y} = 8$

$2 = 8y$

$\dfrac{2}{8} = y$

Therefore $\dfrac{1}{4} = y$

Substituting these values for $x - y$ gives $\dfrac{1}{2} - \dfrac{1}{4} = \dfrac{2}{4} - \dfrac{1}{4} = \dfrac{1}{4}$

Therefore, $x - y = \dfrac{1}{4}$, and the correct answer is (B).

18. (A) b = Bob's age
      c = Jane's age
      d = Jim's age

Since Bob is older than Jane, we have c < b.
Since Bob is younger than Jim, we have b < d.
Hence, c < b and b < d, or c < b < d.

19. (D) Breaking the figure into squares of side x by adding lines gives

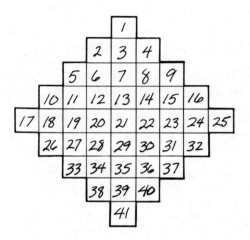

Remember each square has area x^2
then the total area is $41x^2$.

Choices (A), (B), and (E) are not possible as area must be in square units.

20. (C) Distance = rate × time

d = rt
k = rn

$r = \dfrac{k}{n}$ miles per hour

Hence d = rt

$$d = \left(\frac{k}{n}\right)(x) = \frac{kx}{n}$$

21. (D) A rectangular solid consists of six rectangular faces. This one in particular has two 7 × 6, two 6 × 3, and two 7 × 3 rectangles with areas of 42, 18, and 21, respectively. Hence the total surface area will be 2(42) + 2(18) + 2(21) = 84 + 36 + 42 = 162 square meters.

22. (B)   (A) $\frac{1}{8}$ = .125   (D) $\sqrt{.36}$ = .6

     (B) $(.3)^2$ = .09   (E) $\frac{11}{100}$ = .11

     (C) $\frac{1}{.3} = \frac{\frac{1}{3}}{10} = \frac{10}{3}$ = 3.33 . . .

Hence $(.3)^2$ = .09 is the smallest number.

23. (D) There were 4 days where the maximum temperature exceeded the average, thus 4/7 is approximately 57%.

24. (C) The increase was 94 − 84 = 10. The percent increase is found by dividing the increase by the *original* or *from* amount. Thus 10/84 = 11.9%.

25. (D) Set up the equation as follows: Let t be the length of time it will take the plane to overtake the bus, then t + 4 is the time that the bus has traveled before the plane starts. The distance that the bus has traveled by 1:00 P.M. is 50(t + 4), since distance equals rate times time ($d = rt$). The distance the plane will travel is 300t. Now equating these two (they will have to travel the same distance for one to overtake the other), gives 50(t + 4) = 300t.

Solve the equation as follows:

$$50(t + 4) = 300\,t$$
$$50t + 200 = 300t$$
$$200 = 250t$$

Therefore $\frac{4}{5} = t$

$\frac{4}{5}$ of an hour ($\frac{4}{5}$ × 60) is 48 minutes. Hence it will take 48 minutes for the plane to overtake the bus, and since the plane is starting at 1:00 P.M., it will overtake the bus at 1:48 P.M.

26. (C) x + y = 180 (x plus y form a straight line, or straight angle) since x = ($\frac{2}{3}$)y, and substituting gives ($\frac{2}{3}$)y + y = 180, multiplying by 3 leaves 2y + 3y = 540

and solving 5y = 540
                     y = 108

27. (D) Perimeter of $\triangle$MNP = $\frac{1}{2}$ (perimeter of $\triangle$XYZ)

$$= \frac{1}{2}(XY + YZ + XZ)$$
$$= \frac{1}{2}(10 + 15 + 17)$$
$$= \frac{1}{2}(42)$$

Perimeter of $\triangle$MNP = 21

28. (C) For $(a^2 - b^2)/(a - b) = a + b$ to be true, the denominator $a - b$ cannot equal zero, therefore a cannot equal b; $a > b$ is sufficient for this.

29. (D) Circumference = πd

$16\pi = \pi d$
$d = 16$

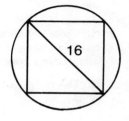

diameter of circle = diagonal of square
area of square = $\frac{1}{2}$ (product of diagonals)

$= \frac{1}{2}d_1 \times d_2$
$= \frac{1}{2}(16)(16) = 128$

30. (D) Let x = the missing number.
Since the average of x and z is y, we have

$\frac{1}{2}(x + z) = y$
$2 \cdot \frac{1}{2}(x + z) = 2y$
$x + z = 2y$
$x + z - z = 2y - z$
$x = 2y - z$

SECTION IV: QUANTITATIVE ABILITY

Quantitative Comparison

1. (A) Changing column A to decimals

$$\frac{1}{3} \times \frac{2}{5} \times \frac{1}{8}$$

gives .33⅓ × .4 × .125 which by inspection is greater than column B. Another method would be to change column B to all fractions and then compare.

2. (D) Since two dimensions, length and width, are necessary to find the area of a rectangle, and only one dimension is given in each case, then no comparison is possible. The correct answer is (D).

3. (C) This comparison should be made without any actual computation as follows:

    35% of 50   50% of 25
    .35 × 50   .50 × 35

    Since 35 × 50 is on each side, and then each column's answer has two decimal places, the quantities are equal.

    Or   35/100 × 50   50/100 × 35
           1/100 × 35 × 50 = 1/100 × 50 × 35

4. (A) Since $a = 3b$ and $b = -2$, then $a = 3(-2) = -6$, substituting into the numerator of each expression (since the denominators are positive and alike, they can be eliminated)

    $$\frac{a^2 + b}{ab} \qquad \frac{a + b^2}{ab}$$

    $(-6)^2 + -2 \qquad -6 + (-2)^2$
    $36 + -2 \qquad\qquad -6 + 4$

    Therefore   34 $>$ -2

5. (A) To find the number of ways four books can be arranged on a shelf, you multiply $4 \times 3 \times 2 \times 1$ and get 24, which is greater than column B.

6. (A) The following diagrams show eight ways of going from A to B, and there are more.

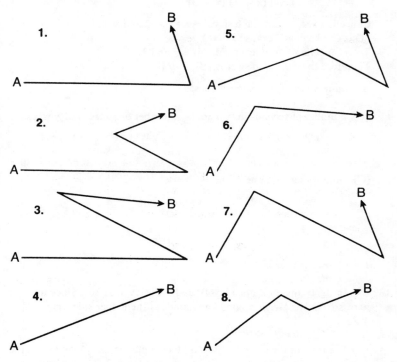

7. (C) Simplifying columns A and B leaves $x^{16}y^{24} = x^{16}y^{24}$. Note that when you have a number with an exponent to a power, you simply multiply the exponents together.

8. (B) Since d is above the x axis, it must be positive and c, being to the left of the y axis, must be negative. Therefore c < d, since all negatives are less than all positives.

9. (A) Since point P is above the line containing points $(-2, 2)$, then d (actual distance) is greater than $|c|$; therefore c + d is a positive number. Point Q is on the line, therefore e and f are additive inverses of each other, totaling 0. All positive numbers are greater than 0, then c + d > e + f.

10. **(B)** Simplifying column A by using the distributing property, leaves

   $(x + 1) (x + 2)$ and $(x + 1) (x + 3)$

   Canceling $x + 1$ from each side, leaves $x + 2$ and $x + 3$.
   (This can be done because $x > 0$.)
   Then canceling x from each side gives 2 and 3.
   Therefore the correct answer is **(B)**, $2 < 3$.

   Alternate method: Try some values.

11. **(B)** Number of seconds in two hours   Number of hours in fifty weeks

   $$60^{min} \times 60^{sec} \times 2 \text{ hrs} \qquad\qquad 24^{hrs} \times 7^{days} \times 50 \text{ weeks}$$
   $$7200 \qquad\qquad < \qquad\qquad 8400$$

12. **(C)** Simplifying columns A and B gives

   $$\sqrt{3^{18}} \qquad\qquad (\sqrt{27^3})^2$$
   $$27^3$$
   $$(3 \cdot 3 \cdot 3)^3$$
   $$3^9 \qquad = \qquad (3^3)^3$$

   The correct answer is **(C)**.

13. **(A)** In the triangle $\angle Z$ must be 60° and $\angle X$ is given as 30°. Since the side across from the larger angle in a triangle is the longer side, then $XY > YZ$.

14. **(B)** The ratio of the sides of a 30-60-90 triangle is 1, 2, $\sqrt{3}$, and since the side across from 30° is 2, the side across from 60° is $2\sqrt{3}$. Compare each column by squaring the number outside and multiply by the numbers under the radical.

   $$2\sqrt{3} \qquad\qquad 3\sqrt{2}$$
   $$\sqrt{3 \cdot 4} \qquad\qquad \sqrt{2 \cdot 9}$$
   $$\sqrt{12} \qquad < \qquad \sqrt{18}$$

15. **(C)** Cross multiplying the values in each column gives

   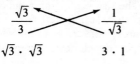

   $$\sqrt{3} \cdot \sqrt{3} \qquad\qquad 3 \cdot 1$$
   Therefore $3 \qquad\qquad = \qquad\qquad 3$

Math Ability

16. (B) Substituting:

If $x = -2$, $x^3 - x^2 - x - 1 = (-2)^3 - (-2)^2 - (-2) - 1$
$$= -8 - 4 + 2 - 1$$
$$= -12 + 2 - 1$$
$$= -10 - 1$$
$$= -11$$

Hence $x^3 - x^2 - x - 1 = -11$

17. (A) Since the sum of the angles is 180° we have

$$m + n + 72 + 25 = 180$$
$$m + n + 97 = 180$$
$$m + n = 180 - 97$$
$$m + n = 83$$

Hence the sum of $m + n$ is 83°.

18. (B) Since the square of a positive number is a positive number, choice (B) is the correct answer.

19. (C) In this type of problem (weighted average) you must multiply the number of students times their respective scores and divide this total by the number of students as follows:

$$\begin{array}{r} 15 \times 80 = 1200 \\ 10 \times 90 = \underline{900} \\ \text{total} \quad 25 \qquad 2100 \end{array}$$

Now divide 25 into 2100. This leaves an average of 84%, therefore the correct answer is (C).

20. (D) Since it takes the pipe t hours to drain the tank completely, it will drain $1/t$ part of the tank each hour.
Hence in three hours, it will drain $3(1/t)$, or $3/t$, part of the tank.

21. (E) Let x equal the length of a side of the cube. The volume $V = x^3$ and the surface area $S = 6x^2$.

Since $V = S$
$x^3 = 6x^2$
Hence $x = 6$

22. **(C)** If you are unfamiliar with the rules, try simple numbers for each situation that will make them false.

    I. The sum of 2 even integers is even.
       $2 + 2 = 4$ $4 + 4 = 8$ (always true)

    II. The product of 2 even integers is even.
       $4 \times 2 = 8$ $2 \times 8 = 16$ (always true)

    III. The sum of 2 odd integers is old.
       $3 + 3 = 6$ (the statement is false)

    IV. The sum of 3 odd integers is even.
       $3 + 5 + 7 = 15$ (the statement is false)

The correct answer is (C), III and IV are false.

23. **(A)** From the bottom graph we see that make B amounted to about 60% of the total domestic sales in July. Thus, 60% of 1,220,000 is about 732,000.

24. **(D)** If you thought the answer was June, look again at the graph. The bottom of the graph is cut off, so the domestic portion of the column appears shorter than it really is.

25. **(C)** From the upper graph, we see that all the columns except one are more than 1,000,000, and all the columns except two are less than 1,200,000. Thus the average is between 1.0 and 1.2 million. Taking the time to add up all the months' totals and divide by 12 is not a good use of time.

26. **(B)** Percent increase is figured by dividing the difference of the two months' sales by the starting month's sales. June is approximately 1100 and December is approximately 1400, hence

$$\frac{1400 - 1100}{1100} = \frac{300}{1100} \approx 30\%$$

27. **(C)** Let

    x = length of equal sides in feet
    x + 8 = length of base in feet

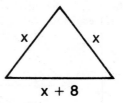

Since the perimeter is 89 feet, we have

$$x + x + (x + 8) = 89$$
$$3x + 8 = 89$$
$$3x + 8 - 8 = 89 - 8$$
$$3x = 81$$
$$\frac{3x}{3} = \frac{81}{3}$$
$$x = 27$$

Hence the length of the base is x + 8, or 35 feet.

28. **(B)** Check each possible pair of numbers for common divisions. For example:

    I.   3 ⎤ Only common divisor 1;
   II. 4 ⎦ these are relatively prime.

    I.   3 ⎤ Only common divisor 1;
  III. 7 ⎦ these are relatively prime.

    I.   3 ⎤ Common divisors are 1 and 3;
  IV. 12 ⎦ these are *not* relatively prime.

29. **(A)** $(-2, 3) \otimes (4, -1) = [(-2)(4) - (3)(-1), (-2)(-1)]$
$$= [(-8) - (-3), (2)]$$
$$= (-5, 2)$$

30. **(C)** Since ABCD is a rhombus, all sides are equal; therefore BC = CD = 6 and BC + CD = 12. AB = 6, minus AE ≈ 4, leaves 6 − 4 ≈ 2, which is the approximate length of BE. Adding 12 + 2 = 14, gives the distance around the rhombus that will be traveled. Now using the formula for circumference of a circle = $2\pi r$, or πd, leaves 6π as the circumference of the complete circle. Because the inscribed angle is 45°, arc DE is 90° (inscribed angle is half of the arc it intercepts). This 90° will not be traveled, as it is in the interior of the figure, therefore only 270° of the 360° in the complete circle will be traveled, or ¾ of the circle. ¾ × 6π = 9π/2. This added to the original 14 gives answer (C) 14 + 9π/2.

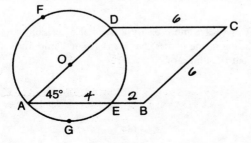

SECTION V: ANALYTICAL ABILITY

Questions 1 to 5 are most easily solved by first making a simple chart from the information given.

	Mon.	Tues.	Wed.	Thurs.
Liz	N	N	N	AD*
Jenni	N	AD	N	N
Jolie	AD	AF	N	N
Rick	AF	AD	AD	AD

*all day

1. (C) Wednesday and Thursday, by referring to the chart.

2. (D) Since they could all study together on Wednesday and Thursday, Monday and Tuesday are the only possible days. Choice (A) is incorrect because they could study together more than twice on the two days.

3. (C) By referring to the chart.

4. (D) I is false, because they could all study together on Wednesday. II is true because the only afternoon Liz could study was Thursday. III is true because Jolie and Jenni could study together Monday, Tuesday, and Wednesday. Therefore, II and III are true.

5. (A) Since the four could study together on Wednesday night and Thursday night, Dan would have to be available on one of those two nights. The only choice given is Wednesday night, (A).

6. (D) This passage implies that the lie detector is sometimes worthless. If the lie detector can be fooled in certain instances, then in those instances it is worthless.

7. (D) The argument is "It has been *proven* that the 'lie detector' can be easily fooled." The best choice is the one which provides such proof—(D). (A) and (B) are too general, and (C) weakens the argument.

8. (D) Only this choice both presents a *strong* point *and* is not contradictory. (A), (C), and (E) contradict the argument, and (B) is not a relatively strong point.

Questions 9 to 13 are more easily answered after constructing a simple diagram and filling in the places. Notice that you could answer some of the questions without the diagram.

From statement 1, place Bernard across from the dentist.

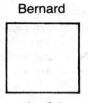

Bernard

dentist

(Bernard is now obviously not the dentist.)

From statement 7, you could tentatively place the general practitioner and the optometrist.

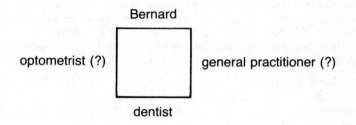

Bernard

optometrist (?)   general practitioner (?)

dentist

Statement 4 tells you that Carla is the general practitioner. Now you can deduce that Bernard must be the surgeon, and since Doug is not across from the surgeon (statement 2), then Doug must be the optometrist.

The final placement can be made from statement 3, because Amy must be the dentist, and the optometrist (Doug) must be on Amy's left.

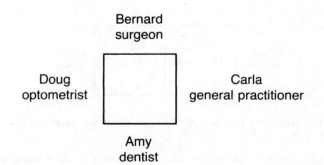

Bernard
surgeon

Doug   Carla
optometrist   general practitioner

Amy
dentist

9. (C) Statement 4 says that Carla is the general practitioner, therefore you already knew that the general practitioner could not be on Carla's left (statement 6).

10. (D) I is false from statement 1. II is false from statement 5. III is true. Since statement 7 tells you that the general practitioner is across from the optometrist, the dentist must be across from the surgeon. This question could have been answered easily from the diagram.

11. (A) I must be true by looking at the diagram.

12. (C) It is evident that both I and II are true, by referring to the diagram.

13. (B) Once again, this is evident from the diagram. You could have eliminated (A), (C), and (D) easily from statements 3 and 4.

14. (A) Bacon advocates retaining dignity without intruding upon liberty. The author implies that retaining dignity is impossible without intruding upon another's liberty by stating that not intruding upon liberty is impossible. (B), (C), and (D) contradict the author's argument, and (E) presents an irrelevant issue.

15. (E) I and II only. The author both relies on his interpretation of Bacon's statement and discusses liberty and dignity in absolute terms; I and II subvert such reliance. III supports, reiterates in fact, the author's argument.

The answers to questions 16 to 20 are not hard to find if an accurate map is constructed. It is important to realize that as one moves to the left, one is going west, and to the right, going east. When traveling to the west, a person will come across the eastern border first. The map should look something like this:

	Bongo	Congo	
West Water	D B E	C F A G	East Water

16. (D) Traveling east to west, the cities would be reached in this order: G, A, F, C, E.

17. (A) The sun rises in the east. The first city to see it would be the easternmost city, "G."

18. (E) The sun sets in the west. The last city to see it would be the westernmost city, "D."

19. (D) As the map shows, "B" is the capital of Bongo and "A" is the capital of Congo. City "C" is a Congo city, not a Bongo city.

20. (C) City "E" is the city on the eastern border of Bongo, the westernmost country.

From the information given, the following chart may be constructed, which would enable you to more easily answer questions 21 to 25.

	FLOOR NUMBER	PEOPLE ON	PEOPLE GET ON	PEOPLE GET OFF
STOP AT	5			
	4			
	3			
STOP AT	2		3	at least 1
	1	3		

Note that there must be at least one more stop to add to get 3 stops.

21. (A) for 3 people to get on the elevator at the 2nd floor, at least 1 person must first get off because the elevator can accommodate only 5 people at any one time.

22. (D) Since the elevator stops at the 5th floor with five people and the total weight may not exceed 1,000 pounds, then the average weight of the people at the 5th floor must not exceed 200 pounds.

23. (B) Only statement II *must* be false. The elevator may make a stop at the 3rd floor, and it is possible that no one gets on at the 4th floor. But someone *must* get off at the 2nd floor to accommodate the 3 people getting on.

24. (E) If the elevator stops at the 2nd floor, the 3rd floor, and finally at the 5th floor, it has made its 3 stops and must therefore not stop at the 4th floor.

25. (A) If the elevator doesn't stop at the 2nd floor and no one gets off at the 3rd or 4th floors, then a total of 2 people must get on at floors 3 and 4 for the total to be 5 people by the 5th floor. Then statement I must be true.

SECTION VI: ANALYTICAL ABILITY

To help answer questions 1 to 7, you may have constructed the following chart.

	X	Y	Z
X	Y	Y	X
Y	Y	Y	Y
Z	X	Y	Z

1. **(B)** II only must be true. From the chart you will observe that I is false (when X reacts with Z, the result is X) and III is false (when Y reacts with Y, the result is Y). Only II is true.

2. **(E)** If the result is Y, then X may have been reacting with X, which is neither I nor II. The key words in the statements are "*had* to be." Y and Z *could* be in the reaction but didn't necessarily have to be.

3. **(B)** The result of X and Z is X. The result of Y and Z is Y. When X reacts with Y, the result is Y.

4. **(A)** Only statement I is false; when X reacts with X, the result is Y.

5. **(E)** The only way X may be the result is if X reacts with Z. Thus X and Z both had to be in the reaction, and therefore Y could not be. Statements I, II, and III are true.

6. **(B)** The result of X and X is Y. The result of Z and Z is Z. Thus the result of Y and Z is Y.

7. **(E)** Since Y is involved in the reaction, the result must be Y; therefore, it is *not* W, X, or Z. Although answers (A) and (C) contain two of these letters, neither answer is as complete as (E). You could have expanded the chart like this:

	X	Y	Z	W
X	Y	Y	X	W
Y	Y	Y	Y	Y
Z	X	Y	Z	W
W	W	Y	W	W

148

From the chart, the result of W and Z is W, and the result of W and Y is Y. The result of W and Y again is Y.

8. (E) Choices (A) and (B) are not implied; they are explicitly stated. (C) is vague; the meaning of *consequentiality* is not clear. (D) is incorrect because the author is arguing that doing nothing has no consequences. Choice (E) is correct. This author says that doing nothing keeps us safe from consequences; this could be true only in light of the implication that doing nothing is not an act.

9. (B) According to the author, the alternative to experiencing consequences is playing it "safe"; this can mean only that consequences are dangerous.

From the information given for questions 10 to 15, you could have constructed the following charts, which may be helpful in enabling you to answer. (Note that the circled books must be positioned as shown.)

```
   1. B B M M (M)            1. B B B B (M)
   2.(S S S S  M)            2.(S S S S  M)
   3. B B B M  M    or       3. B B M M  M
   4. B B B M (M)            4. B B M M (M)
```

10. (C) From the given information, at least 1 mystery book must be on shelf number 3, and all the science fiction books are on shelf number 2. Thus none can be on shelf number 3.

11. (D) There is never only one biography on a shelf.

12. (E) Shelves 1 and 4 together contain over half of the biographies and no science fiction.

13. (C) There is no possible way that shelf number 4 could contain equal numbers of each book. Since 5 books are on the shelf, they cannot be evenly divided.

14. (B) Shelf number 4 must contain either 3 biographies and 2 mysteries or 3 mysteries and 2 biographies. Either way, the ratio is 3 to 2.

15. (E) Shelf number 1 has either 4 biographies and 1 mystery or 2 biographies and 3 mysteries.

16. (A) If only squares are two-dimensional, then anything that is two-dimensional must then be a square.

17. (C) By agreeing that fear is acceptable, we can also agree that fearing fear is nonsense. (D), the only other choice that corresponds at all

with the argument of the passage, is a weak choice because the author is arguing that fearing fear is nonsense and that fear itself is acceptable.

18. (A) Choices (B) and (E) support the author's argument by stressing further the importance of fear. (C) could either support or weaken the argument, depending upon whether it is taken to refer to the blanket generalization that the author attacks, or to the further generalization that the author presents. (D) is irrelevant to the argument, which does not stress the importance of the source of fear.

To construct your chart for questions 19 to 25, it may be easiest to list the letters A, B, C, and D consecutively, leaving room between them to place in numbers. Your chart should then have looked like this:

    4 6 A 5 B 2 C 1 D 3   or   4 6 A 5 B 2 C 3 D 1

19. (B) B is between 1 and A, but *not* next to either.

20. (D) Both I and II must be true.

21. (D) If 3 is the last figure, then 1 is before D, which puts it next to C.

22. (E) The numbers next to B are 2 and 5, which total to 7.

23. (C) To add two more letters to the list, they must go after D to stay in alphabetical order. But then they don't have a number between them to abide by the rules. Thus, the answer is (C).

24. (B) B is in the fifth position. The nearest other letters are third and seventh.

25. (E) The first two numbers in the list total 10, which is twice 5 and greater than the total of the last 3 numbers, 6.

SECTION VII: QUANTITATIVE ABILITY

Quantitative Comparison

1. **(A)** There are 8 ones in 48. There are 6 tens in 68. Thus there are more ones in 48 than tens in 68.

2. **(B)** $\sqrt{48}$ is slightly less than $\sqrt{49}$. $\sqrt{49}$ is actually 7. Thus 7 is greater than $\sqrt{48}$.

3. **(D)** There are no conditions on which values we may plug in for x or y. Thus, if we use 0 for x and 1000 for y, then column B is greater. But if we use 1000 for x and 0 for y, column A is greater. So the answer is **(D)**.

4. **(C)** There is no need to do any calculations for this problem. Column A can be written $(40/100) \times 60$. Column B can be written $(60/100) \times 40$. You should then note that both columns have $(40 \times 60)/100$.

5. **(B)** Subtracting in Column A, we get $.05 - .125 = -.075$. Our difference is a negative number. Thus the positive value in column B must be greater.

6. **(D)** The angles in column A (x, y, c) sum to the total of both vertical angles running up and down. The angles in column B (a, z, b) sum to the total of both vertical angles running side to side.

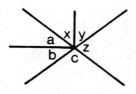

As the diagram is not drawn to scale, it may look like this, in which case column A would be greater.

Or like this, in which case column B would be greater.

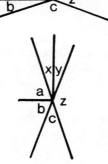

Or they could be equal.

7. (A) In any triangle, the largest side is opposite the largest angle. Side x is opposite the right angle (90°), so it must be the largest side.

8. (C) The triangle is a 30°, 60°, 90° triangle, which means its sides are in proportion 1, $\sqrt{3}$, 2. Since the smallest side (opposite the smallest angle, 30°) equals 2, then the other sides must be $2\sqrt{3}$ and 4. Thus x equals 4. So column B, x/2, equals 4/2 or 2.

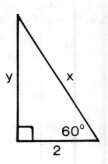

9. (C) 1/20 equals 5/100, which is equal to 5%.

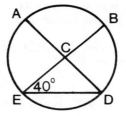

10. (C) ∠CED is given as 40°. Note that $\overset{\frown}{BD}$ is the arc that ∠CED intercepts. A rule in geometry states that any inscribed angle equals half the arc it intercepts, so column A equals column B.

11. (D) We have no way of knowing what the measures of the angles of the circle (∠ACB or ∠ACE) are. Thus we cannot know the values of $\overset{\frown}{AE}$ or $\overset{\frown}{AB}$.

12. (A) Since ∠BCD is an exterior angle of ∆CED, then it is equal to the sum of the remote angles (∠CED + ∠CDE). Therefore, it must be greater than one of them.

13. (A) There are 9 diagonals in a hexagon, but only 6 sides.

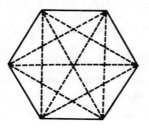

14. (D) A rhombus is a parallelogram with all sides equal. Column A (length of side AB) then equals 5 because the area of a rhombus equals *bh* (20 = 4 × base). But we have no way of knowing whether diagonal AC is the "long" diagonal or the "short" diagonal. (See the alternate drawings that follow.)

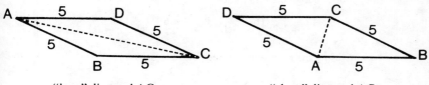

"long" diagonal AC   "short" diagonal AC

15. (B) Since T is greater than x, and m is greater than y, then T + m must always be greater than x + y.

Math Ability

16. (A) If $x - 4 = y$ then $y - x = -4$
    Hence $(y - x)^3 = (-4)^3 = -64$

17. (C) City E cast 60% of its 4000 votes (2400) for candidate R.
    City C cast 55% of its 6000 votes (3300) for candidate R.

18. (C) City B and city E are closer to the 100% point of candidate S than candidate T.

19. (E) Cities A and B cast the same percentage of votes for candidate R but different numbers of votes.

20. (E) For city D, 75% of 7000 = 5250. For city A, 50% of 5000 = 2500. For city B, 25% of 4000 = 1000. For city C, 25% of 6000 = 1500. Therefore 5250 plus 2500 plus 1000 plus 1500 equals 10,250.

21. (B) Only city D cast *more* than two-thirds for one candidate.

22. (D) If $a/b = c/d$ then, by cross multiplying, we get ad = bc.

 If $d/b = c/a$ then we get the same result by cross multiplying,
 ad = bc.

 Hence if $a/b = c/d$, then $d/b = c/a$

23. (C) Since two-thirds of the students are boys we have ⅔ (36) = 24 boys in the class.
 Out of the 24 boys in the class, three-fourths of them are under six feet tall or ¾ (24) = 18 boys under six feet tall.

24. (B) This problem is most easily solved by working from the answers. Divide each of the answers by 5 and notice that choice (C) is eliminated, since it does not give a remainder of 1.

$$\frac{12}{5} = 2r2; \quad \frac{16}{5} = 3r1; \quad \frac{21}{5} = 4r1; \quad \frac{6}{5} = 1r1; \quad \frac{11}{5} = 2r1$$

Now dividing the remaining choices by 3 gives

$$\frac{16}{3} = 5r1; \quad \frac{21}{3} = 7; \quad \frac{6}{3} = 2; \quad \frac{11}{3} = 3r2$$

The correct choice is (B), 11, which when divided by 5 has a remainder of 1 and when divided by 3 has a remainder of 2.

25. (A) If 15 gumballs are picked from the bag it is possible that 8 of them are red and 7 are green. On the next pick however (the 16th), one is assured of having one gumball of each color.

26. (D) Since $x/y = ¾$, and $y/z = ^{12}/_{13}$, cross multiplying gives $4x = 3y$ and $12z = 13y$. Now solving each for x and z, respectively, $x = 3y/4$ and $z = 13y/12$. Hence

$$\frac{x}{z} = \frac{3y/4}{13y/12} = \frac{9y}{13y} = 9/13$$

27. (B) In the right triangle, if c = 2a, then angle a = 30° and c = 60°. Since angle f is supplementary to angle c, angle f must be 120°. If angle f is 120°, then there are 60° left to be divided between angles d and b (remember there are 180° in a triangle). Since d > 2b, then b must be less than 30; therefore the correct answer is (B), angle a (30°) is greater than angle b (less than 30°). Notice the way you should have marked the diagram to assist you.

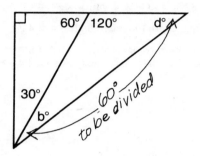

28. (B) Area of larger circle = 144π

    Since area = πr², then

    πr² = 144π
    r² = 144
    r = 12

    Radius of larger circle = 12
    Diameter of smaller circle = 12
    Radius of smaller circle = 6

    Area of smaller circle = πr²
    = π(6)²
    = 36π

29. (D) The only reasonable answer is 5⁵⁄₉ since 85¢ per pound is slightly closer to 93¢ per pound than 75¢ per pound, then slightly more than half of the 10 pounds must be 93¢ per pound.

    Algebraically, let x stand for the pounds of 93¢ tea, then 10 − x is the 75¢ tea. This leads to the equation

    $$.93x + .75 (10 − x) = .85 (10)$$

    Solving gives 93 x + 750 − 75x = 850
    18x = 100
    $$x = \frac{100}{18}$$

    Therefore   x = 5⁵⁄₉

30. **(B)** Since the surface area of side ABFE is 16, then each side is 4. Now use the Pythagorean theorem to find the length of the diagonal that is also the length of the rectangle.

$$4^2 + 4^2 = AH^2$$
$$16 + 16 = AH^2$$
$$32 = AH^2$$
$$\sqrt{32} = AH$$

Simplifying $\sqrt{32} = \sqrt{16 \times 2} = \sqrt{16} \times \sqrt{2} = 4\sqrt{2}$

Now multiplying length times width gives $4 \times 4\sqrt{2} = 16\sqrt{2}$

Notice you may have recognized the ratio of a 45°:45°:90° triangle as $1:1:\sqrt{2}$ and found the diagonal quickly using $4:4:4\sqrt{2}$.

PRACTICE TEST 2

ANSWER SHEET FOR PRACTICE TEST 2
(Remove This Sheet and Use It to Mark Your Answers)

SECTION I

1	Ⓐ	Ⓑ	Ⓒ	Ⓓ	Ⓔ
2	Ⓐ	Ⓑ	Ⓒ	Ⓓ	Ⓔ
3	Ⓐ	Ⓑ	Ⓒ	Ⓓ	Ⓔ
4	Ⓐ	Ⓑ	Ⓒ	Ⓓ	Ⓔ
5	Ⓐ	Ⓑ	Ⓒ	Ⓓ	Ⓔ
6	Ⓐ	Ⓑ	Ⓒ	Ⓓ	Ⓔ
7	Ⓐ	Ⓑ	Ⓒ	Ⓓ	Ⓔ
8	Ⓐ	Ⓑ	Ⓒ	Ⓓ	Ⓔ
9	Ⓐ	Ⓑ	Ⓒ	Ⓓ	Ⓔ
10	Ⓐ	Ⓑ	Ⓒ	Ⓓ	Ⓔ
11	Ⓐ	Ⓑ	Ⓒ	Ⓓ	Ⓔ
12	Ⓐ	Ⓑ	Ⓒ	Ⓓ	Ⓔ
13	Ⓐ	Ⓑ	Ⓒ	Ⓓ	Ⓔ
14	Ⓐ	Ⓑ	Ⓒ	Ⓓ	Ⓔ
15	Ⓐ	Ⓑ	Ⓒ	Ⓓ	Ⓔ
16	Ⓐ	Ⓑ	Ⓒ	Ⓓ	Ⓔ
17	Ⓐ	Ⓑ	Ⓒ	Ⓓ	Ⓔ
18	Ⓐ	Ⓑ	Ⓒ	Ⓓ	Ⓔ
19	Ⓐ	Ⓑ	Ⓒ	Ⓓ	Ⓔ
20	Ⓐ	Ⓑ	Ⓒ	Ⓓ	Ⓔ
21	Ⓐ	Ⓑ	Ⓒ	Ⓓ	Ⓔ
22	Ⓐ	Ⓑ	Ⓒ	Ⓓ	Ⓔ
23	Ⓐ	Ⓑ	Ⓒ	Ⓓ	Ⓔ
24	Ⓐ	Ⓑ	Ⓒ	Ⓓ	Ⓔ
25	Ⓐ	Ⓑ	Ⓒ	Ⓓ	Ⓔ
26	Ⓐ	Ⓑ	Ⓒ	Ⓓ	Ⓔ
27	Ⓐ	Ⓑ	Ⓒ	Ⓓ	Ⓔ
28	Ⓐ	Ⓑ	Ⓒ	Ⓓ	Ⓔ
29	Ⓐ	Ⓑ	Ⓒ	Ⓓ	Ⓔ
30	Ⓐ	Ⓑ	Ⓒ	Ⓓ	Ⓔ

31	Ⓐ	Ⓑ	Ⓒ	Ⓓ	Ⓔ
32	Ⓐ	Ⓑ	Ⓒ	Ⓓ	Ⓔ
33	Ⓐ	Ⓑ	Ⓒ	Ⓓ	Ⓔ
34	Ⓐ	Ⓑ	Ⓒ	Ⓓ	Ⓔ
35	Ⓐ	Ⓑ	Ⓒ	Ⓓ	Ⓔ
36	Ⓐ	Ⓑ	Ⓒ	Ⓓ	Ⓔ
37	Ⓐ	Ⓑ	Ⓒ	Ⓓ	Ⓔ
38	Ⓐ	Ⓑ	Ⓒ	Ⓓ	Ⓔ

SECTION II

1	Ⓐ	Ⓑ	Ⓒ	Ⓓ	Ⓔ
2	Ⓐ	Ⓑ	Ⓒ	Ⓓ	Ⓔ
3	Ⓐ	Ⓑ	Ⓒ	Ⓓ	Ⓔ
4	Ⓐ	Ⓑ	Ⓒ	Ⓓ	Ⓔ
5	Ⓐ	Ⓑ	Ⓒ	Ⓓ	Ⓔ
6	Ⓐ	Ⓑ	Ⓒ	Ⓓ	Ⓔ
7	Ⓐ	Ⓑ	Ⓒ	Ⓓ	Ⓔ
8	Ⓐ	Ⓑ	Ⓒ	Ⓓ	Ⓔ
9	Ⓐ	Ⓑ	Ⓒ	Ⓓ	Ⓔ
10	Ⓐ	Ⓑ	Ⓒ	Ⓓ	Ⓔ
11	Ⓐ	Ⓑ	Ⓒ	Ⓓ	Ⓔ
12	Ⓐ	Ⓑ	Ⓒ	Ⓓ	Ⓔ
13	Ⓐ	Ⓑ	Ⓒ	Ⓓ	Ⓔ
14	Ⓐ	Ⓑ	Ⓒ	Ⓓ	Ⓔ
15	Ⓐ	Ⓑ	Ⓒ	Ⓓ	Ⓔ
16	Ⓐ	Ⓑ	Ⓒ	Ⓓ	Ⓔ
17	Ⓐ	Ⓑ	Ⓒ	Ⓓ	Ⓔ
18	Ⓐ	Ⓑ	Ⓒ	Ⓓ	Ⓔ
19	Ⓐ	Ⓑ	Ⓒ	Ⓓ	Ⓔ
20	Ⓐ	Ⓑ	Ⓒ	Ⓓ	Ⓔ
21	Ⓐ	Ⓑ	Ⓒ	Ⓓ	Ⓔ
22	Ⓐ	Ⓑ	Ⓒ	Ⓓ	Ⓔ
23	Ⓐ	Ⓑ	Ⓒ	Ⓓ	Ⓔ
24	Ⓐ	Ⓑ	Ⓒ	Ⓓ	Ⓔ
25	Ⓐ	Ⓑ	Ⓒ	Ⓓ	Ⓔ
26	Ⓐ	Ⓑ	Ⓒ	Ⓓ	Ⓔ
27	Ⓐ	Ⓑ	Ⓒ	Ⓓ	Ⓔ
28	Ⓐ	Ⓑ	Ⓒ	Ⓓ	Ⓔ
29	Ⓐ	Ⓑ	Ⓒ	Ⓓ	Ⓔ
30	Ⓐ	Ⓑ	Ⓒ	Ⓓ	Ⓔ

31	Ⓐ	Ⓑ	Ⓒ	Ⓓ	Ⓔ
32	Ⓐ	Ⓑ	Ⓒ	Ⓓ	Ⓔ
33	Ⓐ	Ⓑ	Ⓒ	Ⓓ	Ⓔ
34	Ⓐ	Ⓑ	Ⓒ	Ⓓ	Ⓔ
35	Ⓐ	Ⓑ	Ⓒ	Ⓓ	Ⓔ
36	Ⓐ	Ⓑ	Ⓒ	Ⓓ	Ⓔ
37	Ⓐ	Ⓑ	Ⓒ	Ⓓ	Ⓔ
38	Ⓐ	Ⓑ	Ⓒ	Ⓓ	Ⓔ

ANSWER SHEET FOR PRACTICE TEST 2
(Remove This Sheet and Use It to Mark Your Answers)

SECTION III	SECTION IV	SECTION V
1 Ⓐ Ⓑ Ⓒ Ⓓ Ⓔ	1 Ⓐ Ⓑ Ⓒ Ⓓ Ⓔ	1 Ⓐ Ⓑ Ⓒ Ⓓ Ⓔ
2 Ⓐ Ⓑ Ⓒ Ⓓ Ⓔ	2 Ⓐ Ⓑ Ⓒ Ⓓ Ⓔ	2 Ⓐ Ⓑ Ⓒ Ⓓ Ⓔ
3 Ⓐ Ⓑ Ⓒ Ⓓ Ⓔ	3 Ⓐ Ⓑ Ⓒ Ⓓ Ⓔ	3 Ⓐ Ⓑ Ⓒ Ⓓ Ⓔ
4 Ⓐ Ⓑ Ⓒ Ⓓ Ⓔ	4 Ⓐ Ⓑ Ⓒ Ⓓ Ⓔ	4 Ⓐ Ⓑ Ⓒ Ⓓ Ⓔ
5 Ⓐ Ⓑ Ⓒ Ⓓ Ⓔ	5 Ⓐ Ⓑ Ⓒ Ⓓ Ⓔ	5 Ⓐ Ⓑ Ⓒ Ⓓ Ⓔ
6 Ⓐ Ⓑ Ⓒ Ⓓ Ⓔ	6 Ⓐ Ⓑ Ⓒ Ⓓ Ⓔ	6 Ⓐ Ⓑ Ⓒ Ⓓ Ⓔ
7 Ⓐ Ⓑ Ⓒ Ⓓ Ⓔ	7 Ⓐ Ⓑ Ⓒ Ⓓ Ⓔ	7 Ⓐ Ⓑ Ⓒ Ⓓ Ⓔ
8 Ⓐ Ⓑ Ⓒ Ⓓ Ⓔ	8 Ⓐ Ⓑ Ⓒ Ⓓ Ⓔ	8 Ⓐ Ⓑ Ⓒ Ⓓ Ⓔ
9 Ⓐ Ⓑ Ⓒ Ⓓ Ⓔ	9 Ⓐ Ⓑ Ⓒ Ⓓ Ⓔ	9 Ⓐ Ⓑ Ⓒ Ⓓ Ⓔ
10 Ⓐ Ⓑ Ⓒ Ⓓ Ⓔ	10 Ⓐ Ⓑ Ⓒ Ⓓ Ⓔ	10 Ⓐ Ⓑ Ⓒ Ⓓ Ⓔ
11 Ⓐ Ⓑ Ⓒ Ⓓ Ⓔ	11 Ⓐ Ⓑ Ⓒ Ⓓ Ⓔ	11 Ⓐ Ⓑ Ⓒ Ⓓ Ⓔ
12 Ⓐ Ⓑ Ⓒ Ⓓ Ⓔ	12 Ⓐ Ⓑ Ⓒ Ⓓ Ⓔ	12 Ⓐ Ⓑ Ⓒ Ⓓ Ⓔ
13 Ⓐ Ⓑ Ⓒ Ⓓ Ⓔ	13 Ⓐ Ⓑ Ⓒ Ⓓ Ⓔ	13 Ⓐ Ⓑ Ⓒ Ⓓ Ⓔ
14 Ⓐ Ⓑ Ⓒ Ⓓ Ⓔ	14 Ⓐ Ⓑ Ⓒ Ⓓ Ⓔ	14 Ⓐ Ⓑ Ⓒ Ⓓ Ⓔ
15 Ⓐ Ⓑ Ⓒ Ⓓ Ⓔ	15 Ⓐ Ⓑ Ⓒ Ⓓ Ⓔ	15 Ⓐ Ⓑ Ⓒ Ⓓ Ⓔ
16 Ⓐ Ⓑ Ⓒ Ⓓ Ⓔ	16 Ⓐ Ⓑ Ⓒ Ⓓ Ⓔ	16 Ⓐ Ⓑ Ⓒ Ⓓ Ⓔ
17 Ⓐ Ⓑ Ⓒ Ⓓ Ⓔ	17 Ⓐ Ⓑ Ⓒ Ⓓ Ⓔ	17 Ⓐ Ⓑ Ⓒ Ⓓ Ⓔ
18 Ⓐ Ⓑ Ⓒ Ⓓ Ⓔ	18 Ⓐ Ⓑ Ⓒ Ⓓ Ⓔ	18 Ⓐ Ⓑ Ⓒ Ⓓ Ⓔ
19 Ⓐ Ⓑ Ⓒ Ⓓ Ⓔ	19 Ⓐ Ⓑ Ⓒ Ⓓ Ⓔ	19 Ⓐ Ⓑ Ⓒ Ⓓ Ⓔ
20 Ⓐ Ⓑ Ⓒ Ⓓ Ⓔ	20 Ⓐ Ⓑ Ⓒ Ⓓ Ⓔ	20 Ⓐ Ⓑ Ⓒ Ⓓ Ⓔ
21 Ⓐ Ⓑ Ⓒ Ⓓ Ⓔ	21 Ⓐ Ⓑ Ⓒ Ⓓ Ⓔ	21 Ⓐ Ⓑ Ⓒ Ⓓ Ⓔ
22 Ⓐ Ⓑ Ⓒ Ⓓ Ⓔ	22 Ⓐ Ⓑ Ⓒ Ⓓ Ⓔ	22 Ⓐ Ⓑ Ⓒ Ⓓ Ⓔ
23 Ⓐ Ⓑ Ⓒ Ⓓ Ⓔ	23 Ⓐ Ⓑ Ⓒ Ⓓ Ⓔ	23 Ⓐ Ⓑ Ⓒ Ⓓ Ⓔ
24 Ⓐ Ⓑ Ⓒ Ⓓ Ⓔ	24 Ⓐ Ⓑ Ⓒ Ⓓ Ⓔ	24 Ⓐ Ⓑ Ⓒ Ⓓ Ⓔ
25 Ⓐ Ⓑ Ⓒ Ⓓ Ⓔ	25 Ⓐ Ⓑ Ⓒ Ⓓ Ⓔ	25 Ⓐ Ⓑ Ⓒ Ⓓ Ⓔ
26 Ⓐ Ⓑ Ⓒ Ⓓ Ⓔ	26 Ⓐ Ⓑ Ⓒ Ⓓ Ⓔ	
27 Ⓐ Ⓑ Ⓒ Ⓓ Ⓔ	27 Ⓐ Ⓑ Ⓒ Ⓓ Ⓔ	
28 Ⓐ Ⓑ Ⓒ Ⓓ Ⓔ	28 Ⓐ Ⓑ Ⓒ Ⓓ Ⓔ	
29 Ⓐ Ⓑ Ⓒ Ⓓ Ⓔ	29 Ⓐ Ⓑ Ⓒ Ⓓ Ⓔ	
30 Ⓐ Ⓑ Ⓒ Ⓓ Ⓔ	30 Ⓐ Ⓑ Ⓒ Ⓓ Ⓔ	

ANSWER SHEET FOR PRACTICE TEST 2
(Remove This Sheet and Use It to Mark Your Answers)

SECTION VI   SECTION VII

SECTION VI	SECTION VII
1 Ⓐ Ⓑ Ⓒ Ⓓ Ⓔ	1 Ⓐ Ⓑ Ⓒ Ⓓ Ⓔ
2 Ⓐ Ⓑ Ⓒ Ⓓ Ⓔ	2 Ⓐ Ⓑ Ⓒ Ⓓ Ⓔ
3 Ⓐ Ⓑ Ⓒ Ⓓ Ⓔ	3 Ⓐ Ⓑ Ⓒ Ⓓ Ⓔ
4 Ⓐ Ⓑ Ⓒ Ⓓ Ⓔ	4 Ⓐ Ⓑ Ⓒ Ⓓ Ⓔ
5 Ⓐ Ⓑ Ⓒ Ⓓ Ⓔ	5 Ⓐ Ⓑ Ⓒ Ⓓ Ⓔ
6 Ⓐ Ⓑ Ⓒ Ⓓ Ⓔ	6 Ⓐ Ⓑ Ⓒ Ⓓ Ⓔ
7 Ⓐ Ⓑ Ⓒ Ⓓ Ⓔ	7 Ⓐ Ⓑ Ⓒ Ⓓ Ⓔ
8 Ⓐ Ⓑ Ⓒ Ⓓ Ⓔ	8 Ⓐ Ⓑ Ⓒ Ⓓ Ⓔ
9 Ⓐ Ⓑ Ⓒ Ⓓ Ⓔ	9 Ⓐ Ⓑ Ⓒ Ⓓ Ⓔ
10 Ⓐ Ⓑ Ⓒ Ⓓ Ⓔ	10 Ⓐ Ⓑ Ⓒ Ⓓ Ⓔ
11 Ⓐ Ⓑ Ⓒ Ⓓ Ⓔ	11 Ⓐ Ⓑ Ⓒ Ⓓ Ⓔ
12 Ⓐ Ⓑ Ⓒ Ⓓ Ⓔ	12 Ⓐ Ⓑ Ⓒ Ⓓ Ⓔ
13 Ⓐ Ⓑ Ⓒ Ⓓ Ⓔ	13 Ⓐ Ⓑ Ⓒ Ⓓ Ⓔ
14 Ⓐ Ⓑ Ⓒ Ⓓ Ⓔ	14 Ⓐ Ⓑ Ⓒ Ⓓ Ⓔ
15 Ⓐ Ⓑ Ⓒ Ⓓ Ⓔ	15 Ⓐ Ⓑ Ⓒ Ⓓ Ⓔ
16 Ⓐ Ⓑ Ⓒ Ⓓ Ⓔ	16 Ⓐ Ⓑ Ⓒ Ⓓ Ⓔ
17 Ⓐ Ⓑ Ⓒ Ⓓ Ⓔ	17 Ⓐ Ⓑ Ⓒ Ⓓ Ⓔ
18 Ⓐ Ⓑ Ⓒ Ⓓ Ⓔ	18 Ⓐ Ⓑ Ⓒ Ⓓ Ⓔ
19 Ⓐ Ⓑ Ⓒ Ⓓ Ⓔ	19 Ⓐ Ⓑ Ⓒ Ⓓ Ⓔ
20 Ⓐ Ⓑ Ⓒ Ⓓ Ⓔ	20 Ⓐ Ⓑ Ⓒ Ⓓ Ⓔ
21 Ⓐ Ⓑ Ⓒ Ⓓ Ⓔ	21 Ⓐ Ⓑ Ⓒ Ⓓ Ⓔ
22 Ⓐ Ⓑ Ⓒ Ⓓ Ⓔ	22 Ⓐ Ⓑ Ⓒ Ⓓ Ⓔ
23 Ⓐ Ⓑ Ⓒ Ⓓ Ⓔ	23 Ⓐ Ⓑ Ⓒ Ⓓ Ⓔ
24 Ⓐ Ⓑ Ⓒ Ⓓ Ⓔ	24 Ⓐ Ⓑ Ⓒ Ⓓ Ⓔ
25 Ⓐ Ⓑ Ⓒ Ⓓ Ⓔ	25 Ⓐ Ⓑ Ⓒ Ⓓ Ⓔ
	26 Ⓐ Ⓑ Ⓒ Ⓓ Ⓔ
	27 Ⓐ Ⓑ Ⓒ Ⓓ Ⓔ
	28 Ⓐ Ⓑ Ⓒ Ⓓ Ⓔ
	29 Ⓐ Ⓑ Ⓒ Ⓓ Ⓔ
	30 Ⓐ Ⓑ Ⓒ Ⓓ Ⓔ

SECTION I: VERBAL ABILITY

Time: 30 Minutes
38 Questions

In this section, choose the best answer for each question and blacken the corresponding space on the answer sheet.

Sentence Completion

DIRECTIONS

Each blank in the following sentences indicates that something has been omitted. Considering the lettered words beneath the sentence, choose the word or set of words that best fits the whole sentence.

1. The thought of a nuclear _____ sparked by a misunderstanding poses an awesome _____.
   - (A) device . . . reverberation
   - (B) holocaust . . . specter
   - (C) endanger . . . spectacle
   - (D) liaison . . . probability
   - (E) explosion . . . calamity

2. Rural dwellers who hold _____ values may, at times, be altogether uncritical of various federal programs aimed at the regulation and _____ of agriculture.
   - (A) rigorous . . . legalization
   - (B) conventional . . . subsidization
   - (C) ludicrous . . . obfuscation
   - (D) rhythmic . . . communization
   - (E) similarity . . . decimation

3. Truman tried to continue Roosevelt's _____ approach to the Soviet Union, but by 1946, he had adopted a much tougher policy toward the Russians.
   - (A) cursory
   - (B) strict
   - (C) obligatory
   - (D) uncompromising
   - (E) conciliatory

4. As the controversial argument continued, the debaters became more _____ and their remarks became more _____.
   - (A) subdued . . . hostile
   - (B) vehement . . . acrimonious
   - (C) reticent . . . cliché
   - (D) affable . . . adverse
   - (E) emotional . . . adroit

5. My wealthy aunt exceeds the trait of being economical. She is so
_____ that she washes paper plates to be used again.
   - (A) affluent
   - (B) parsimonious
   - (C) indigent
   - (D) impoverished
   - (E) selfish

6. In spite of competition, the newspaper _____ remains among the
best _____ of communication between advertisers and customers.
   - (A) cannot . . . medium
   - (B) never . . . means
   - (C) still . . . media
   - (D) often . . . measure
   - (E) consistently . . . standard

7. In the 1850s the Republicans arose, a sectional _____ whose
cohesiveness was provided by _____ opposition to the extension of
slavery.
   - (A) territory . . . township
   - (B) amalgam . . . uncompromising
   - (C) sect . . . fragmentary
   - (D) conglomeration . . . moneyed
   - (E) region . . . technological

8. _____ must be distinguished from _____, which is the
recognition of different categories of people without the imputing of any
differences in rank.
   - (A) Totalitarianism . . . brotherhood
   - (B) Modification . . . ossification
   - (C) Classification . . . ramification
   - (D) Stratification . . . differentiation
   - (E) Finitude . . . infinitude

Analogies

DIRECTIONS

In each question below, you are given a related pair of words or phrases.
Select the lettered pair that *best* expresses a relationship similar to that in
the original pair of words.

9. SANCTUARY : CHURCH : :
   - (A) lobby : theater
   - (B) door : building
   - (C) stage : curtain
   - (D) boudoir : house
   - (E) mountain : cave

10. JAUNTY : PERKY ::
    (A) closet : coterie
    (B) caustic : witty
    (C) lackluster : vital
    (D) notion : nation
    (E) par : equal

11. MESA : VALLEY ::
    (A) plate : food
    (B) saucer : cup
    (C) mountain : ravine
    (D) table : chair
    (E) rock : plateau

12. CURSORILY : CIRCUMSPECTLY ::
    (A) caution : haste
    (B) angrily : roundabout
    (C) superficially : watchfully
    (D) intolerably : acceptably
    (E) painfully : hurt

13. THIEF : SURREPTITIOUS ::
    (A) doctor : perfunctory
    (B) teacher : explanatory
    (C) woman : flagrant
    (D) remark : inane
    (E) Cadillac : plebeian

13. CHIMERICAL : DRAGON ::
    (A) chemical : penicillin
    (B) fantasy : monster
    (C) fictional : theme
    (D) musical : recording
    (E) leaden : pencil

15. DISQUIET : FEARS ::
    (A) dampen : spirit
    (B) imprison : criminal
    (C) agitate : mob
    (D) mitigate : pain
    (E) mollify : exacerbation

16. DEMAGOGUE : POPULACE ::
    (A) pariah : following
    (B) orator : speech
    (C) rabble-rouser : crowd
    (D) demigod : deity
    (E) teacher : pupils

17. DOCTOR : DISEASE
    (A) dentist : drill
    (B) gardener : lawnmower
    (C) policeman : criminal
    (D) politician : electorate
    (E) teacher : ignorance

Reading Comprehension

DIRECTIONS

Questions follow each of the passages below. Using only the stated or implied information in each passage, answer the questions.

Laboratory evidence indicates that life originated through chemical reactions in the primordial mixture (water, hydrogen, ammonia, and hydrogen cyanide) which blanketed the earth at its formation. These reactions were brought about by the heat, pressure, and radiation conditions then prevailing. One suggestion is that nucleosides and amino acids were formed from the primordial mixture, and the nucleosides produced nucleotides which produced the nucleic acids (DNA, the common denominator of all living things, and RNA). The amino acids became polymerized (chemically joined) into proteins, including enzymes, and lipids were formed from fatty acids and glycerol-like molecules. The final step appears to have been the gradual accumulation of DNA, RNA, proteins, lipids, and enzymes into a vital mass which began to grow, divide, and multiply.

The evolution of the various forms of life from this biochemical mass must not be considered a linear progression. Rather, the fossil record suggests an analogy between evolution and a bush whose branches go every which way. Like branches, some evolutionary lines simply end, and others branch again. Many biologists believe the pattern to have been as follows: bacteria emerged first and from them branched viruses, red algae, blue-green algae, and green flagellates. From the latter branched green algae, from which higher plants evolved, and colorless rhizoflagellates, from which diatoms, molds, sponges, and protozoa evolved. From ciliated protozoa (ciliophora) evolved multinucleate (syncytial) flatworms. These branched into five lines, one of which leads to the echinoderms and chordates. The remaining lines lead to most of the other phyla of the animal kingdom.

18. Which of the following best expresses the analogy between evolution and a bush?
    (A) species : evolution :: bush : branching
    (B) species : branching :: bush : evolution
    (C) evolution : species :: bush : branched viruses
    (D) evolution : species :: bush : branches
    (E) evolution : species :: branches : bush

19. Nucleosides are predecessors of
    (A) polymers   (D) proteins
    (B) amino acids   (E) lipids
    (C) nucleic acids

20. The primordial mixture did not include
    (A) ammonia   (D) hydrogen cyanide
    (B) hydrogen   (E) water
    (C) heat

In economics, demand implies something slightly different from the common meaning of the term. The layman, for example, often uses the term to mean the amount that is demanded of an item. Thus, if the price were to decrease and individuals wanted more of the item, it is commonly said that demand increases. To an economist, demand is a relationship between a series of prices and a series of corresponding quantities that are demanded at these prices. If one reads the previous sentences carefully, it should become apparent that there is a distinction between the quantity demanded and demand. This distinction is often a point of confusion and we all should be aware of and understand the difference between these two terms. We repeat, therefore, that demand is a relationship between price and quantities demanded, and therefore suggests the effect of one (e.g., price) on the other (e.g., quantity demanded). Therefore, knowledge of the demand for a product enables one to predict how much more of a good will be purchased if price decreases. But the increase in quantity demanded does not mean demand has increased, since the relationship between price and quantity demanded (i.e., the demand for the product) has not changed. Demand shifts when there is a change in income, expectations, taste, etc., such that a different quantity of the good is demanded at the same price.

In almost all cases, a consumer wants more of an item if the price decreases. This relationship between price and quantity demanded is so strong that it is referred to as the "law of demand." This "law" can be explained by the income and substitution effects. The income effect occurs because price increases reduce the purchasing power of the individual and, thus, the quantity demanded of goods must decrease. The substitution effect reflects the consumer's desire to get the "best buy." Accordingly, if the price of good A increases, the individual will tend to substitute another good and purchase less of good A. The negative correlation between price and quantity demanded is also explained by the law of diminishing marginal utility. According to this law, the additional utility the consumer gains from consuming a good decreases as successively more units of the good are consumed. Because the additional units yield less utility or satisfaction, the consumer is willing to purchase more only if the price of the good decreases.

Economists distinguish between individual and market demand. As the term implies, individual demand concerns the individual consumer and illustrates the quantities that individuals demand at different prices. Market demand includes the demand of all individuals for a particular good and is found by summing the quantities demanded by all individuals at the various prices.

The other side of the price system is supply. As in the case of demand, supply is a relationship between a series of prices and the associated quantities supplied. It is assumed that as price increases the individual or firm will supply greater quantities of a good. There is a positive correlation between quantity supplied and product price.

Economists also distinguish between a change in supply and quantity supplied. The distinction is similar to the one made with respect to demand. Also, as in the case of demand, economists distinguish between individual firm supply and market supply, which is the summation of individual supply.

Taken together, supply and demand yield equilibrium price and quantity. Equilibrium is a state of stability, with balanced forces in which prices and quantity will remain constant. Moreover, there are forces in the market that will act to establish equilibrium if changes in demand or supply create disequilibrium. For example, if prices are above equilibrium, the quantity supplied exceeds quantity demanded and surpluses occur that have a downward pressure on prices. These pressures will persist until equilibrium is established. If prices are below equilibrium, the good will become scarce and there will be an upward pressure on price.

In reality, equilibrium is seldom attained, for the factors affecting the market are constantly changing. In a dynamic market of this kind, there is a continual process of adjustment as the market searches or gropes for equilibrium. The rapidity of adjustment will depend to a large extent on the quality of information that is available to firms and consumers.

Through the market interaction of demand and supply, a "market price" is established. This price serves two very important roles of rationing and allocating goods. Since wants far exceed resources, there must be a device by which to determine who gets the goods. In the market system, price plays this rationing role by supplying goods to all who pay the price of the product. As an allocator of goods, price insures that resources are utilized in their most valuable uses. In short, in a market system, price serves both a demand-inhibiting and a supply-eliciting function. Naturally, the market system does not work perfectly.

In most economies, the government plays a role in the market system. Governments enforce the "rules of the game," impose taxes, and may control prices through price ceilings or price supports. These actions necessarily may create shortages or surpluses. In most developed and interdependent economies, the necessity of the government playing some role in the economy seldom is disputed.

21. Assume that firms develop an orange-flavored breakfast drink high in vitamin C that is a good substitute for orange juice but sells for less. Based upon assertions in the passage, which of the following would occur with respect to the demand for orange juice?
    (A) health food stores would resurrect the law of diminishing marginal utility
    (B) assuming that the price of fresh orange juice remained constant, more orange juice would be consumed
    (C) the law of demand would prevail
    (D) assuming that the price of fresh orange juice remained constant, the demand would not change
    (E) there is not enough information in the passage to answer this question

22. According to the passage, a group of individuals will
    (A) derive less satisfaction from a product
    (B) exert individual demand under appropriate conditions
    (C) shift the demand line to the right
    (D) constitute a market
    (E) emphasize supply over demand

23. According to the passage, a change in demand would occur in which of the following situations?
    (A) the gasoline price increases, resulting in the increased sale of Datsuns (whose price remains stable)
    (B) the gasoline price increases, resulting in the increased sale of Datsuns (which go on sale in response to increased gas prices)
    (C) the gasoline price decreases on the same day that a new 43-mpg car enters the market
    (D) a federal order imposes a price ceiling on gasoline
    (E) a federal order lifts price regulations for gasoline

24. Assume that the demand for houses increases. Drawing from the passage, decide which of the following would most likely cause such a shift.
    (A) interest rates on mortgages increase
    (B) the government predicts a large increase in the extent of unemployment
    (C) in a poverty area, a new government program provides jobs for all who need them
    (D) announcement of a low-priced type of mobile home which is a good substitute for houses
    (E) the increased cost of lumber

25. According to the passage, quantity supplied and product price are not
    (A) correlative   (D) symbiotic
    (B) disjunctive   (E) consequential
    (C) related

26. The final sentence in the passage hints that
    (A) interdependence goes hand in hand with development
    (B) there are underdeveloped countries whose attitude toward govern-
        ment control may be hostile
    (C) disputes over government control usually come from an illiterate
        populace
    (D) socialism is a sophisticated achievement
    (E) capitalism is a sophisticated achievement

27. According to the final paragraph, the government's intervention in the
    economy may cause
    (A) higher prices
    (B) disequilibrium
    (C) lower prices
    (D) the market to tend toward socialism
    (E) the market to tend toward capitalism

28. According to the passage, when most people use the term "demand,"
    they are usually referring to
    (A) an aggressive personality
    (B) a run on the banks
    (C) a collective public action
    (D) a desire to acquire more for less
    (E) the relationship between "quantity demanded" and "demand"

Antonyms

DIRECTIONS

Each word in CAPITAL LETTERS is followed by five words or phrases.
The correct choice is the word or phrase whose meaning is most nearly
opposite to the meaning of the word in capitals. You may be required to
distinguish fine shades of meaning. Look at all choices before marking your
answer.

29. COVENANT
    (A) condemnation   (D) inference
    (B) breach   (E) argument
    (C) disillusion

30. PRECARIOUS
    (A) carnivorous   (D) soluble
    (B) caring   (E) certain
    (C) equivocal

31. CONTUMACIOUS
    (A) compliant   (D) obdurate
    (B) reciprocal   (E) dogged
    (C) pertinacious

32. CONCLAVE
    (A) marriage   (D) display
    (B) ritual   (E) divorce
    (C) public assembly

33. TRACTABLE
    (A) retractable   (D) retrainable
    (B) refractory   (E) retrenched
    (C) refreshing

34. VAPID
    (A) loquacious   (D) translatable
    (B) engaging   (E) succinct
    (C) remarkable

35. GLIBLY
    (A) plaintively   (D) didactically
    (B) ominously   (E) disparagingly
    (C) haltingly

36. ARGOT
    (A) cant   (D) extremism
    (B) colloquialism   (E) standard
    (C) vulgarism

37. PLETHORA
    (A) supply   (D) modicum
    (B) alliance   (E) shortage
    (C) enigma

38. SUPPLICATION
    (A) regard   (D) condemnation
    (B) query   (E) inculcation
    (C) grant

STOP. IF YOU FINISH BEFORE TIME IS CALLED, CHECK YOUR WORK ON THIS SECTION ONLY. DO NOT WORK ON ANY OTHER SECTION IN THE TEST.

SECTION II: VERBAL ABILITY

Time: 30 Minutes
38 Questions

In this section, choose the best answer for each question and blacken the corresponding space on the answer sheet.

Sentence Completion

DIRECTIONS

Each blank in the following sentences indicates that something has been omitted. Considering the lettered words beneath the sentence, choose the word or set of words that best fits the whole sentence.

1. When one is thrust into an unknown world, he is careful to note the conditions in which he finds himself, _____ them with his _____.

   (A) bemusing . . . daydreams
   (B) refuting . . . expertise
   (C) congealing . . . observations
   (D) concurring . . . thoughts
   (E) comparing . . . expectations

2. In his large, _____ home, he was able to _____ himself from the rigors of urban life.

   (A) palatial . . . sequester
   (B) rambunctious . . . isolate
   (C) colonial . . . dignify
   (D) inconsiderable . . . hide
   (E) dashing . . . stigmatize

3. A(n) _____ is a number of persons who are in close proximity with one another but who are not in sustained communication.

   (A) aggregate   (D) mob
   (B) category   (E) set
   (C) group

4. Another _____ function of the political institution is the protection of the society from _____ forces.

   (A) expendable . . . natural
   (B) inherent . . . political
   (C) conservative . . . governmental
   (D) liberal . . . conservative
   (E) salient . . . external

5. In _____ nature, myths use _____ reasoning, relating the unfamiliar to the familiar by means of likeness.
   - (A) observing . . . logical
   - (B) appreciating . . . irrational
   - (C) disclosing . . . metonymic
   - (D) interpreting . . . analogical
   - (E) seizing . . . fanciful

6. Phoenician seamen were primarily interested in commerce and may have been the first people to _____ Africa.
   - (A) circumnavigate
   - (B) demystify
   - (C) trudge
   - (D) mispronounce
   - (E) expropriate

7. One cannot _____ to be impressed by the structural and _____ differences between the United States as a federal union in 1789 and the United States as a federal union today.
   - (A) deteriorate . . . legal
   - (B) stop . . . attitudinal
   - (C) begin . . . politically
   - (D) fail . . . operational
   - (E) start . . . classical

8. Generally, Babylonian mythology lacks the _____ quality of the myth of Osiris; it is more earthbound and more materialistic.
   - (A) ancient
   - (B) anthropological
   - (C) metaphysical
   - (D) experiential
   - (E) transcendental

9. The _____ of Darwin's theory of evolution on Victorian religion was to create a bitter _____ of ideas and beliefs.
   - (A) result . . . moderation
   - (B) effect . . . conflict
   - (C) extension . . . growth
   - (D) origin . . . compromise
   - (E) influence . . . solidarity

Analogies

DIRECTIONS

Each blank in the following sentences indicates that something has been omitted. Considering the lettered words beneath the sentence, choose the word or set of words that best fits the whole sentence.

10. VIGILANTE : POLICEMAN : :
   (A) posse : sheriff
   (B) judge : jury
   (C) villain : criminal
   (D) lynching : execution
   (E) quack : doctor

11. TRESS : TUFT : :
   (A) grass : blade
   (B) modicum : iota
   (C) profusion : magnitude
   (D) curl : hair
   (E) bushel : ton

12. CHARTER : CORPORATION : :
   (A) oath : allegiance
   (B) patent : monopoly
   (C) copyright : song
   (D) contract : liability
   (E) vow : marriage

13. MEGALOMANIAC : BRAGGADOCIO : :
   (A) general : commands
   (B) egoist : opinions
   (C) writer : paper
   (D) musician : score
   (E) home : family

14. FINCH : ORNITHOLOGY : :
   (A) fetus : etymology
   (B) rain : geology
   (C) skull : archaeology
   (D) mind : philology
   (E) word : embryology

15. THEOLOGY : ANTHROPOLOGY : :
   (A) ontology : epistemology
   (B) philanthropy : philology
   (C) belief : speculation
   (D) Heaven : Earth
   (E) virtue : vice

16. WANTON : ASCETIC : :
   (A) soup : acid
   (B) wicked : good
   (C) fertile : sterile
   (D) free : chained
   (E) fed : hungry

17. SERVANT : SERVILITY : :
   (A) storyteller : exaggeration
   (B) waitress : wait
   (C) overweight : fat
   (D) drunk : alcohol
   (E) lawful : sheriff

18. DIFFIDENT : SHYNESS : :
   (A) talented : song
   (B) recalcitrant : ambivalence
   (C) gratified : gifts
   (D) brave : courage
   (E) polite : cocktails

Reading Comprehension

DIRECTIONS
Questions follow each of the passages below. Using only the stated or implied information in each passage, answer the questions.

Concerning the origin of the soul Augustine's view differs from that of the Greek philosophers. He does not believe that souls are eternal or that they have an existence prior to their union with the body. He holds that souls are created by God, although it is not entirely clear whether he means that a soul is created simultaneously with the birth of each infant or the soul of the newborn child is generated from the souls of the parents at the same time when the new body is developed. In either case it is the creative activity of God that is involved. Although the souls do not exist prior to their union with the body, they will survive the death of the physical body, in which case they will again be united with some other type of body, the nature of which we do not know. It is in this sense only that Augustine believes in the immortality of the soul. His argument in support of this belief is similar to the one used by Plato. Because the soul is capable of knowing truth which is eternal it must possess qualities that are more than merely temporal.

Souls are free insofar as they have the power to choose between right and wrong courses of action. Hence man is to some degree at least responsible for his fate. He cannot place the blame for his sins on God, nature, or even Satan as the Manicheans were inclined to do. The responsibility lies in himself. The temptations are there through no fault of his own but yielding to these temptations is another matter and one for which he can justly be blamed. The nature of man's freedom was, however, a very difficult one for him to explain and he was never able to do so without becoming involved in inconsistencies. One of the reasons for this was his belief in predestination along with the idea that God knows what man will do in the future.

Although man was created in the image of God and without any evil being present in this nature, he now finds himself in a miserable predicament. As Augustine contemplates his own nature as well as that of his fellow men he sees wickedness and corruption on every hand. Man is a sinful creature and there is nothing that is wholly good about him. How did this come about? The answer is to be found in original sin which mankind inherited from Adam. In what sense can it be said that Adam's descendants are responsible for what he did long ago? It is in this connection that Augustine makes use of the Platonic relationship between the universal and the individual. If Adam is regarded as a particular human being it would make no sense at all to blame his descendants for the mistakes that he made. But Adam is interpreted to mean the universal man rather than a particular individual. Since the universal necessarily includes all of the particulars belonging to the class they are involved in whatever the universal does.

The total corruption of human nature as taught by Augustine did not mean that man is incapable of doing any good deeds. It meant that each part of his nature is infected with an evil tendency. In contrast to the Greek notion of a good mind and an evil body, he held that both mind and body had been made corrupt as a result of the fall. This corruption is made manifest in the lusts of the flesh and also in the activities of the mind. So far as the mind is concerned the evil tendency is present in both the intellect and in the will. In the intellect it is expressed in the sin of pride and in the will there is the inclination to follow that which is pleasant at the moment rather than to obey the demands of reason.

19. According to Augustine, one of the symptoms of human corruption is
   (A) man's exclusive pursuit of pleasure
   (B) man's periodic attempts to do good deeds
   (C) man's refusal to connect the universal with the particular
   (D) Adam
   (E) Eve

20. Augustine thinks that the soul is
   (A) eternal
   (B) eternal, but not immortal
   (C) immortal, but not eternal
   (D) transient
   (E) capable of sin

21. Augustine could not declare man to be wholly free because
   (A) man is shackled by Adam's sin
   (B) God knows man's every move before it is made
   (C) the question of freedom is a political one
   (D) he himself was not free
   (E) anything that is free is not worth much

22. According to the passage, the desires of the flesh are controlled by
   (A) Augustine's theory   (D) the will
   (B) the intellect   (E) none of these
   (C) God

23. Pride is a function of
    (A) Augustine's theory   (D) the soul
    (B) the intellect   (E) the will
    (C) God

Malinowski and other anthropologists have noted that some people, notably the Trobriand Islanders and the Australian Aborigines, are unaware of the role of the father in procreation. Most anthropologists accept the fact that almost universally social paternity is considered to be more important than the biological. Some peoples believe that the mother is but the carrier of the developing embryo, its actual flesh and blood coming from the father. Others believe that the menstrual flow nourishes the embryo; still others that it is the semen. In parts of Oceania, where the birthrate is low, a woman may be required to give proof that she is fertile before she is permitted to marry.

Once pregnancy occurs, a woman may be required to eat certain foods that are believed to strengthen the baby within her or may have to perform certain activities to influence the growth of the baby. In the West, a pregnant woman is usually thought to be in a "delicate" condition whereas in other parts of the world she may be considered to be especially strong.

Men and unmarried females are frequently kept away from the vicinity of a birth. Often a woman returns to her mother's village for assistance during accouchement. Not all babies born are allowed to live. Infanticide is in many societies a factor in group survival, a technique of population control. Some peoples believe that twins are unnatural, thus they may be killed at birth. In some patrilineal groups, a baby without recognized paternity is not permitted to live. If a baby is born with the caul, he may be killed or perhaps be given a special status.

The couvade is a custom found among the Basques and in some parts of South America in which the father of a newborn child takes to bed and symbolically goes through the motions of parturition. In South America, the father's friends will pay him a visit, bringing him gifts and inquiring solicitously about his health. They are waited upon by the new mother.

Russians swaddle their babies because they believe that the babies are so strong and violent they might do harm to themselves unless secured in this way. Some American Indians think their babies will not grow up with straight, sturdy legs unless they are strapped to a board. In some societies babies are not allowed to cry. They are picked up immediately and satisfied or distracted. Other people consider that crying is a healthy exercise for the baby and allow him to cry for protracted periods.

A child learns about the ways of the society in which he was born from his playgroup. He will later transfer the experience gained in the primary group to the society at large. Very often patterns of authority are consistent throughout a culture, from parental to political to spiritual. A child is often disciplined by depriving him of that which he (or his society) prizes. Thus, one may learn what is held of value in a society. Rules of punishment teach much about the dominance-submission (superordination-subordination) attitudes of a society. In some societies every adult has authority over every child. In others the parent-child relationship is exclusive and not to be interfered with in any way.

In parts of the world where the life spans are short, forty may be regarded as an advanced age. People who live longer are believed to possess special powers. These elders are sometimes treated with a deference based on fear rather than love.

In some societies, when death approaches, the dying person is moved out of the living quarters as a precaution against spiritual pollution. A corpse may be washed and dressed, perhaps painted and decorated, before being disposed of. In some cultures, corpses are placed where animals and the natural elements can get rid of the soft parts. In India bodies are usually cremated. The body may be buried in a seated or fetal position, facing camp or eastward, etc. Burial may be directly in the ground or in a coffin, tree trunk, large basket or pottery urn. Some people practice an initial interment of a year or so followed by a disinterment, the bones being collected at this time and placed elsewhere.

24. According to the passage, many societies regard certain types of childbearing as
   (A) sacred
   (B) joyful
   (C) unfortunate
   (D) harmless
   (E) normal

25. Which of the following might be most usefully supplied between paragraph 6 and paragraph 7?
   (A) a subtitle to indicate the beginning of an entirely new section
   (B) a transitional sentence indicating the author's shift from considering birth and life to considering age and death
   (C) a remention of specific practices of the Trobriand Islanders and the Australian Aborigines
   (D) a summary statement which particularly defines the unfamiliar words which have come before
   (E) an opinion by the author on the relative consequences of the beliefs he has sketched

26. The passage suggests that some areas try to assure population expansion by encouraging
    (A) premarital sex
    (B) polygamy
    (C) menstruation
    (D) patrilinearity
    (E) couvade

27. In some societies, infanticide is analogous to which of the following practices in our society?
    (A) murder
    (B) vasectomy
    (C) social Darwinism
    (D) black magic
    (E) parturition

28. At least one form of burial mentioned in the passage suggests a symbolic connection between
    (A) mother and father
    (B) birth and death
    (C) infanticide and genocide
    (D) embalming and cremation
    (E) civilization and primitivism

Antonyms

DIRECTIONS

Each word in CAPITAL LETTERS is followed by five words or phrases. The correct choice is the word or phrase whose meaning is most nearly *opposite* to the meaning of the word in capitals. You may be required to distinguish fine shades of meaning. Look at all choices before marking your answer.

29. OBSEQUIOUS
    (A) rough-hewn
    (B) rustic
    (C) antique
    (D) rude
    (E) parasitic

30. BELLICOSE
    (A) varicose
    (B) fretful
    (C) ringing
    (D) peaceful
    (E) calm

31. PEDANT
    (A) egoist
    (B) esthete
    (C) sycophant
    (D) demagogue
    (E) pluralist

32. CADAVEROUS
    (A) recriminating   (D) mortal
    (B) salubrious   (E) livid
    (C) cantankerous

33. PIQUANT
    (A) basic   (D) strong
    (B) indigestible   (E) svelt
    (C) insipid

34. INSOUCIANT
    (A) condoned   (D) concerned
    (B) insistent   (E) defaulted
    (C) slovenly

35. YAW
    (A) askew   (D) narrow
    (B) steadfast   (E) constant
    (C) destined

36. PERFIDY
    (A) faithfulness   (D) fallaciousness
    (B) treachery   (E) loving
    (C) infidelity

37. PALINGENESIS
    (A) devotion   (D) vitality
    (B) stability   (E) omnipotence
    (C) pleasantry

38. HIE
    (A) undulate   (D) heave
    (B) heddle   (E) gnaw
    (C) saunter

STOP. IF YOU FINISH BEFORE TIME IS CALLED, CHECK YOUR WORK ON THIS SECTION ONLY. DO NOT WORK ON ANY OTHER SECTION IN THE TEST.

SECTION III: QUANTITATIVE ABILITY

Time: 30 Minutes
30 Questions

Quantitative Comparison

DIRECTIONS

In this section you will be given two quantities, one in column A and one in column B. You are to determine a relationship between the two quantities and mark

- (A) if the quantity in column A is greater than the quantity in column B
- (B) if the quantity in column B is greater than the quantity in column A
- (C) if the quantities are equal
- (D) if the comparison cannot be determined from the information that is given

Common Information:

Information centered above both columns refers to one or both columns.

All numbers used are real numbers.

Figures are intended to provide useful positional information, but are not necessarily drawn to scale and should not be used to estimate sizes by measurement.

Lines that appear straight can be assumed to be straight.

	Column A	**Column B**
1.	$\dfrac{3}{7} \times \dfrac{2}{5} \times \dfrac{5}{8}$	$\dfrac{2}{5} \times \dfrac{4}{11} \times \dfrac{5}{8}$

$$x < y < z$$

2.	$x + y + z$	xyz

a, b, c, all greater than 0

3.	$(b + c)a$	$ac + ab$

$$x\sqrt{.09} = 2$$

4.	7	x

181

	Column A	**Column B**
5.	Number of degrees in the interior angles of a pentagon	500°

$$x < y$$

	Column A	**Column B**
6.	$(x - y)^2$	$x^2 - y^2$

	Column A	**Column B**
7.	$\dfrac{1}{71} - \dfrac{1}{151}$	$\dfrac{1}{65} - \dfrac{1}{153}$

$$a = b$$
$$a < c$$

	Column A	**Column B**
8.	$2a$	$b + c$

Questions 9–12 refer to the diagram.

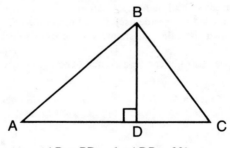

AD = BD = 6, ∠ADB = 90°

9.	AB	BC
10.	∠ BAD	∠ ABD
11.	∠ DBC + ∠ BCD	90°
12.	AB + BC	AC

Column A	Column B

$$3x - 12y = 36$$

13. $2x - 8y$ 21

$$1 > x > 0$$

14. x^{-2} x^{-3}

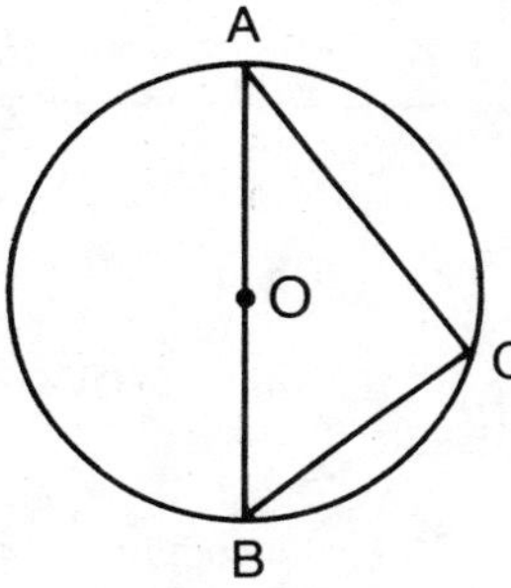

AB is a diameter

15. $\angle ACB$ $180° - (\angle CAB + \angle ABC)$

Math Ability

DIRECTIONS

Solve each problem in this section by using the information given and your own mathematical calculations. Then select the *one* correct answer of the five choices given. Use the available space on the page for scratchwork. NOTE: Some problems may be accompanied by figures or diagrams. These figures are drawn as accurately as possible, *except* when it is stated in a specific problem that the figure is not drawn to scale. The figure is meant to provide information useful in solving the problem or problems. Unless otherwise stated or indicated, all figures lie in a plane. All numbers used are real numbers.

16. $\dfrac{\frac{2}{3} - \frac{1}{2}}{\frac{1}{6} + \frac{1}{4} + \frac{2}{3}} =$

   (A) $\frac{2}{13}$ (B) $\frac{2}{9}$ (C) $\frac{13}{20}$ (D) $1\frac{1}{13}$ (E) $3\frac{1}{4}$

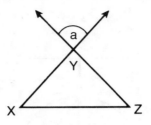

17. In $\triangle XYZ$, $XY = 10$, $YZ = 10$, and $\angle a = 84°$. Find the degree measure of $\angle Z$.

   (A) $42°$ (B) $48°$ (C) $84°$ (D) $96°$
   (E) cannot be determined

18. If it takes 18 minutes to fill $\frac{2}{3}$ of a container, how long will it take to fill the rest of the container at the same rate?

   (A) 6 minutes   (B) 9 minutes   (C) 12 minutes
   (D) 27 minutes   (E) 36 minutes

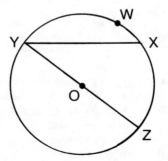

19. On the circle with center O, arc YWX equals $100°$. Find the degree measure of $\angle$ XYZ.

   (A) $40°$ (B) $50°$ (C) $80°$ (D) $100°$ (E) $130°$

20. The average of 9 numbers is 7 and the average of 7 other numbers is 9. What is the average of all 16 numbers?
    (A) 8   (B) 7⅞   (C) 7½   (D) 7¼
    (E) cannot be determined

21. Bob can paint a house in 5 days and Fred can paint the same house in 6 days. How many days would it take to paint the house if they work together?
    (A) 1   (B) 2⁸⁄₁₁   (C) 3²⁄₉   (D) 4   (E) 5½

22. If $n! = n \cdot (n - 1) \cdot (n - 2) \cdot (n - 3) \ldots 2 \cdot 1$, find the value of

$$\frac{(6!)\,(4!)}{(5!)\,(3!)}$$

    (A) ⁵⁄₄   (B) ⁸⁄₅   (C) 10   (D) 24   (E) 1152

23. If x, y, and z are consecutive positive integers greater than 1, not necessarily in that order, then which of the following is (are) true?

    I. $x > z$ III. $yz > xz$
    II. $x + y > z$ IV. $xy > y + z$

    (A) I   (B) II   (C) II and III   (D) III and IV
    (E) II and IV

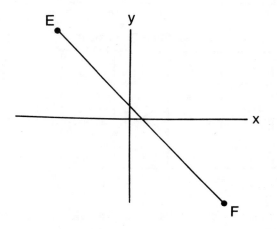

24. If point E has coordinates $(-3, 5)$ and point F has coordinates $(6, -7)$, then length of EF =
    (A) 21   (B) 15   (C) 7   (D) 5   (E) 3

Questions 25–28 refer to the graphs.

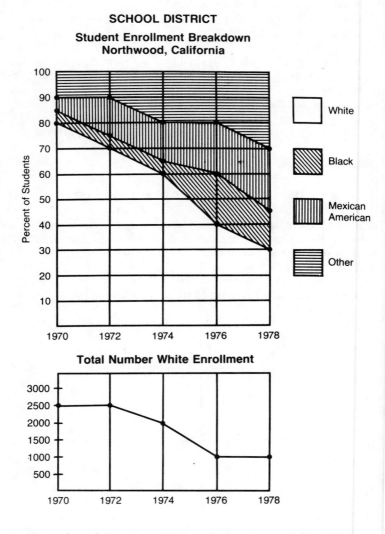

SCHOOL DISTRICT

Student Enrollment Breakdown
Northwood, California

Total Number White Enrollment

25. Approximately how many black students were enrolled in 1974?
    (A) 100   (B) 167   (C) 224   (D) 300   (E) 500

26. What was the total student enrollment in 1976?
    (A) 1000   (B) 2400   (C) 2500   (D) 4000
    (E) none of these

27. Which of the indicated groups showed the largest percent change in
    percent breakdown from 1970 to 1978?
    (A) white   (B) black   (C) Mexican American   (D) other
    (E) cannot be determined

28. What happened to the number of "other" students from 1974 to 1976?
    (A) same   (B) up by less than 100   (C) down by less than 100
    (D) up by more than 100   (E) down by more than 100

29. What is the area of a square in square inches if its perimeter is 10 feet?
    (A) 6.25   (B) 25   (C) 60   (D) 600   (E) 900

30. Mr. Smitherly leaves Beverly Hills at 8:00 A.M. and drives north on the
    highway at an average speed of 50 miles per hour. Mr. Dinkle leaves
    Beverly Hills at 8:30 A.M. and drives north on the same highway at an
    average speed of 60 miles per hour. Mr. Dinkle will
    (A) overtake Mr. Smitherly at 9:30 A.M.
    (B) overtake Mr. Smitherly at 10:30 A.M.
    (C) overtake Mr. Smitherly at 11:00 A.M.
    (D) be 30 miles behind at 8:35 A.M.
    (E) never overtake Mr. Smitherly

STOP. IF YOU FINISH BEFORE TIME IS CALLED, CHECK YOUR
WORK ON THIS SECTION ONLY. DO NOT WORK ON ANY
OTHER SECTION IN THE TEST.

SECTION IV: QUANTITATIVE ABILITY

Time: 30 Minutes
30 Questions

Quantitative Comparison

DIRECTIONS

In this section you will be given two quantities, one in column A and one in column B. You are to determine a relationship between the two quantities and mark
- (A) if the quantity in column A is greater than the quantity in column B
- (B) if the quantity in column B is greater than the quantity in column A
- (C) if the quantities are equal
- (D) if the comparison cannot be determined from the information that is given

Common Information:

Information centered above both columns refers to one or both columns.

All numbers used are real numbers.

Figures are intended to provide useful positional information, but are not necessarily drawn to scale and should not be used to estimate sizes by measurement.

Lines that appear straight can be assumed to be straight.

	Column A	Column B
1.	$\dfrac{.89 \times 57}{.919}$	58

$x < 0$

2.	$x^3 - 1$	0

3.	Number of prime numbers between 3 and 19	5

$\dfrac{a}{6} = \dfrac{b}{4}$

4.	$2a$	$3b$

Column A	Column B

Questions 5–6 refer to the diagram.

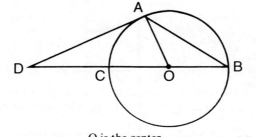

O is the center

	Column A	Column B
5.	$\overset{\frown}{AC}$	$2(\angle B)$
6.	$\angle AOB$	$\angle ADB$

$$2x + 5y > 4$$

	Column A	Column B
7.	x	y

8.	Number of inches in one mile	Number of minutes in one year
9.	Area of circle with diameter 8	Area of square with side 7
10.	$3\sqrt{2}$	$\sqrt{17}$

$$5x + y = 2$$
$$x + 3y = 6$$

11.	x	y

$$n \neq 0$$
$$n \neq -\tfrac{1}{2}$$
$$n \neq -1$$

12.	$\dfrac{1}{1 + \dfrac{1}{1 + 1/n}}$	$\dfrac{n + 1}{2n + 1}$

	Column A	Column B

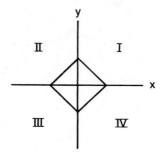

Point (x, y) is a point in quadrant II on the quadrilateral

13.	x	y

14.	$5 + 4 \cdot 10^2 + 8 \cdot 10^3$	8405

Alice is taller than Hilda, Joan is taller than
Alice, and Jill is taller than Hilda

15.	Jill's height	Joan's height

Math Ability

DIRECTIONS

Solve each problem in this section by using the information given and your own mathematical calculations. Then select the *one* correct answer of the five choices given. Use the available space on the page for scratchwork. NOTE: Some problems may be accompanied by figures or diagrams. These figures are drawn as accurately as possible, *except* when it is stated in a specific problem that the figure is not drawn to scale. The figure is meant to provide information useful in solving the problem or problems. Unless otherwise stated or indicated, all figures lie in a plane. All numbers used are real numbers.

16. If $2x - 5 = 9$, then $3x + 2 =$

    (A) 7   (B) 14   (C) 16   (D) 23   (E) 44

17. In the series 8, 9, 12, 17, 24, . . . the next number would be

    (A) 29   (B) 30   (C) 33   (D) 35   (E) 41

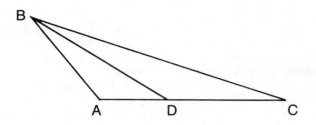

18. In the figure AB = AD and BD = CD. If ∠ C measures 19°, what is the measure of ∠ A in degrees?
    (A) 75   (B) 94   (C) 104   (D) 142
    (E) cannot be determined

Questions 19–20 refer to the graph.

AVERAGE FAMILY'S EXPENSES

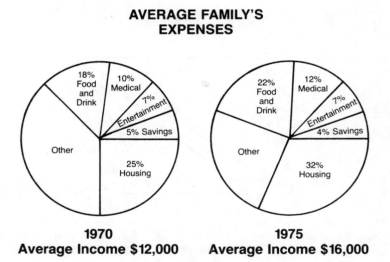

19. How much more money did the average family spend on medical expenses in 1975 than in 1970?
    (A) $500–$600   (B) $600–$700   (C) $700–$800
    (D) $800–$900   (E) $900–$1000

20. What was the percent increase from 1970 to 1975 in the percentage spent on food and drink?
    (A) 4%   (B) 18%   (C) 22%   (D) 40%   (E) 50%

21. What is the ratio of $\frac{3}{10}$ to $\frac{5}{8}$?

(A) $\frac{3}{16}$ (B) $\frac{12}{25}$ (C) $\frac{37}{40}$ (D) $\frac{25}{12}$ (E) $\frac{16}{3}$

22. If it takes a machine $\frac{2}{3}$ of a minute to produce one item, how many items will it produce in 2 hours?

(A) $\frac{1}{3}$ (B) $\frac{4}{3}$ (C) 80   (D) 120   (E) 180

23. If Tom leaves home and travels west for 3 miles and then north for 4 miles, how far is he from home?

(A) 7 miles   (B) 5 miles   (C) 4 miles

(D) $3\frac{1}{2}$ miles   (E) 1 mile

24. If $a = p + prt$, then $r =$

(A) $\dfrac{a - 1}{t}$ (B) $\dfrac{a - p}{pt}$ (C) $a - p - pt$ (D) $\dfrac{a}{t}$

(E) $\dfrac{a + p}{pt}$

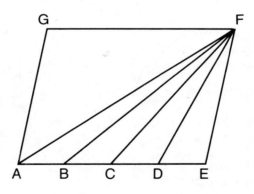

25. In the parallelogram, if $AB = BC = CD = DE$, then what is the ratio of the area of triangle CDF to the area of triangle ABF?

(A) 1:4   (B) 1:1   (C) 2:1   (D) 4:1

(E) cannot be determined

26. If m and n are integers and $\sqrt{mn} = 10$, which of the following cannot be a value of $m + n$?

(A) 25   (B) 29   (C) 50   (D) 52   (E) 101

27. The denominator of a fraction is 5 greater than the numerator. If the numerator and the denominator are increased by 2, the resulting fraction is equal to $\frac{7}{12}$. What is the value of the original fraction?
    (A) $\frac{5}{12}$ (B) $\frac{1}{2}$ (C) $\frac{9}{14}$ (D) $\frac{2}{3}$ (E) $\frac{12}{17}$

28. If a book costs $5.70 after a 40% discount, what was its original price?
    (A) $2.28   (B) $6.10   (C) $7.98   (D) $9.12
    (E) $9.50

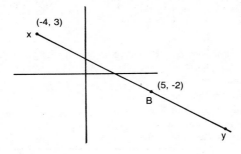

29. The midpoint of xy is B. The coordinates of x are $(-4, 3)$ and the coordinates of B are $(5, -2)$. What are the coordinates of y?
    (A) $(\frac{1}{2}, \frac{1}{2})$ (B) $(1, 1)$ (C) $(6, -7)$
    (D) $(14, -3)$ (E) $(14, -7)$

30. The average of three numbers is 55. The second is 1 more than twice the first, and the third is 4 less than three times the first. Find the largest number.
    (A) 165   (B) 88   (C) 80   (D) 57
    (E) cannot be determined

STOP. IF YOU FINISH BEFORE TIME IS CALLED, CHECK YOUR WORK ON THIS SECTION ONLY. DO NOT WORK ON ANY OTHER SECTION IN THE TEST.

SECTION V: ANALYTICAL ABILITY

Time: 30 Minutes
25 Questions

DIRECTIONS

The following questions or group of questions are based on a passage or set of statements. Choose the best answer for each question and blacken the corresponding space on your answer sheet. It may be helpful to draw rough diagrams or simple charts in attempting to answer these question types.

Questions 1–4

> Al, Paul, Jim, Sam, and Bob have an average height of six feet.
> Sam is taller than Al.
> Bob is shorter than Jim.
> Paul is shorter than Sam.
> Bob is taller than Paul.
> Sam is shorter than Jim.
> Paul is the shortest of the five.

1. The tallest boy is
   (A) Al   (B) Bob   (C) Sam   (D) Jim
   (E) cannot be determined

2. Al is not necessarily

   I. taller than Paul
   II. taller than Bob

   (A) I only   (D) both I and II
   (B) II only   (E) neither I nor II
   (C) either I or II

3. Which of the following must be true?

   I.   Jim is taller than Al.
   II. Sam is taller than Bob.
   III. Bob is taller than Al.

   (A) I   (B) II   (C) III   (D) I and II   (E) II and III

194

4. If Harold joins the group and is taller than Bob, but shorter than Al, then which of the following must be true?

   I. Sam is taller than Harold.
   II. Al is taller than Bob.

   (A) I only
   (B) II only
   (C) either I or II

   (D) both I and II
   (E) neither I nor II

Questions 5–6

   Recent studies indicate that more violent crimes are committed during hot weather than cold weather. Thus, if we could control the weather, the violent crime rate would drop.

5. The argument above makes which of the following assumptions?

   I. The relationship between weather conditions and crime rate is merely coincidental.
   II. The relationship between weather conditions and crime rate is causal.
   III. The relationship between weather conditions and crime rate is controllable.

   (A) I and II   (B) II and III   (C) I, II, and III
   (D) I only   (E) none of these

6. The argument would be strengthened if it pointed out that
   (A) the annual crime statistics for New York are higher than those for Los Angeles
   (B) in laboratory tests, increased heat alone accounted for increased aggressive behavior between members of the test group
   (C) poor socioeconomic conditions, more uncomfortable in hot weather than in cold, are the direct causes of increased crime
   (D) weather control will be possible in the near future
   (E) more people leave their doors and windows open during hot weather

Questions 7–8

1. Julie is 23 years old.
2. Alice is not the youngest.
3. Carol is not 25 years old.
4. Julie is 2 years younger than Alice.
5. Alice and Carol are 3 years apart.
6. Carol is younger than Julie.
7. Alice is not 3 years older than Julie.
8. Julie is one year older than Carol.

7. Which of the following must be true?

I. The difference in age between Alice and Julie is greater than the difference in age between Julie and Carol.
II. Carol is younger than 22 years old.

(A) I   (B) II   (C) both I and II   (D) either I or II, but not both
(E) neither I nor II

8. If another girl, Sheila, is younger than Alice, but not older than Julie, then
(A) she must be younger than Carol
(B) she must be older than Carol
(C) she is 24 years old
(D) she could be the same age as Julie
(E) she could be 4 years older than Carol

Questions 9–10

The shortsightedness of our government and our scientists has virtually nullified all of their great discoveries because of their failure to consider the environmental impact. The situation is far from hopeless, but our government agencies must become better watchdogs.

9. This argument fails to place any blame on

I. consumers who prefer new technology to clean air
II. the ability of government to actually police industry
III. legal loopholes which allow industry abuse of government regulations

(A) I only   (B) II only   (C) III only   (D) I, II, and III
(E) I and III only

10. Which of the following is (are) false?

   I. The argument emphasizes the importance of government regulation.
   II. The argument chastizes both scientists and government workers.
   III. The author argues on behalf of a better environment.

   (A) I, II, and III   (B) I and II   (C) II only   (D) I only
   (E) none of these

Questions 11–15

   The government is arranging an expedition to an under-developed area of the world and has to select a four-member team. Two of the members must be engineers. The following professionals applied for the expedition:

A is an architect.   E is an engineer.
B is a biologist.   F is a field engineer.
C is a chemist.   G is a general engineer.
D is a doctor.

The architect and the engineer will not go together.
The doctor and the general engineer will not go together.
The biologist and the architect will not go together.

11. If A is selected, the rest of the expedition would be composed of
    (A) C, D, and F   (B) B, F, and G   (C) C, F, and G
    (D) C, E, and F   (E) E, F, and G

12. If the field engineer is rejected, then the others rejected would be
    (A) the chemist only
    (B) the chemist or the biologist
    (C) the architect, chemist, and engineer
    (D) the architect and doctor
    (E) the biologist, chemist, and doctor

13. If the general engineer is selected, then which of the following must be true?

    I. The biologist is selected.
    II. The architect is not selected.

    (A) I only   (D) either I or II, but not both
    (B) II only   (E) neither I nor II
    (C) both I and II

14. Which of the following must be true?

    I. G and A can never be on the expedition together.
    II. C and E can never be on the expedition together.
    III. F and C will always be on the expedition together.

    (A) I   (D) all of these
    (B) II   (E) none of these
    (C) III

15. If the doctor is selected and the chemist is not selected, then the expedition will be composed of

    (A) A, E, and F   (B) B, E, and F   (C) A, F, and G
    (D) B, E, and G   (E) A, B, and F

Questions 16–19

Five children in a family of six children have freckles.
Three children in the family are girls.
Four children in the family have blue eyes.

16. Which of the following must be true?

    I. All of the girls have freckles.
    II. At least one girl has blue eyes.

    (A) I   (D) both I and II
    (B) II   (E) neither I nor II
    (C) either I or II, but not both

17. Which of the following must be false?

    I. All the blue-eyed girls have freckles.
    II. No children with freckles have blue eyes.

    (A) I   (D) both I and II
    (B) II   (E) neither I nor II
    (C) either I or II, but not both

18. Which of the following can be deduced from the statements?
    (A) None of the girls have freckles.
    (B) Three of the blue-eyed children have freckles.
    (C) One girl has no freckles.
    (D) All of the girls have blue eyes.
    (E) none of the above

19. Which of the following must be false?
    (A) One of the children does not have freckles.
    (B) Three of the children are boys.
    (C) All of the boys have blues eyes.
    (D) Three children have brown eyes.
    (E) none of the above

Questions 20–25

Strawberries are grown in California, Oregon, Washington, and Idaho.
Blueberries are grown in Nevada, Oregon, Washington, and Arizona.
Boysenberries are grown in California, Nevada, Utah, Washington, and Idaho.
Blackberries are grown in Arizona, Nevada, Utah, and Colorado.
Raspberries are grown in Arizona, Washington, Oregon, and California.
Gooseberries are grown in Oregon, Washington, Idaho, and Utah.

20. The berry that grows in the most states is
    (A) strawberry   (D) blackberry
    (B) blueberry   (E) all are the same
    (C) boysenberry

21. The state that has the most different kinds of berries growing in it is
    (A) California   (D) Nevada
    (B) Oregon   (E) Utah
    (C) Washington

22. If one wanted to grow boysenberries, gooseberries, and blackberries, then one should live in
    (A) Oregon   (D) Nevada
    (B) Arizona   (E) Utah
    (C) Washington

23. Which of the following must be true?

    I. Arizona is the only state to grow gooseberries, but not boysenberries.
    II. Oregon is the only state to grow strawberries, but not boysenberries.

    (A) I only   (D) either I or II, but not both
    (B) II only   (E) neither I nor II
    (C) both I and II

24. Blackberries can be grown in
    (A) Utah, where boysenberries cannot be grown
    (B) Nevada, where strawberries cannot be grown
    (C) California, where boysenberries cannot be grown
    (D) Washington, where blueberries cannot be grown
    (E) Arizona, where raspberries cannot be grown

25. If someone wanted to make preserves from both blueberries and black-berries that were freshly picked, then the person would have to live in
    (A) California or Utah   (D) Washington or Colorado
    (B) Oregon or Arizona   (E) Idaho or Utah
    (C) Arizona or Nevada

STOP. IF YOU FINISH BEFORE TIME IS CALLED, CHECK YOUR WORK ON THIS SECTION ONLY. DO NOT WORK ON ANY OTHER SECTION IN THE TEST.

SECTION VI: ANALYTICAL ABILITY

Time: 30 Minutes
25 Questions

DIRECTIONS

The following questions or group of questions are based on a passage or set of statements. Choose the best answer for each question and blacken the corresponding space on your answer sheet. It may be helpful to draw rough diagrams or simple charts in attempting to answer these question types.

Questions 1–6

Row	*Column*			
	1	2	3	4
I	hill	lock	team	step
II	pill	flock	seem	stop
III	dill	clock	ream	stand
IV	still	block	beam	strand
V	mill	stock	deem	store

Each word in the first three columns rhymes with the other words in that column.

There are no words with more than five letters.

Each word in a column except column 4 starts with a different letter.

Other rules can be drawn from words in the columns.

1. Which of the following words could not be in column 2?
   - (A) mock
   - (B) sock
   - (C) knock
   - (D) dock
   - (E) rock

2. Which of the following words could be added to column 4 without breaking any rules?
   - (A) subtle
   - (B) stumped
   - (C) simple
   - (D) stove
   - (E) steeple

3. Which of the columns does not follow all of the rules?
   - (A) 1 (B) 2 (C) 3 (D) 4 (E) none

4. If column 1 must end in *ill,* which of the following words could not be added to column 1?

    I. fill   II. will   III. spill   IV. instill

  (A) I and II   (D) I and III
  (B) II and III   (E) II and IV
  (C) III and IV

5. It can be deduced from the word chart that
  (A) each word in column 3 ends in *am*
  (B) each word in column 2 includes the word *lock*
  (C) each word in column 4 has one vowel
  (D) each word in column 3 has two vowels
  (E) none of the above

6. Which of the following could be row VI?
  (A) kill, mock, fume, start
  (B) fill, soak, mean, still
  (C) mild, crock, seam, sold
  (D) spill, mock, steam, stone
  (E) bill, dock, cream, stow

Questions 7–8

    "The department store owned by my competitor sells green necklaces that glow in the dark. Only customers of mine wearing those necklaces must be giving business to the competition."

7. This statement could best be strengthened by
  (A) deleting *that glow in the dark*
  (B) changing *sells* to *has sold*
  (C) changing *the competition* to *my competitor*
  (D) inserting *only* as the first word in sentence one
  (E) changing *wearing* to *owning*

8. The author foolishly assumes that
  (A) the customers might find the necklaces attractive
  (B) customers are not buying other products from the competition
  (C) customers will wear the necklaces in daylight
  (D) a department store should not sell necklaces
  (E) the competition is outselling the author

Questions 9–14

Five students (Rich, Ron, Holly, Maria, and Sheila) receive different grades on an algebra test (A, B, C, D, and F, but not necessarily respectively).

Maria gets a lower grade than Holly.

Holly gets a lower grade than Rich.

Ron and Sheila do not get F's.

Rich gets the top grade.

Ron's grade is the average of Maria's and Rich's grades.

9. Which of the following must be true?

   I. Ron does not get an A.

   II. Sheila does not get a B.

   (A) I only   (D) both I and II

   (B) II only   (E) neither I nor II

   (C) either I or II, but not both

10. Which of the following must be false?

   I. Rich cannot get a C.

   II. Maria gets an F.

   (A) I only   (D) both I and II

   (B) II only   (E) neither I nor II

   (C) either I or II, but not both

11. Which statement is not deducible from the given information?

   (A) Rich gets an A.

   (B) Ron gets a C.

   (C) Sheila gets a lower grade than Holly.

   (D) Maria gets a lower grade than Sheila.

   (E) Holly does not get an A.

12. If Holly gets a B, then

   I. Maria gets a C

   II. Sheila gets a D

   III. Ron gets an F

   (A) I   (D) I and II

   (B) II   (E) II and III

   (C) III

13. Which of the following must be true?

    I. Sheila cannot get a C.
    II. Maria cannot get a B.

  (A) I only   (D) either I or II, but not both
  (B) II only   (E) neither I nor II
  (C) both I and II

14. Which of the following is determined by Sheila getting a B?
  (A) Rich getting an A   (D) Maria getting an F
  (B) Ron getting a C   (E) none of these
  (C) Holly getting a D

Questions 15–18

    "The older we get, the less sleep we should desire. This is because our advanced knowledge and capabilities are most enjoyable when used; therefore, 'mindless' sleep becomes a waste of time."

15. Which of the following distinctions is not expressed or implied by the author?
  (A) between sleep and wakefulness
  (B) between youth and maturity
  (C) between productivity and waste
  (D) between a desire and a requirement
  (E) between more sleep and less sleep

16. The author of this statement assumes that
  (A) less sleep is not desirable
  (B) sleep advances knowledge and capabilities
  (C) mindlessness coincides with wakefulness
  (D) knowledge and capabilities naturally improve with age
  (E) sleep is only for the young

17. This author's statement might be strengthened if he or she pointed out that
  (A) advanced knowledge is often manifested in creative dreams
  (B) the mind is quite active during sleep
  (C) few empirical studies have concluded that sleep is an intellectual stimulant
  (D) advanced capabilities are not necessarily mind-associated
  (E) dreams teach us how to use waking experiences more intelligently

18. The author's statement might be weakened by pointing out that
    (A) eight hours of sleep is a cultural, not a physical, requirement
    (B) the most capable people rarely sleep
    (C) rest is a positive contribution to knowledge and capability
    (D) young children enjoy themselves less than knowledgeable adults
    (E) people rarely waste time during their waking hours

Questions 19–25

Sam is getting dressed to go to a party, but is having trouble deciding on what clothes to wear.
Sam will not wear colors that do not go well together.
He has two pairs of slacks, brown and blue; three dress shirts, white, aqua, and gray; four pairs of socks, red, black, brown, and blue; and two pairs of shoes, black and brown.
Blue slacks cannot be worn with red or brown socks.
Gray does not go well with brown.
Black does not go well with brown.
Assuming that Sam can wear only one pair of shoes, slacks, socks, and one shirt at a time, answer the following questions.

19. If Sam wears black shoes he will not wear
    (A) blue socks   (D) blue slacks
    (B) a white shirt   (E) red socks
    (C) brown slacks

20. If Sam wears brown slacks and a white shirt, then

    I.   he will not wear blue socks
    II. he will not wear black socks
    III. he could wear blue socks

    (A) I   (D) I and II
    (B) II   (E) II and III
    (C) III

21. Sam will never wear
    (A) blue and red together
    (B) blue and brown together
    (C) white and black together
    (D) gray and blue together
    (E) white and red together

22. If color combinations did not matter, how many possible clothing combinations could Sam have?
    (A) 6   (B) 8   (C) 11   (D) 18   (E) 48

23. Sam buys a brown tie. Now he could wear

    I. a blue shirt   III. blue socks
   II. brown slacks   IV. black shoes

  (A) I, III, and IV   (D) I, II, and III
  (B) I, II, and IV   (E) all of these
  (C) II, III, and IV

24. If Sam wears blue slacks, a white shirt, and brown shoes, then

    I. he cannot wear red socks
   II. he must wear blue socks
  III. he cannot wear black socks

  (A) I   (D) I and III
  (B) II   (E) I, II, and III
  (C) III

25. If Sam doesn't wear black socks or a gray shirt, then he could wear
  (A) red socks and blue slacks
  (B) brown socks and black shoes
  (C) brown shoes and brown slacks
  (D) brown slacks and black shoes
  (E) brown socks and blue slacks

STOP. IF YOU FINISH BEFORE TIME IS CALLED, CHECK YOUR WORK ON THIS SECTION ONLY. DO NOT WORK ON ANY OTHER SECTION IN THE TEST.

SECTION VII: QUANTITATIVE ABILITY

Time: 30 Minutes
30 Questions

Quantitative Comparison

DIRECTIONS

In this section you will be given two quantities, one in column A and one in column B. You are to determine a relationship between the two quantities and mark
- (A) if the quantity in column A is greater than the quantity in column B
- (B) if the quantity in column B is greater than the quantity in column A
- (C) if the quantities are equal
- (D) if the comparison cannot be determined from the information that is given

Common Information:
Information centered above both columns refers to one or both columns.
All numbers used are real numbers.
Figures are intended to provide useful positional information, but are not necessarily drawn to scale and should not be used to estimate sizes by measurement.
Lines that appear straight can be assumed to be straight.

	Column A	Column B
1.	76.088	76.10

$$x + y = 0$$

2.	x	y

Circle O has radius 1 unit

3.	Number of units in area of circle O	Number of units in circumference of circle O

2.2 pounds in 1 kilogram

4.	Number of kilograms in 50 pounds	Number of pounds in 50 kilograms

Column A   **Column B**

Questions 5–7 refer to the diagram.

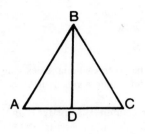

△ABC is equilateral
BD is a median

	Column A	Column B
5.	∠ABC + ∠BAC	∠CDB
6.	AD	DC
7.	AB + BD	BC

x and y are different prime numbers
x is even

8.	xy	x + y

Questions 9–10 refer to the diagram.

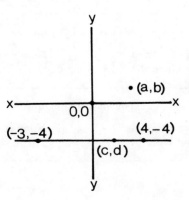

	Column A	**Column B**
9.	a	b
10.	c + d	a + b

$$x + y = 4$$
$$xy = 0$$

11.	x	y

12.	5^3	2^7

$$x^4 - 1 = 0$$

13.	x	x^2

$$x = \frac{4 - y}{y}$$
$$y \neq 0$$

14.	y	$\dfrac{4}{x + 1}$

30¢ per pound tea X and
40¢ per pound tea Y were
mixed to give 10 pounds
of tea costing $3.60

15.	Number of pounds of tea X	Number of pounds of tea Y

Math Ability

DIRECTIONS

Solve each problem in this section by using the information given and your own mathematical calculations. Then select the *one* correct answer of the five choices given. Use the available space on the page for scratchwork. NOTE: Some problems may be accompanied by figures or diagrams. These figures are drawn as accurately as possible, *except* when it is stated in a specific problem that the figure is not drawn to scale. The figure is meant to provide information useful in solving the problem or problems. Unless otherwise stated or indicated, all figures lie in a plane. All numbers used are real numbers.

16. The closest approximation of $\dfrac{69.28 \times .004}{.03}$ is

   (A) .092   (B) .92   (C) 9.2   (D) 92   (E) 920

17. Mary will be y years old x years from now. How old will she be z years from now?

   (A) $y - x + z$ (B) $y + x + z$ (C) $y + x - z$

   (D) $y - x - z$ (E) $x + z - y$

18. Evaluate: $3 + \cfrac{3}{3 + \cfrac{3}{3 + \cfrac{3}{3 + 3}}}$

   (A) $3\frac{23}{27}$ (B) $3\frac{7}{9}$ (C) $3\frac{19}{27}$ (D) $3\frac{17}{27}$

   (E) none of these

19. If $6x - 3y = 30$ and $4x = 2 - y$, then find $x + y$.

   (A) 2   (B) -4 (C) -6 (D) -8

   (E) none of these

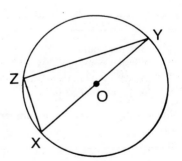

20. In circle O, XY is a diameter, OX = 8.5 and YZ = 15. What is the area of $\triangle XYZ$ in square units?

   (A) 127.5   (B) 120   (C) 60   (D) 40

   (E) cannot be determined

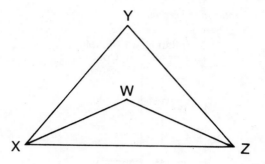

21. WX and WZ are angle bisectors of the base angles of isosceles △XYZ. If ∠Y = 80°, find the degree measure of ∠XWZ.
    (A) 65   (B) 80   (C) 100   (D) 130
    (E) cannot be determined

22. If D is between A and B on $\overrightarrow{AB}$, which of the following must be true?
    (A) AD = DB   (B) DB = AB − AD   (C) AD = AB + DB
    (D) DB = AD + AB (E) AB = AD = BD

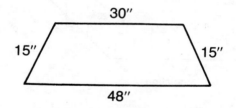

23. Find the area of the given trapezoid in square inches.
    (A) 585   (B) 468   (C) 234   (D) 108
    (E) cannot be determined

24. If 12 < 2x < 18 and −9 < 3y < 6, then which of the following are true?

    I. 3 < x + y < 11
    II. −12 < y − x < −4
    III. x > 7

    (A) I only   (D) I and III only
    (B) III only   (E) I and II only
    (C) II and III only

Questions 25–27 refer to the graph.

U.S. Indian Head Nickels
Average Retail Cost

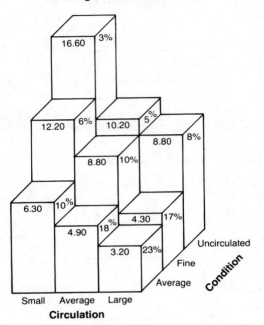

Percentages indicate percent of total coins available for sale.

Other numbers indicate average price of each coin.

25. Which of the following coin classifications represented the most coins?
    (A) large circulation
    (B) average circulation
    (C) average condition
    (D) fine condition
    (E) none of these

26. If 10,000 uncirculated coins were available for sale, what would be the average cost per coin?
    (A) $9.01–$9.50
    (B) $9.51–$10.00
    (C) $10.01–$10.50
    (D) $10.51–$11.00
    (E) $11.01–$11.50

27. If 20,000 total coins are available for sale, how many of them would be from coins of average circulation?
    (A) 3500–5000   (B) 5001-6500   (C) 6501–8000
    (D) 8001–9500   (E) 9501–11,000

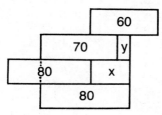

28. The horizontal length of each rectangle is marked within. What is the total horizontal length of x + y?
    (A) 40   (B) 50   (C) 80   (D) 90
    (E) cannot be determined

29. Which of the following is the largest?
    (A) half of 30% of 280   (D) three times 40% of 40
    (B) one-third of 70% of 160   (E) 60% of 60
    (C) twice 50% of 30

30. The product of x and y is a constant. If the value of x is increased by 50%, by what percentage must the value of y be decreased?
    (A) 50%   (B) 40%   (C) 33⅓%   (D) 25%
    (E) none of these

STOP. IF YOU FINISH BEFORE TIME IS CALLED, CHECK YOUR WORK ON THIS SECTION ONLY. DO NOT WORK ON ANY OTHER SECTION IN THE TEST.

ANSWER KEY FOR PRACTICE TEST 2

Section I Verbal Ability	Section II Verbal Ability	Section III Quantitative Ability	Section IV Quantitative Ability
1. B	1. E	1. A	1. B
2. B	2. A	2. D	2. B
3. E	3. A	3. C	3. C
4. B	4. E	4. A	4. C
5. B	5. D	5. A	5. C
6. C	6. A	6. D	6. A
7. B	7. D	7. B	7. D
8. D	8. E	8. B	8. B
9. D	9. B	9. D	9. A
10. E	10. D	10. C	10. A
11. B	11. B	11. C	11. B
12. C	12. C	12. A	12. C
13. B	13. A	13. A	13. B
14. A	14. C	14. B	14. C
15. C	15. D	15. C	15. D
16. C	16. D	16. A	16. D
17. E	17. A	17. B	17. C
18. D	18. D	18. B	18. C
19. C	19. A	19. A	19. C
20. C	20. C	20. B	20. C
21. C	21. B	21. B	21. B
22. D	22. E	22. D	22. E
23. A	23. B	23. B	23. B
24. C	24. C	24. B	24. B
25. B	25. B	25. B	25. B
26. B	26. A	26. C	26. C
27. B	27. B	27. C	27. B
28. D	28. B	28. E	28. E
29. B	29. D	29. E	29. E
30. E	30. D	30. C	30. C
31. A	31. E		
32. C	32. B		
33. B	33. C		
34. B	34. D		
35. C	35. E		
36. E	36. A		
37. E	37. B		
38. C	38. C		

ANSWER KEY FOR PRACTICE TEST 2

Section V Analytical Ability	Section VI Analytical Ability	Section VII Quantitative Ability
1. D	1. B	1. B
2. B	2. D	2. D
3. A	3. D	3. B
4. D	4. C	4. B
5. E	5. D	5. A
6. B	6. E	6. C
7. A	7. D	7. A
8. D	8. B	8. A
9. E	9. A	9. D
10. E	10. E	10. B
11. C	11. C	11. D
12. D	12. B	12. B
13. E	13. C	13. D
14. E	14. C	14. C
15. B	15. D	15. B
16. B	16. D	16. C
17. B	17. C	17. A
18. E	18. C	18. B
19. D	19. C	19. B
20. C	20. E	20. C
21. C	21. A	21. D
22. E	22. E	22. B
23. B	23. D	23. B
24. B	24. E	24. E
25. C	25. C	25. C
		26. D
		27. C
		28. E
		29. D
		30. C

HOW TO SCORE YOUR EXAM

1. Add the total number of correct responses for Sections I and II.
2. This total would be scaled to give a Verbal Ability score ranging from 200 to 800.
3. Repeat this process by adding the total correct responses for Sections III and IV.
4. This total would be scaled to give a Quantitative Ability score ranging from 200 to 800.
5. Repeat this process once again by adding the total correct responses for Sections V and VI.
6. This total would be scaled to give an Analytical Ability score ranging from 200 to 800.

NOTE: On this practice test we are assuming that Section VII is experimental and does not count on your score, although this is not always the case.

ANALYZING YOUR TEST RESULTS

The charts on the following pages should be used to carefully analyze your results and spot your strengths and weaknesses. The complete process of analyzing each subject area and each individual problem should be completed for each Practice Test. These results should then be reexamined for trends in types of errors (repeated errors) or poor results in specific subject areas. THIS REEXAMINATION AND ANALYSIS IS OF TREMENDOUS IMPORTANCE TO YOU IN ASSURING MAXIMUM TEST PREPARATION BENEFIT.

PRACTICE TEST 2: VERBAL ABILITY ANALYSIS SHEET

SECTION I

	Possible	Completed	Right	Wrong
Sentence Completion	8			
Analogies	9			
Reading Comprehension	11			
Antonyms	10			
SUBTOTALS	38			

SECTION II

	Possible	Completed	Right	Wrong
Sentence Completion	9			
Analogies	9			
Reading Comprehension	10			
Antonyms	10			
SUBTOTALS	38			
OVERALL VERBAL ABILITY TOTALS	76			

PRACTICE TEST 2: QUANTITATIVE ABILITY ANALYSIS SHEET

SECTION III

	Possible	Completed	Right	Wrong
Quantitative Comparison	15			
Math Ability	15			
SUBTOTALS	30			

SECTION IV

	Possible	Completed	Right	Wrong
Quantitative Comparison	15			
Math Ability	15			
SUBTOTALS	30			
OVERALL QUANTITATIVE ABILITY TOTALS	60			

SECTION VII

NOTE: For this practice test, do not include Section VII in your overall Quantitative Ability score.

	Possible	Completed	Right	Wrong
Quantitative Comparison	15			
Math Ability	15			
TOTALS	30			

PRACTICE TEST 2: ANALYTICAL ABILITY ANALYSIS SHEET

	Possible	Completed	Right	Wrong
Section V	25			
Section VI	25			
OVERALL ANALYTICAL ABILITY TOTALS	50			

WHY??????????????????????????????????

ANALYSIS: TALLY SHEET FOR PROBLEMS MISSED

One of the most important parts of test preparation is analyzing WHY! you missed a problem so that you can reduce the number of mistakes. Now that you have taken the practice test and corrected your answers, carefully tally your mistakes by marking them in the proper column.

REASON FOR MISTAKE

	Total Missed	Simple Mistake	Misread Problem	Lack of Knowledge
SECTION I: VERBAL ABILITY				
SECTION II: VERBAL ABILITY				
SUBTOTALS				
SECTION III: QUANTITATIVE ABILITY				
SECTION IV: QUANTITATIVE ABILITY				
SUBTOTALS				
SECTION V: ANALYTICAL ABILITY				
SECTION VI: ANALYTICAL ABILITY				
SUBTOTALS				
TOTAL VERBAL, QUANTITATIVE, AND ANALYTICAL				

Reviewing the above data should help you determine WHY you are missing certain problems. Now that you have pinpointed the type of error, focus on avoiding your most common type.

COMPLETE ANSWERS AND EXPLANATIONS FOR
PRACTICE TEST 2

SECTION I: VERBAL ABILITY

Sentence Completion

1. (B) Working from the second blank first, notice that you are looking for a word coinciding with "thought." Only *specter* is a type of thought (something that haunts or perturbs the mind), and along with it, *holocaust* (destruction by fire) makes good sense.

2. (B) Those who are "uncritical" of "regulation" would tend to hold *conventional* values. Along with this, *subsidization* (support) makes good sense.

3. (E) The correct answer is *conciliatory*. The sentence sets up a contrast situation with the word "but." Truman tried to do something but ended up adopting a "tougher policy." *Conciliatory* is the only choice which suggests a previous "weaker" approach.

4. (B) The answer is *vehement . . . acrimonious*. The signal words "controversial" and "more" and "more" suggest a conflict which increases or intensifies. The only pair which supports these context clues is *vehement . . . acrimonious*. Even if you are not certain of the definition of *acrimonious,* the other choices can be eliminated because none of them suggests the intensification of the controversy.

5. (B) The correct answer is *parsimonious*. The context provides a definition for the correct choice in "exceeds the trait of being economical." The context also suggests the trait of being excessively frugal by the word "so." Choices (C) and (D) would not apply because they mean "poor" and the aunt, we know, is wealthy. Choice (A) is not excessive. (E) does not fit with the example of washing paper plates.

6. (C) The correct answer is *still . . . media*. "In spite of" suggests an enduring situation, unchanged by competition. The second word is practically defined by the phrase "communication between advertisers and customers."

7. (B) The first blank must refer to a group of people, the Republicans. (A), (D), and (E) do not do so. (C) is a useless repetition of the meaning of sectional." Therefore, *amalgam* (a mixture of different elements) is left, and makes good sense along with *uncompromising* (making no concessions).

8. (D) In this case, the second blank is easier to fill because it is followed by a definition. *Differentiation* is "the recognition of different categories of people," etc. *Stratification* which *does* imply the differences in rank which *differentiation* does not, is also appropriate.

Analogies

9. (D) *Sanctuary* is to *church* in the same way *boudoir* is to *house*. An interior room of a building is compared to the entire structure in this analogy. A part-to-whole relationship is characteristic of all the choices, but only (D) satisfies the interior room to structure relationship.

10. (E) *Jaunty* is to *perky* in the same way as *par* is to *equal*. The relationship here is one of synonymous words. *Jaunty* and *perky* are synonyms, as are *par* and *equal*. None of the other choices presents a set of synonyms. In choice (B) the word "caustic" has a bitter connotation which it does not share with the more neutral word, "witty." Thus, choice (B) does not present a set of synonyms. The best choice is (E), *par: equal*.

11. (B) *Mesa* is to *valley* in the same way *saucer* is to *cup*. The relationship here is one of flat plane to concave shape. A *saucer* is a flat surface compared to a concave shape, a *cup;* in the same way a *mesa* (flat land) is compared to a *valley* (land curved inward, or concave).

12. (C) To do something *cursorily* is to do it *superficially,* in the same way as to do something *circumspectly* is to do it *watchfully* or carefully. Although (A) presents a similar distinction between meanings, its terms are not the same part of speech as the original and are in the wrong order.

13. (B) In order to be successful, a *thief* must be *surreptitious* (acting in a secret, stealthy way). In the same way, a successful *teacher* must be *explanatory*.

14. (A) A *dragon* is a *chimerical* (fanciful) product in the same way as *penicillin* is a *chemical* product. This is an "origin-product" analogy.

15. (C) *Disquiet* is to *fears* in the same way *agitate* is to *mob*. The relationship here is one of restless activity disturbing something. The verb *disquiet* ("to disturb") is related to *fears* in the same way *agitate* ("to stir up") is related to *mob*. All other choices involve verbs which subdue, hide, or decrease the effectiveness of the second term.

16. (C) *Demagogue* is to *populace* in the same way *rabble-rouser* is to *crowd*. The relationship here is one of a person (in this case one who stirs up people by appealing to emotion) to a group. A *demagogue* stirs up the emotions of a *populace* in the same way a *rabble-rouser* appeals to the emotions of a *crowd*.

17. (E) *Doctor* is to *disease* in the same way *teacher* is to *ignorance*. Here the person and the thing the person works to eliminate are compared. Choice (C) is close but a policeman would have to be compared to crime, not

criminal, if the analogy were to satisfy the relationship of the original pair. In choices (A) and (B) tools are compared to persons who use them and are therefore incorrect.

Reading Comprehension

18. (D) *Evolution* is to *species* in the same way as *bush* is to *branches*. Just as the branches of a bush reach out every which way in varying lengths, the results of evolution (forms of life, species) have developed in irregular "branches." This is the main point of paragraph 2.

19. (C) A "predecessor" is that which comes before. Since, according to paragraph 1, "nucleosides produced nucleotides," *nucleosides* came before (are predecessors of) *nucleic acids*.

20. (C) The first paragraph lists water, hydrogen, ammonia, and hydrogen cyanide as the only members of the primordial mixture.

21. (C) This situation establishes a relationship between price and quantity which parallels the paragraph 2 explanation of the "law of demand." This section discusses "the consumer's desire to get the 'best buy,'" and goes on to say that "if the price of good A increases, the individual will tend to substitute another good and purchase less of good A." Since the appearance of a lower-priced breakfast drink makes orange juice more "expensive," in relation, the law of demand as so described would prevail.

22. (D) The third paragraph distinguishes between "individual demand" and "market demand"; the former is exercised by a single person, whereas the latter is exerted by a *group* of individuals. With this distinction in mind, we may conclude that a group of individuals constitutes a market. (B) contradicts the paragraph. (A), (C), and (E) might be true under certain conditions, but those conditions are not specified in the question or in the passage.

23. (A) Initially, the passage emphasizes a distinction between "demand" and "quantity demanded," concluding that "demand shifts when there is a change in income, expectations, taste, etc., such that a different quantity of the good is demanded at the *same* price." This statement fits (A) precisely. All other choices include or allow for a *changing* price.

24. (C) The passage says that "demand shifts when there is a change in income, expectations, taste, etc., such that a different quantity of the good is demanded at the same price." (A), (D), and (E) all involve a *changing* price, and (B) would reduce income so that demand would *decrease*.

25. **(B)** Paragraph 4 states, "there is a positive correlation between quantity supplied and product price." Since that means that quantity and price are related, any choice (in this case all choices except B) with a relational connotation does not tell us what the two items are *not*.

26. **(B)** The last sentence says that it is "developed" or "interdependent" economies that acquiesce to the idea that government must control economy to some extent. This leaves underdeveloped countries unspoken for and raises the possibility they might *not* acquiesce to government control.

27. **(B)** The paragraph states that government action "may create shortages or surpluses." Shortages and surpluses are associated with disequilibrium in paragraph 6.

28. **(D)** The third sentence in the passage supports this answer. (C) may be true, but is too general to be the best answer.

Antonyms

29. **(B)** A *covenant* (*co* = together; *ven* = come) is a solemn mutual agreement. A *breach* is a violation of such an agreement.

30. **(E)** *Precarious* describes an uncertain, often dangerous, situation. The most nearly opposite choice is *certain*.

31. **(A)** *Contumacious* refers to defiance of authority. Its opposite is *compliant*, which refers to agreeing or giving in.

32. **(C)** A *conclave* (*con* = with, together) is a secret gathering. The most nearly opposite choice is *public assembly*.

33. **(B)** *Tractable* (*tract* = to draw or pull) means easy to manage. Its opposite is *refractory*, which means difficult to manage, stubborn, obstinate. "Retractable" means capable of being withdrawn or denied.

34. **(B)** *Vapid* is often used to refer to talk which is extremely dull; it is quite the opposite of *engaging*, which suggests an "interesting" quality more strongly than any of the other choices.

35. **(C)** *Glibly* refers to someone who speaks readily and easily. The opposite is someone who speaks *haltingly*.

36. **(E)** *Argot* is a type of slang; the opposite of slang language is *standard* language.

37. (E) *Plethora* generally means an overabundance; therefore the opposite is *shortage*. "Modicum" is a possibility, but is not as extreme as *shortage*.

38. (C) *Supplication (supple* = flexible; *pli* = to bend) is a humble request, often delivered on bended knee. The action most nearly opposite to a *supplication*, which *asks*, is a *grant*, which *gives*.

SECTION II: VERBAL ABILITY

Sentence Completion

1. (E) The best choice is *comparing . . . expectations.* The signal clues are "unknown world" and "careful to note." "Careful to note" suggests careful thought or *comparing,* while "unknown world" suggests a meaning in this sentence that is best fulfilled by the word *expectations.* In choice (B), the word "refuting" is negative and does not convey the intended meaning of "careful to note."

2. (A) The best choice is *palatial . . . sequester.* The phrase "from the rigors" requires that the second word in our choice convey a meaning of escape or hiding. The words "large" and "home" require a positive word that describes a home. Choice (A) is the only choice which meets those requirements.

3. (A) The sentence is, in effect, a definition of *aggregate.*

4. (E) It makes good sense to conclude that a political institution would "protect" society from *external* forces; that is, those forces which threaten society as a whole. *Salient* (conspicuous, prominent) fits this meaning too.

5. (D) In this case, the second blank is easier to fill because it is followed by a definition; "relating the unfamiliar to the familiar by means of likeness" is a definition of "analogy." Linking *analogical* with *interpreting,* we note that myths do indeed interpret nature, that is, the beginnings of cultures and societies.

6. (A) The signal word is "seamen." *Circumnavigate* (sail around) is something only a seaman could do. None of the other choices has any relationship to either "commerce" or "seamen."

7. (D) The best choice is *fail . . . operational.* The signal here is "cannot _____ to be impressed," which should be a negative word, while the second choice should be a complement to "structural," which is *operational.*

8. (E) The blank must be the opposite of "earthbound" and "materialistic." The best choice, therefore, is *transcendental* (transcending material existence).

9. (B) The answer is *effect . . . conflict.* A cause and effect relationship is set up in this sentence with a negative term required for the second blank suggested by the term "bitter."

Analogies

10. (D) *Vigilante* is to *policeman* in the same way as *lynching* is to *execution*. The first term in the original pair is an extralegal (outside the law) counterpart of the second. A *lynching* is an illegal version of an *execution*, suggesting that the law has been taken into the hands of private citizens. This same relationship is true of a *vigilante* (a member of a group organized without legal authorization) and a *policeman*.

11. (B) *Tress* is to *tuft* in the same way as *modicum* is to *iota*. The comparison here is of small amounts. A *tress* (lock or curl) is a small amount of hair and a *tuft* is a small amount of grass. (C) and (E) are comparisons of large amounts, while (A) and (D) are not related in terms of amounts at all, only whole-to-part and part-to-whole.

12. (C) *Charter* is to *corporation* in the same way as *copyright* is to *song*. A *charter* is a written legal document protecting and establishing the rights and limitations of a *corporation* in a similar manner to a *copyright* protecting the rights of a *song*. Both documents are written and legally binding in their relationship to the *corporation* and *song*.

13. (A) A *megalomaniac* (suffering from abnormally strong egomania) characteristically engages in *braggadocio* (empty boasting) in the same way as a *general* characteristically issues *commands*.

14. (C) A *finch* (type of bird) is an interest of *ornithology* (study of birds) in the same way as a *skull* is an interest of *archaeology* (study of ancient peoples).

15. (D) *Theology* (the study of God and religion) is to *anthropology* (the study of the origins of man on earth) in the same way as *Heaven* (the province of God) is to *Earth* (the province of man). This is a "high-low" analogy.

16. (D) *Wanton* (reckless) is to *ascetic* (self-constrained, self-denying) in the same way as *free* is to *chained*. This is an "opposites" analogy and (D) is a better choice than (B), (C), and (E) because the terms in (D) correspond most closely to the meaning of the original.

17. (A) *Servant* is to *servility* in the same way as *storyteller* is to *exaggeration*. The relationship expressed here is one of a person compared to a characteristic. The best choice in this case is (A), *storyteller : exaggeration*, since *exaggeration* is a characteristic a *storyteller* might possess in the same way a *servant* might behave with *servility*. Both *servility* and *exaggeration* are extreme characteristics. Choice (B), "waitress : wait," is not appropriate, as to wait is not an extreme characteristic. Choice (C),

"overweight : fat" is not appropriate, as overweight does not title a person in the same way as a *servant*, which, along with *storyteller*, is clearly a noun. Choice (E) is in the wrong order.

18. (D) *Diffidence* (the noun form of diffident) is a synonym for *shyness* in the same way as *bravery* (the noun form of brave) is a synonym for *courage*.

Reading Comprehension

19. (A) The fourth paragraph describes Augustine's ideas about man's evil tendency, which contributes to the "corruption of human nature." This evil tendency is associated "in the will" with "the inclination to follow that which is pleasant." Adam (D) and Eve (E) became corrupt, but they cannot be described as "symptoms" because they are people.

20. (C) Paragraph 1 says that Augustine does not "believe that souls are eternal," and later states that souls are immortal, that "they will survive the death of the physical body." (E) is incorrect because it is the intellect and the will which are capable of sin, not the soul. (See paragraph 4.)

21. (B) Paragraph 2 states that one of the difficulties Augustine had explaining "the nature of man's freedom" involved "the idea that God knows what man will do in the future." (A) is correct according to certain religions, but is not stated in the passage as an obstacle to man's freedom.

22. (E) According to the passage (paragraph 4) the intellect and the will (B and D) are parts of the mind, not the flesh. (A) and (C) are obviously inconsistent with the passage.

23. (B) Paragraph 4 says, "In the intellect it [the evil tendency] is expressed in the sin of pride."

24. (C) This answer is supported by paragraph 3, which mentions several reasons for infanticide; in general, each infanticide is justified insofar as the birth is unfortunate for the society as a whole. In all cases infanticide is "a technique of population control." (A) is a possible choice, but the religious implications of infanticide are more implicit than explicit in the passage.

25. (B) Paragraph 7 abruptly leaves the topic of birth and childhood and concentrates on age and death. A transitional sentence would be useful for eliminating such abruptness. (A) is inconsistent with the form of the passage; there are no subtitles anywhere. (C) would call for information which may or may not be relevant at that point. (D) would be out of place and useless insofar as it supplies definitions long *after* the words have been used. (E) is inconsistent with the author's straightforward, nonopinionated presentation.

26. (A) This is true of Oceania, which in some parts requires a woman "to give proof that she is fertile before she is permitted to marry." She could give such proof only by becoming pregnant; menstruation (C) is not itself proof of fertility.

27. (B) The passage states that infanticide is used in many societies "as a technique of population control." Only (B) is such a technique although (A) may control population without meaning to. (C) refers to an economic, rather than psychological, phenomenon.

28. (B) Near the end of the passage, burial in the fetal position is mentioned. So a connection is suggested between the fetus (unborn child) and the corpse, between birth and death.

Antonyms

29. (D) *Obsequious* means extremely submissive and polite (*ob* = upon; *sequor* = follow). The most nearly opposite is *rude*.

30. (D) *Bellicose (bell* = war) means inclined to fighting, hostile, quarrelsome. Its opposite, then, is *peaceful*. "Calm" is not correct because a calm person is not necessarily a nonhostile person.

31. (E) A *pedant* emphasizes narrow and minute details of scholarship and constantly corrects petty errors. A *pluralist* is a liberal thinker who entertains wide-ranging points of view.

32. (B) *Cadaverous* means pale or ghostly (a cadaver is a corpse). *Salubrious* means healthful or wholesome (*salus* = health).

33. (C) *Piquant* means pungent or flavorful. *Insipid* means without sufficient taste.

34. (D) *Insouciant* means carefree or without concern. *Concerned* is the nearest opposite.

35. (E) A *yaw* implies deviation from a direct course. A *constant* implies lack of deviation.

36. (A) *Perfidy* means a breach of faith, or treachery. *Faithfulness* would be its opposite.

37. (B) *Palingenesis* means a transformation from one state to another. *Stability* would be the opposite.

38. (C) *Hie* means to move with haste. *Saunter* is to linger or move slowly.

SECTION III: QUANTITATIVE ABILITY

Quantitative Comparison

1. (A) Since both sides have the factors $\frac{2}{5}$ and $\frac{5}{8}$, you may eliminate them from each column. Now compare

   $\frac{3}{7}$ and $\frac{4}{11}$ by

   cross multiplying upward and you get

   $$\frac{3}{7} \times \frac{4}{11}$$

   Since 33 is greater than 28, $\frac{3}{7} > \frac{4}{11}$

2. (D) Substituting 0 for x, 1 for y, and 2 for z, gives

   $(0) + (1) + (2)$ $(0)(1)(2)$
   Therefore $3 > 0$

   Now substituting -1 for x, 0 for y, and 1 for z gives

   $(-1) + (0) + (1)$ $(-1)(0)(1)$
   Therefore $0 = 0$

   Since different values give different comparisons, the correct answer is (D).

3. (C) This is really an example of the distributive property of multiplication over addition. By multiplying $(b + c)a$ you would get $ab + ac$. Therefore the correct answer is (C).

4. (A) Solving the equation

   $x\sqrt{.09} = 2$
   $x(.3) = 2$

   dividing by .3,

   $$\frac{x(.3)}{(.3)} = \frac{2}{.3}$$

   $x = \frac{20}{3} = 6\frac{2}{3}$

   Therefore $7 > 6\frac{2}{3}$

5. (A) To find the number of degrees in the interior angles of a pentagon use the formula $180 \times (n - 2)$, where n is the number of sides. Therefore $180 \times (5 - 2) = 180 \times 3 = 540$.

$540° > 500°$

Another method would be to draw the pentagon and break it into triangles connecting vertices, (lines cannot cross) as shown below.

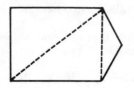

Multiplying the number of triangles (3) by 180 (degrees in a triangle) gives the same result, 540°.

6. (D) Substituting $x = 0$ and $y = 1$

$(x - y)^2$	$x^2 - y^2$
$(0 - 1)^2$	$(0)^2 - (1)^2$
then 1 >	-1

Now substituting $x = -1$ and $y = 0$

gives

$(-1 - 0)^2$	$(-1)^2 - (0)^2$
$(-1)^2$	$(-1)^2$
then 1 =	1

Since different values give different comparisons, then no comparison can be made.

7. (B) Finding a common denominator is not necessary here. Make a partial comparison by comparing the first fraction in each column; 1/71 is smaller than 1/65. Now comparing the second fractions that are being subtracted, 1/151 is greater than 1/153. If you start with a smaller number and subtract a greater number, it must be less than starting with a greater number and subtracting a smaller one.

8. (B) If $a = b$ and $a < c$, then the following substitutions make the comparison simpler.

2a	$b + c$
$a + a$	$b + c$

Since $a = b$, then   Now canceling b's from each column

$a + b$ $b + c$ leaves $a < c$.

9. (D) The length of side AB is determinable by using the Pythagorean theorem, but since DC is not known, BC cannot be determined. Note you cannot make a determination by measuring.

10. (C) ∠BAD = ∠ABD, for angles across from equal sides in a triangle are equal.

11. (C) Since there are 180° in a triangle and ∠BDC is 90°, the remaining two angles, ∠DBC and ∠BCD, must total 90°.

12. (A) AB + BC is greater than AC, since the sum of any two sides of a triangle is greater than the third side.

13. (A) Dividing the equation by 3 gives x − 4y = 12; now multiplying this by 2 gives 2x − 8y = 24. Therefore, column A is 24, which is greater than column B.

14. (B) Simplifying each column leaves

$1/x^2$ $1/x^3$

Now substituting simple fractions such as 1/2 gives

$$1/(1/2)^2 \qquad 1/(1/2)^3$$
$$1/(1/4) \qquad 1/(1/8)$$
$$4 \quad < \quad 8$$

Column B will always be greater.

15. (C) Since triangle ABC is inscribed in a semicircle, angle C is 90°. Because there are 180° in a triangle, the sum of the remaining angles, ∠CAB and ∠ABC, must total 90°. Therefore, the correct answer is (C) because 180 − 90 = 90.

Math Ability

16. (A) Multiply numerator and denominator by 12 (lowest common denominator).

$$\frac{12(2/3 - 1/2)}{12(1/6 + 1/4 + 2/3)} = \frac{8 - 6}{2 + 3 + 8} = 2/13$$

17. (B) Since XY = YZ = 10, then △XYZ is an isosceles △ and ∠X = ∠Z. ∠Y = 84°, since it forms a vertical angle with the given angle.

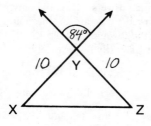

$$\angle X + \angle Y + \angle Z = 180$$
$$\angle X + 84 + \angle Z = 180$$
$$2\,(\angle Z) + 84 = 180$$
$$2\,(\angle Z) = 96$$
$$\angle Z = 48$$

Hence the measure of $\angle Z = 48°$.

18. **(B)** If $\frac{2}{3}$ of the container is full, there remains $\frac{1}{3}$ of the container to fill. The time to fill $\frac{1}{3}$ of the container will be half as long as the time needed to fill $\frac{2}{3}$ of the container. Hence $\frac{1}{2}$ (18 minutes) = 9 minutes.

19. **(A)** Since arc YXZ is a semicircle, its measure is 180°.

$$\text{arc } XZ = \text{arc } YXZ - \text{arc } YWX$$
$$= 180° - 100°$$
$$\text{arc } XZ = 80°$$

Since an inscribed angle = $\frac{1}{2}$ (intercepted arc) we have

$$\angle XYZ = \frac{1}{2} \,(\text{arc } XZ)$$
$$= \frac{1}{2} \,(80°)$$
$$= 40°$$

Hence $\angle XYZ$ has a measure of 40°.

20. **(B)** If the average of 7 numbers is 9, then the sum of these numbers must be 9×7, or 63.
If the average of 7 numbers is 9, then the sum of these numbers must be 7×9, or 63.
The sum of all 16 numbers must be $63 + 63$, or 126.
Hence the average of all 16 numbers must be

$$126 \div 16 = {}^{126}\!/_{16} = 7^{14}\!/_{16} = 7^{7}\!/_{8}$$

21. **(B)** By inspecting the answers, (B) is the only reasonable choice. If Bob and Fred each worked at a rate of one house for every 6 days, then working together, they would be able to complete a house in 3 days. Since Bob works at a slightly faster rate, it would take slightly less than 3 days.

Mathematically,

let x = number of days working together

$$\text{then } \frac{x}{5} + \frac{x}{6} = 1$$

$$30 \left(\frac{x}{5} + \frac{x}{6} \right) = 1 \, (30)$$

$$6x + 5x = 30$$

$$11x = 30$$

Therefore x = $^{30}/_{11}$, or $2^{8}/_{11}$

22. **(D)** $\dfrac{(6!) \, (4!)}{(5!) \, (3!)}$

$$= \frac{(6 \cdot 5 \cdot 4 \cdot 3 \cdot 2 \cdot 1) \cdot (4 \cdot 3 \cdot 2 \cdot 1)}{(5 \cdot 4 \cdot 3 \cdot 2 \cdot 1) \cdot (3 \cdot 2 \cdot 1)}$$

$$= \frac{6 \cdot 4}{1} = 24$$

23. **(B)** Adding any two of three consecutive positive integers greater than 1 will always be greater than the other integer, therefore II is true. The others cannot be determined; as they depend on values and/or the order of x, y, and z.

24. **(B)** If two points have coordinates (x_1, y_1) and (x_2, y_2), the distance, d, between these points is defined to be

$$d = \sqrt{(x_1 - x_2)^2 + (y_1 - y_2)^2}$$

Since E has coordinates $(-3, 5)$ and F had coordinates $(6, -7)$, the distance between E and F is

$$EF = \sqrt{(-3 - 6)^2 + [5 - (-7)]^2}$$
$$= \sqrt{(-9)^2 + (12)^2}$$

$$= \sqrt{81 + 144}$$
$$= \sqrt{225}$$
$$EF = 15$$

25. **(B)** In 1974, there were 60% white and 5% black students. Thus there were 12 times as many whites as blacks. Since there were 2000 whites in 1974, there were 2000/12 or 167 blacks.

26. **(C)** In 1976, there were 1000 white students. This was 40% of the total. Thus, the total must have been 2500.

27. **(C)** Whites declined from 80% to 30%, (50/80), a 62.5% decrease. Blacks increased from 5% to 15%, (10/5), a 200% increase. Mexican Americans increased from 5% to 25%, (20/5), a 400% increase. Others increased from 10% to 30%, (20/10), a 200% increase.

28. **(E)** In 1974 there were 20% other and 60% white. Thus there were three times as many whites as others. Since there were 2000 whites, there were 666 other. In 1976, 40% white and 20% other. Twice as many whites as other. Thus 500 other. Therefore, a decrease of 166.

29. **(E)** Perimeter = 10 feet   Area = s^2
        = (10) (12) inches
        = 120 inches   = $(30)^2$
    Perimeter = 4s (s = length of side)
                                  = (30) (30)

                    4s = 120   = 900 square inches

                    $\dfrac{4s}{4} = \dfrac{120}{4}$

30. **(C)** Let x be the length of time Mr. Dinkle travels, then x + ½ is the time Mr. Smitherly travels. This gives the equation 50(x + ½) = 60x, to see when they will meet. Solving gives

$$50x + 25 = 60x$$
$$25 = 10x$$
$$2.5 = x$$

Therefore, it will take Mr. Dinkle 2½ hours to overtake Mr. Smitherly. Since Mr. Dinkle starts at 8:30 A.M., he will overtake Mr. Smitherly at 11:00 A.M. Note that answers (A), (D), and (E) are not reasonable.

SECTION IV: QUANTITATIVE ABILITY

Quantitative Comparison

1. **(B)** By inspection, if you multiply $(.89/.919) \times 57$, this must be less than 57 (as you are multiplying 57 by a fraction less than 1). Therefore it must be less than 58. The correct answer is **(B)**.

2. **(B)** Substituting -1 for x gives $(-1)^3 - 1 = -1 - 1 = -2$. Now trying -2 for x gives $(-2)^3 - 1 = -8 - 1 = -9$. It is evident that this phrase will always generate negative values if $x < 0$. Therefore, the correct answer is **(B)**. The cube of a negative is negative. One less than a negative is negative. Any negative is less than 0.

3. **(C)** The prime numbers between 3 and 19 are 5, 7, 11, 13, and 17. The correct answer is **(C)**, since there are 5 primes.

4. **(C)** To solve $a/6 = b/4$

   cross multiply, giving $4a = 6b$
   then divide by 2
   leaving $2a = 3b$

5. **(C)** $\overarc{AC} = 2(\angle B)$, since an inscribed angle is half of the arc it subtends (connects to).

6. **(A)** Since $\angle AOB$ is a central angle, it equals the measure of $\overarc{AB}$, and since $\angle ADC$ is outside the circle, but connects to $\overarc{AB}$, it is less than half of $\overarc{AB}$. Therefore

   $\angle AOB > \angle ADC$

   Alternate method: The external angle AOB must be larger than either of the remote interior angles.

7. **(D)** This problem is best solved by inspection or insight. Since there are two variables in this single inequality, there are many possible values for x and y; therefore a comparison cannot be made.

8. **(B)** First set up the numbers for each side:

Number of inches in 1 mile	Number of minutes in 1 year
(12 inches in 1 ft) ×	(60 minutes in 1 hr) ×
(5280 ft in 1 mile)	(24 hrs in 1 day) ×
	(365 days in 1 yr)
12 × 5280	60 × 24 × 365

Now dividing out, a 10 and 12 leaves

1 × 528	6 × 2 × 365
or 528	12 × 365

Column B is obviously greater.

9. **(A)** Area of circle with diameter 8 is computed by finding the radius, which is half of the diameter and substituting into this equation $A = \pi r^2$. Since the radius is 4, and π is about 3.14

$\pi (4)^2$	Area of square with
3.14 × 16	side 7 is
50.24	49

10. **(A)** Changing the form of column A by squaring 3 and multiplying it by 2 to get everything under the radical sign leaves the simple comparison $\sqrt{18} > \sqrt{17}$.

11. **(B)** Solving the systems of equations as follows by first multiplying the bottom equation by -5 gives

$$5x + y = 2$$
$$-5x + -15y = -30$$

Now adding equations leaves

$$-14y = -28$$

Therefore $y = 2$

Substituting $y = 2$ into the original second equation gives

$$x + 3(2) = 6$$
then $x + 6 = 6$
and $x = 0$
Therefore $x < y$

12. **(C)** Simplifying the complex fraction in column A as follows,

$$\cfrac{1}{1 + \cfrac{1}{1 + 1/n}} = \cfrac{1}{1 + \cfrac{1}{n/n + 1/n}} = \cfrac{1}{1 + \cfrac{1}{(n + 1)/n}} = \cfrac{1}{1 + \cfrac{n}{n + 1}}$$

$$= \cfrac{1}{\cfrac{n + 1}{n + 1} + \cfrac{n}{n + 1}} = \cfrac{1}{\cfrac{n + 1 + n}{n + 1}} = \cfrac{1}{\cfrac{2n + 1}{n + 1}} = \cfrac{n + 1}{2n + 1}$$

An alternate method would involve substituting simple numbers into each expression.

13. **(B)** In quadrant II, all y values are positive and all x values are negative. Therefore, y will always be greater than x in quadrant II.

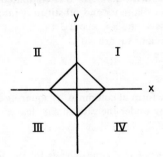

14. **(C)** Simplifying column A by following the rules for priorities of operations (powers, square root, multiply, divide, add, subtract) gives

$$5 + 4 \cdot 10^2 + 8 \cdot 10^3$$
$$5 + 4 \cdot 100 + 8 \cdot 1000$$
$$5 + 400 + 8000 = 8405$$

15. **(D)** We have not been given enough information to compare Jill and Joan.

Math Ability

16. **(D)** Solve for x, $2x - 5 = 9$
$$2x = 14$$
then $$x = 7$$

Now substitute 7 for x.

Hence 3x + 2 = 3(7) + 2
$$= 21 + 2$$
$$= 23$$

17. (C) In the series, 8, 9, 12, 17, 24 . . .

9 − 8 = 1   17 − 12 = 5
12 − 9 = 3   24 − 17 = 7

Hence the difference between the next term and 24 must be 9 or
x − 24 = 9
and x = 33
Hence the next term in the series must be 33.

18. (C) Since BD = CD, ∠CBD = ∠C = 19°
Hence ∠BDC = 180 − (∠CBD − ∠C)
$$= 180 − (19 + 19)$$
$$= 180 − 38$$
∠BDC = 142°

then ∠BDA = 180 − ∠BDC
$$= 180 − 142$$
∠BDA = 38°

Since AB = AD, ∠ABD = ∠BDA = 38°
Hence ∠A = 180 − (∠BDA + ∠ABD)
$$= 180 − (38 + 38)$$
$$= 180 − 76$$
∠A = 104°

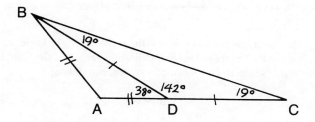

19. (C) In 1970, 10% of $12,000, or $1,200, was spent on medical. In 1975,
12% of $16,000, or $1,920, was spent on medical. Thus, an increase of
$720.

20. (C) There was an increase from 18% to 22%. That is a 4% increase.
Therefore a 4% increase from 18% is a 22% increase in the percent spent
on food and drink.

21. **(B)** Ratio of $^3/_{10}$ to $^5/_8$ = $(^3/_{10})/(^5/_8)$

    Multiply numerator and denominator by 40 (lowest common denominator).

$$\frac{40(^3/_{10})}{40(^5/_8)} = \;^{12}/_{25}$$

Hence the ratio of $^3/_{10}$ to $^5/_8$ = $^{12}/_{25}$

22. **(E)** First change 2 hours into 120 minutes. (Always get a common unit of measurement.) Then dividing 120 by $^2/_3$ gives

$$\overset{60}{\cancel{120}} \times \frac{3}{\cancel{2}} = 180$$

The correct answer is **(E)**, 180 items. Notice choices **(A)** and **(B)** are ridiculous answers.

23. **(B)** Charting Tom's trip would look like this:

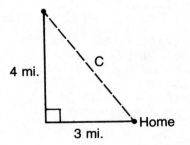

Since the directions are west and north, we have a right angle, allowing us to use the Pythagorean theorem to find the length of the third side of the triangle (which is Tom's actual distance from home).

$$a^2 + b^2 = c^2$$
$$3^2 + 4^2 = c^2$$
$$9 + 16 = c^2$$
$$25 = c^2$$
$$5 = c$$

Therefore, the correct answer is **(B)**. Tom's actual distance from home is 5 miles. (You may have noticed the 3:4:5 common right triangle relationship and avoided using the Pythagorean theorem.).

24. **(B)** Since a = p + prt

$$a - p = p + prt - p$$

$$a - p = prt$$

$$\frac{a - p}{pt} = \frac{prt}{pt}$$

$$\frac{a - p}{pt} = r$$

Hence

$$r = \frac{a - p}{pt}$$

25. **(B)** In parallelogram AEFG if all of the triangles have the same base, and they all meet at F (giving them all the same height), since the formula for area of a triangle is ½ × base × height, then they all have equal areas. Therefore the ratio of the area of triangle CDF to the area of triangle ABF is 1:1 and the correct answer is **(B)**.

26. **(C)** Since $\sqrt{mn}$ = 10, mn = 100 and the possible values for m and n would be:

1 and 100	5 and 20
2 and 50	10 and 10
4 and 25	

Since none of these combinations yield m + n = 50, choice **(C)** is correct.

27. **(B)** Set up the problem as follows:

$$\frac{x + (2)}{x + 5 + (2)} = \frac{7}{12} \text{ or } \frac{x + 2}{x + 7} = \frac{7}{12}$$

By observation x = 5 since $\frac{5 + 2}{5 + 7} = \frac{7}{12}$

Substituting into the original fraction $\frac{x}{x + 5}$ gives $\frac{5}{5 + 5} = \frac{5}{10} = \frac{1}{2}$

A longer method would have been to solve $\frac{x + 2}{x + 7} = \frac{7}{12}$
as follows:

Cross multiplying gives

$$12x + 24 = 7x + 49$$
$$5x = 25$$
$$x = 5$$

and then substitute in $\dfrac{x}{x + 5}$, or $\dfrac{5}{5 + 5} = \dfrac{5}{10} = \dfrac{1}{2}$

Alternate method: Subtract 2 from the numerator and denominator of $7/12$ and then reduce.

28. **(E)** Let x = original price

$$\text{then } x - .40x = 5.70$$
$$.60x = 5.70$$
$$x = 9.50$$

Hence the book originally cost $9.50.

29. **(E)** If the coordinates of two points x and y are (x_1, y_1) and (x_2, y_2), respectively, then the coordinates of the midpoint B (m_1, m_2) of xy are

$$\left(\frac{x_1 + x_2}{2}, \frac{y_1 + y_2}{2} \right) = (m_1, m_2)$$

Hence

$$m_1 = \frac{x_1 + x_2}{2} \text{ and } m_2 = \frac{y_1 + y_2}{2}$$

$$5 = \frac{-4 + x_2}{2} \text{ and } -2 = \frac{3 + y_2}{2}$$

$$(2)(5) = (2) \frac{(-4 + x_2)}{2} \text{ and } (2)(-2) = (2) \frac{(3 + y_2)}{2}$$

$$10 = -4 + x_2 \qquad\qquad -4 = 3 + y_2$$

$$10 + 4 = -4 + x_2 + 4 \qquad -4 - 3 = 3 + y_2 - 3$$

$$14 = x_2 \qquad\qquad -7 = y_2$$

Hence the coordinates of y are $(x_2, y_2) = (14, -7)$.

30. (C) Let x = first number
    2x + 1 = second number
    3x − 4 = third number
    Since the average of the three numbers is 55, we have

$$\frac{x + (2x + 1) + (3x - 4)}{3} = 55$$

Multiplying both sides of our equation by 3, we have

$$x + (2x + 1) + (3x - 4) = 165$$

$$6x - 3 = 165$$

$$6x - 3 + 3 = 165 + 3$$

$$6x = 168$$

$$\frac{6x}{6} = \frac{168}{6}$$

$$x = \frac{168}{6}$$

x = 28 = first number
2x + 1 = 57 = second number
3x − 4 = 80 = third number
Hence the largest number is 80.

SECTION V: ANALYTICAL ABILITY

In questions 1–4, using greater than (>) and less than (<) symbols will help place the boys in some order.

Sam is taller than Al.	S > A
Bob is shorter than Jim.	B < J
Paul is shorter than Sam.	P < S
Bob is taller than Paul.	B > P
Sam is shorter than Jim.	S < J
Paul is the shortest of the five.	

Now putting this information together gives the following relationships:

$$J > S > A > P$$

$$J > \leftarrow B \rightarrow > P$$

Notice that some of the boys cannot be placed in exact order. This is not necessary to answer the questions.

1. **(D)** From the diagram, Jim is obviously the tallest.

2. **(B)** I is false, because Al is necessarily taller than Paul. II is true, because Al and Bob cannot be compared by the information given, therefore Al is not necessarily taller than Bob.

3. **(A)** From the chart, I is the only true statement, because Jim is taller than Al.

4. **(D)** If Harold joins the group and is taller than Bob, but shorter than Al, then the order of the boys must be

$$J > S > A > H > B > P$$

From this chart, I and II must be true.

5. **(E)** The only correct choice is II; it is argued that hot weather *causes* crime. This is not mere coincidence, and the statement does not state that we *can* control the weather. (E) must be chosen because no other choices offer II exclusively.

6. **(B)** The argument posits an exclusive relationship between hot weather and crime. (A), (C), and (E) contradict such an exclusive relationship, (D) is irrelevant to the relationship, and (B) provides evidence supporting and strengthening the heat-crime relationship.

Questions 7–8 are answered by deduction. Since Julie is 2 years younger than Alice (4), and Julie is 23 years old, then Alice is 25. By statements 5 and 6 or by statement 8, Carol must be 22 years old. Therefore,

> Carol is 22.
> Julie is 23.
> Alice is 25.

7. (A) I is true by substituting in the proper ages. Alice minus Julie is $25 - 23 = 2$ and this is greater than Julie minus Carol which is $23 - 22 = 1$. II is false since Carol is 22 years old.

8. (D) If Sheila is younger than Alice, she is younger than 25, but not older than Julie. She is then 23 or below. Sheila could therefore be the same age as Julie.

9. (E) I and III only. Neither consumers nor legal loopholes are mentioned in the statement.

10. (E) Each choice is *true,* relative to the argument, and the question asks for a false choice.

For questions 26–30 a simple connection diagram will be helpful. The lines connect those professionals who would not go together. From the given information the chart is as follows:

11. (C) If A is selected, then F and G are selected, and E and B are not selected. If G is selected, then D is not selected, therefore the team is A, C, F, and G.

12. (D) If the field engineer is rejected, then the engineer and the general engineer are selected, therefore the architect and doctor would be rejected.

13. (E) If the general engineer is selected, then either the engineer or the field engineer is selected. If the engineer is selected, then the biologist is selected, otherwise neither is selected. Therefore, I is not necessarily true. If the engineer is selected, then the architect is not selected. But the engineer is not necessarily selected, therefore II is not necessarily true. The correct answer is (E), neither I nor II must be true.

14. (E) From the diagram, I is not necessarily true, as G and A could possibly go together. II is also not necessarily true. As you can easily deduce

from the diagram, C and E could go together. If F goes on the expedition and E goes on the expedition, then B and C or D could go, therefore III is not necessarily true. The correct answer is (E), none of the above.

15. (B) If the doctor is selected, then the general engineer is not selected, and the engineer and the field engineer are selected. If the engineer is selected, then the architect is not selected, and since the chemist is not selected, then the biologist is selected. Therefore the team would consist of the biologist, doctor, engineer, and field engineer or B, D, E, and F. The other three are therefore B, E, and F.

16. (B) II is true. Since four of the six children have blue eyes and three of the six are girls, then at least one girl has blue eyes. All of the girls do not have to have freckles.

17. (B) II must be false. Since five of the six children have freckles and four of the six children have blue eyes, then some of the freckled children must have blue eyes. Statement I, "all the blue-eyed girls have freckles," could be true.

18. (E) None of the statements can be deduced from the information given.

19. (D) "Three children have brown eyes" must be false. Since four children have blue eyes, that would total seven children. There are only six children in the family.

With the information given for questions 20 to 25, a chart may be constructed.

Berry	*States*							
	CA	OR	WA	AR	NV	CO	ID	UT
Strawberry	X	X	X	—	—	—	X	—
Blueberry	—	X	X	X	X	—	—	—
Boysenberry	X	—	X	—	X	—	X	X
Blackberry	—	—	—	X	X	X	—	X
Raspberry	X	X	X	X	—	—	—	—
Gooseberry	—	X	X	—	—	—	X	X

20. (C) From the chart, it can be seen that boysenberries grow in five states.

21. (C) Washington has five varieties of berries.

22. (E) In Utah you can grow boysenberries, blackberries, and gooseberries.

23. (B) Oregon is the only state that grows strawberries, but does not grow boysenberries.

24. (B) Blackberries grow in Nevada, but strawberries do not.

25. (C) Arizona and Nevada grow both blackberries and blueberries.

SECTION VI: ANALYTICAL ABILITY

1. **(B)** *Sock* could not be in column 2 because it starts with *s*. *Stock* already starts with *s*.

2. **(D)** *Stove* could be added to column 4 because it starts with *st* and is five letters.

3. **(D)** Column 4 contains the word *strand*, which breaks the rule about having only five letters.

4. **(C)** III, *spill*, could not be added to column 1 because it starts with *s* (*still* already starts with *s*), and IV, *instill*, could not be added because it has seven letters.

5. **(D)** By inspection, we can see that each word in column 3 has two vowels.

6. **(E)** *Bill, dock, cream*, and *stow* do not violate any column rules and have no more than five letters.

7. **(D)** Making *only* the first word of sentence 1 does not solve all of the logical problems in the passage, but does strengthen the passage by indicating that customers with green necklaces must have bought them from the competition.

8. **(B)** The author does not realize that customers not wearing green necklaces may have bought other items from the competition.

For questions 9 to 14, constructing a chart would be helpful.

	A	B	C	D	F
Rich	A	—	—	—	—
Ron	—	—	C	—	—
Holly	—	?	—	?	—
Maria	—	—	—	—	F
Sheila	—	?	—	?	—

Use the given information as follows to complete this elimination chart.

If Maria gets a lower grade than Holly, then Maria can't get an A and Holly can't get an F.

If Holly gets a lower grade than Rich, then Holly can't get an A and Rich can't get an F.

Ron and Sheila do not get F's; therefore, you can deduce that Maria gets the F.

If Maria gets the F, she can receive no other grade.
If Rich gets the top grade, an A, then he can get no other grade and no
one else can get an A.
Ron's grade is halfway between Maria's and Rich's and is therefore a
C.
This leaves Holly and Sheila; one gets a B and the other a D, but we do
not know who gets which.

9. (A) Statement I must be true, since Rich gets the A, but we do not
know whether Sheila gets a B or a D.

10. (E) Statement I must be true, since Rich gets an A. Statement II is
true based on the information in the chart. Therefore, neither must be false.

11. (C) From the chart, it is evident that a comparison between Sheila's
grade and Holly's grade cannot be made.

12. (B) The information in the chart tells us that if Holly gets a B, then
Sheila gets a D.

13. (C) From the chart we know that Sheila cannot get a C because Ron
does and Maria gets an F. So both statements are true.

14. (C) Sheila's getting a B means that Holly must get a D. This is
evident from the chart.

15. (D) The author does not address the distinction between how much
sleep we desire and how much our bodies require. Each of the other
distinctions is addressed in the passage.

16. (D) In the passage, becoming older corresponds with "*advanced*
knowledge and capabilities.*" Choices (A), (B), and (C) should be eliminated
because each is contradicted by the assumptions of the passage (the passage
suggests that *more* sleep is undesirable, knowledge and capabilities are
connected with *wakefulness,* and mindlessness is connected with *sleep*).
Choice (E) is a generalization not at all concerned with amount of sleep and
therefore not relevant to the passage.

17. (C) Choices (A), (B), and (E) present information that supports the
value of sleep, and (D) dissociates advanced capabilities from the mind, thus
damaging the author's mind/mindlessness distinction.

18. (C) Only choice (C) asserts the positive value of sleep and thus
weakens the author's stance in favor of decreased sleep.

For questions 19 to 25 you may have constructed a chart.

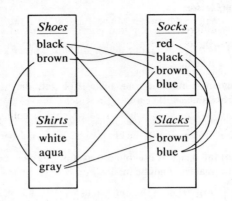

19. (C) Black does not go well with brown.

20. (E) Statements II and III are true, since black does not go well with brown and blue socks may be worn with brown slacks.

21. (A) Blue slacks cannot be worn with red socks.

22. (E) There are 48 possible combinations. 4 socks × 3 shirts × 2 slacks × 2 shoes.

23. (D) Statements I, II, and III are true. Sam could wear a blue shirt, brown slacks, and blue socks. The only general statement is that black does not go with brown.

24. (E) Statements I, II, and III are true. Red socks may not be worn with blue slacks, and brown doesn't go with black. Also, brown socks cannot be worn with blue slacks. Therefore he must wear blue socks.

25. (C) All the other combinations are prohibited.

SECTION VII: QUANTITATIVE ABILITY

Quantitative Comparison

1. **(B)** The only difference in the two numbers occurs after the decimal points, where .10 (column B) is greater than .088 (column A).

2. **(D)** As the only condition for plugging in values for x and y is that together they must equal 0, the values for x and y may vary. For instance, both x and y may equal 0, in which case the answer would be (C). Or x may be 1 and y may be −1, in which case column A would be greater. Thus the answer is (D).

3. **(B)** The area of a circle = πr^2. So column A = $\pi(1^2) = \pi$. The circumference of a circle = $2\pi r$. So column B = $2(\pi)1 = 2\pi$.

4. **(B)** Column A = 50 ÷ 2.2, and column B = 50 × 2.2.

5. **(A)** Since △ABC is an equilateral triangle, ∠ABC = 60° and ∠BAC = 60°. So column A = 120°. Looking at △CDB, ∠CDB must be less than 120° because ∠BCD already equals 60° and there is still another angle (CBD) in △CDB.

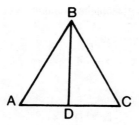

6. **(C)** The definition of a median is that it divides the side it intersects into two equal parts.

7. **(A)** Since △ABC is equilateral, AB = BC. Thus AB + BD must be more than BC alone.

8. (A) 2 is the only even prime number. The lowest odd prime number is 3. So the least possible value of column A is 6, which would be more than column B, 5. Plugging in any other prime numbers will always give A greater than B.

9. (D) The values for a and b must be positive (because of the location in the upper right-hand quadrant. But we cannot be sure whether the x value (a) is greater than the y value (b), or vice versa. (Remember, unless the points plotted fall on a line, their location cannot be precisely pinpointed. We can know only the quadrant.)

10. (B) Point c,d falls on the y = −4 line before point 4, −4. So c is less than 4, and d = −4. So c + d must be negative. a and b must both be positive because of their location in the upper right-hand quadrant.

11. (D) For xy to equal 0, either x or y must be 0. If x = 0, then y = 4. But if y = 0, then x = 4. There is no way of knowing which is which.

12. (B) $5^3 = 5 \times 5 \times 5 = 125$, and $2^7 = 2 \times 2 \times 2 \times 2 \times 2 \times 2 \times 2 = 128$.

13. (D) For $x^4 − 1 = 0$, then x^4 must equal 1. x, however, may then be $+1$ or $−1$. If x = $+1$, then columns A and B will be equal. But if x = $−1$, then column B will be greater than column A. So the answer is (D).

14. (C) Cross multiplying, we get

$$xy = 4 − y$$

$$xy + y = 4$$

$$y(x + 1) = 4$$

$$y = \frac{4}{x + 1}$$

15. (B) Since $3.60 is closer to $4.00, there must have been more 40¢ tea. Or let x equal the number of pounds of tea X and 10 − x equal the number of pounds of tea Y. Then

$$30x + 40(10 - x) = 360$$

$$30x + 400 - 40x = 360$$

$$-10x = -40$$

$$x = 4$$

So there were 4 pounds of tea X and 6 pounds of tea Y.

Math Ability

16. **(C)** This problem is most easily completed by rearranging and approximating as follows:

$$\frac{69.28 \times .004}{.03} \simeq 69 \times \frac{.004}{.03} \simeq 69 \times .1 = 6.9$$

which is the only reasonably close answer to 9.2.

17. **(A)** Since Mary will be y years old x years from now she is $y - x$ years old now.
Hence z years from now she will be $y - x + z$ years old.

18. **(B)** Start solving at the bottom right with the fraction $3/(3 + 3)$ and continue as follows:

$$3 + \cfrac{3}{3 + \cfrac{3}{3 + (3)/(3 + 3)}} \qquad 3 + \cfrac{3}{3 + \frac{6}{7}}$$

$$3 + \cfrac{3}{3 + \cfrac{3}{3 + 3/6}} \qquad 3 + \cfrac{3}{\frac{36}{7}}$$

$$3 + \cfrac{3}{3 + \cfrac{3}{3\frac{1}{2}}} \qquad 3 + \cfrac{3}{\frac{27}{7}}$$

$$3 + \cfrac{3}{3 + \cfrac{3}{\frac{7}{2}}} \qquad 3 + \frac{21}{27}$$

$$3\frac{21}{27} = 3\frac{7}{9}$$

19. **(B)** We solve simultaneously

$$6x - 3y = 30$$
$$4x + y = 2$$

Multiply the bottom equation by 3 and add the two equations together.

$$6x - 3y = 30$$
$$\underline{12x + 3y = 6}$$
$$18x = 36$$

Thus $x = 2$
Substitute back to one of the original equations and we find that $y = -6$.
Thus their sum is -4.

20. **(C)** $\triangle XYZ$ is inscribed in a semicircle and is therefore a right angle. Hence $\triangle XYZ$ is a right triangle and the Pythagorean theorem states

$$(XY)^2 = (XZ)^2 + (YZ)^2$$
$$(17)^2 = (XZ)^2 + (15)^2 \qquad (XY \text{ is a diameter})$$
$$289 = (XZ)^2 + 225$$
$$(XZ)^2 = 64$$
$$XZ = \sqrt{64}$$
$$XZ = 8$$

21. **(D)** In isosceles $\triangle XYZ$, $\angle X = \angle Z$.
Since $\angle Y = 80$, we have

$$\angle X + \angle Y + \angle Z = 180°$$
$$\angle X + 80 + \angle Z = 180$$
$$\angle X + \angle Z = 100$$
$$\angle X = \angle Z = 50°$$

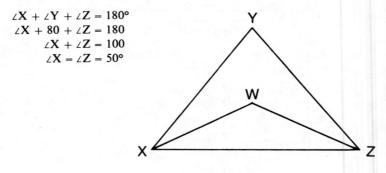

Since WX bisects $\angle YXZ$ and WZ bisects $\angle YZX$, we have $\angle YXW = \angle WXZ = \angle YZW = \angle WZX = 25°$.

Hence on $\triangle XWZ$,

$$\angle XWZ + \angle WXZ + \angle WZX = 180°$$
$$\angle XWZ + 25 + 25 = 180$$
$$\angle XWZ + 50 = 180$$
$$\angle XWZ = 130°$$

22. **(B)**

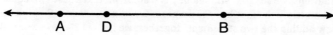

Since D is between A and B on $\overleftrightarrow{AB}$, we know that the sum of the lengths of the smaller segments AD and DB is equal to the length of the larger segment AB.

Hence $AB = AD + DB$
$$AB - AD = AD + DB - AD$$
$$AB - AD = DB$$

23. **(B)** Since the area of a trapezoid $= \frac{1}{2} \cdot h \cdot (b_1 + b_2)$, we need to find the altitude, h.
Draw altitudes in the figure as follows:

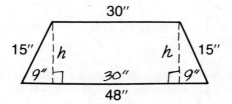

Since the triangles formed are right triangles, we use the Pythagorean theorem, which says

$$c^2 = a^2 + b^2$$
$$15^2 = 9^2 + h^2$$
$$225 = 81 + h^2$$
$$h^2 = 225 - 81$$
$$h^2 = 144$$
$$h = \sqrt{144} = 12 \text{ inches}$$

Hence the area of the trapezoid will be

$$\frac{1}{2} \cdot h \cdot (b_1 + b_2) = \frac{1}{2} \cdot 12 \cdot (30 + 48)$$
$$= (6)(78)$$
$$= 468 \text{ square inches}$$

24. (E) Divide the first equation by 2 and we get $6 < x < 9$. Divide the second equation by 3 and we get $-3 < y < 2$. If we add these two equations, we see that statement I is true. If we take these two equations and multiply the first by -1, we get $-6 > -x > -9$ or $-9 < -x < -6$. Now adding the two statements together, we get $-12 < y - x < -4$. So II is true.

25. (C) Adding the percentages, the large circulation coins represent (23%, 17%, 8%), 48%, while the average condition coins represent (23%, 18%, 10%), 51%.

26. (D) The number of coins is irrelevant. Since 3%, 5%, and 8% add to 16%, we have the following:

    $16.60 \times 3\%$ plus $10.20 \times 5\%$ plus $8.80 \times 8\% = 1.712$,

    and $1.712/.16 = 10.70$ which is the average price.

27. (C) There are (5%, 10%, 18%), 33%, in this category. Thus 33% of 20,000 is 6600.

28. (E) The length of x cannot be determined because there is no indication of the overlapping length of the rectangle to the left of x. If x cannot be determined, then x + y cannot be determined.

29. (D) Let us calculate the value of each:

    (A) $(.5)(.3)(280) = 42$ (D) $(3)(.4)(40) = 48$
    (B) $(.33)(.7)(160) = 36.96$ (E) $(.6)(60) = 36$
    (C) $(2)(.5)(30) = 30$

30. (C) If x is increased by 50%, we can represent it by $\frac{3}{2}$ x. We must multiply this by $\frac{2}{3}$ y in order to keep the product equal to xy. Since $\frac{2}{3}$ is a $\frac{1}{3}$ reduction, answer (C) is the correct response.

FINAL PREPARATION: "The Final Touches"

1. Make sure that you are familiar with the testing center location and nearby parking facilities.
2. The last week of preparation should be spent primarily on reviewing strategies, techniques, and directions for each area.
3. Don't *cram* the night before the exam. It's a waste of time!
4. Remember to bring the proper materials to the test—identification, admission ticket, three or four sharpened Number 2 pencils, a watch, and a good eraser.
5. Start off crisply, working the ones you know first, and then coming back and trying the others.
6. Be sure to mark an answer for each question because THERE IS NO PENALTY FOR GUESSING.
7. Mark in reading passages, underline key words, write out information, make notations on diagrams, take advantage of being permitted to write in the test booklet.
8. Make sure that you are answering "what is being asked" and that your answer is reasonable.
9. Using the OVERALL POSITIVE APPROACH is the key to getting the ones right that you should get right—resulting in a good score on the GRE.

GET CLIFFS NOTES
FOR HELP IN LITERATURE.
Select the titles you need from this list.

Absalom, Absalom!
The Aeneid
Agamemnon
Alice in Wonderland
All the King's Men
All Quiet on the Western
  Front
All's Well That Ends Well
  & Merry Wives of
  Windsor
The American
American Tragedy
Animal Farm
Anna Karenina
Antony and Cleopatra
Aristotle's Ethics
Arrowsmith
As I Lay Dying
The Assistant
As You Like It
Auto. of Ben Franklin
Auto. of Malcolm X
The Awakening
Babbitt
The Bear
The Bell Jar
Beowulf
Billy Budd & Typee
Black Boy
Black Like Me
Bleak House
Brave New World &
  Brave New World
  Revisited
Brothers Karamazov
Call of the Wild &
  White Fang
Candide
Canterbury Tales
Catch-22
Catcher in the Rye
The Color Purple
Comedy of Errors, Love's
  Labour's Lost & Two
  Gentlemen of Verona
Connecticut Yankee
Coriolanus & Timon
  of Athens
The Count of Monte Cristo
Crime and Punishment
The Crucible
Cry, the Beloved Country
Cymbeline & Pericles
Cyrano de Bergerac
Daisy Miller & Turn
  of the Screw
David Copperfield
Death of a Salesman
The Deerslayer

Demian
Diary of Anne Frank
Divine Comedy-I.
  Inferno
D.C.-II. Purgatorio
D.C.-III. Paradiso
Doctor Faustus
Dr. Jekyll and Mr. Hyde
Don Juan
Don Quixote
Dracula
Dune & Other Works
Emerson's Essays
Emily Dickinson:
  Selected Poems
Emma
Ethan Frome
Euripides' Electra
  & Medea
The Faerie Queene
Far from the
  Madding Crowd
A Farewell to Arms
Fathers and Sons
Faust Pt. I & Pt. II
The Federalist
For Whom The Bell Tolls
Frankenstein
The French Lt.'s.
  Woman
Giants in the Earth
Glass Menagerie &
  Streetcar
Go Down, Moses
The Good Earth
Grapes of Wrath
Great Expectations
Great Gatsby
Greek Classics
Gulliver's Travels
Hamlet
Hard Times
Heart of Darkness &
  Secret Sharer
Henry IV Part 1
Henry IV Part 2
Henry V
Henry VI Parts 1, 2, 3
Henry VIII
House of the
  Seven Gables
Huckleberry Finn
Ibsen's Plays I, A
  Dolls House &
  Hedda Gabler
Ibsen's Plays II,
  Ghosts, An Enemy
  of the People & The
  Wild Duck
The Idiot

Idylls of the King
The Iliad
Invisible Man
Ivanhoe
Jane Eyre
Joseph Andrews
Jude the Obscure
Julius Caesar
The Jungle
Kafka's Short Stories
Keats & Shelley
King Lear
Last of the Mohicans
Le Morte Darthur
Leaves of Grass
Les Miserables
Light in August
Lord Jim
Lord of the Flies
Lord of the Rings
Lost Horizon
Lysistrata & Other
  Comedies
Macbeth
Madame Bovary
Main Street
Manchild in the
  Promised Land
Mayor of
  Casterbridge
Measure for Measure
Merchant of Venice
Middlemarch
Midsummer Night's
  Dream
Mill on the Floss
Miss Lonelyhearts &
  Day of the Locust
Moby Dick
Moll Flanders
Mrs. Dalloway
Much Ado About
  Nothing
My Antonia
Mythology
Native Son
New Testament
Nineteen Eighty-four
No Exit and The Flies
Notes from
  Underground
O'Connor's Short
  Stories
The Odyssey
Oedipus the King
  Oedipus at Colonus
  and Antigone
Of Human Bondage
(Continued on next page)

(Titles continued)

Of Mice and Men
Old Man and the Sea
Old Testament
Oliver Twist
One Day in the Life
 of Ivan Denisovich
One Flew Over the
 Cuckoo's Nest
100 Years of Solitude
O'Neill's Plays
Othello
Our Town
Ox-Bow Incident
Paradise Lost
A Passage to India
The Pearl
Pickwick Papers
Pilgrim's Progress
The Plague
Plato's Dialogues
Plato's The Republic
Poe's Short Stories
Portrait of the Artist
 as a Young Man
Portrait of a Lady
Power and the Glory
The Prelude
Pride and Prejudice
The Prince
The Prince and the Pauper
Red Badge of Courage
The Red and the Black
Red Pony

Return of the Native
Richard II
Richard III
Rise of Silas Lapham
Robinson Crusoe
Roman Classics
Romeo and Juliet
Scarlet Letter
A Separate Peace
Shakespeare's Sonnets
Shane
Shaw's
 Major Barbara &
 St. Joan
Shaw's
 Man and Superman &
 Caesar and Cleopatra
Shaw's
 Pygmalion & Arms
 and the Man
Silas Marner
Sir Gawain and the Green
 Knight
Sister Carrie
Sons and Lovers
The Sound and the Fury
Steppenwolf &
 Siddhartha
The Stranger
The Sun Also Rises
T.S. Eliot's Major Poems
 and Plays
Tale of Two Cities
Taming of the Shrew

Tartuffe, Misanthrope &
 Bourgeois Gentleman
Tempest
Tender is the Night
Tess of the D'Urbervilles
Titus Andronicus &
 King John
To Kill A Mockingbird
Tom Jones
Tom Sawyer
Treasure Island &
 Kidnapped
The Trial
Tristram Shandy
Troilus and Cressida
Twelfth Night
Ulysses
Uncle Tom's Cabin
The Unvanquished
Utopia
Vanity Fair
Victory
Vonnegut's Major
 Works
Waiting for Godot
Walden
Walden Two
War and Peace
Who's Afraid of
 Virginia Woolf?
Winesburg, Ohio
The Winter's Tale
Worldly Philosophers
Wuthering Heights

Cliffs Notes = $2.25 and up
Check with your local bookstore or send for current information.

Please send me information on these Cliffs Notes Publications

☐ **Cliffs Notes**
☐ **Cliffs Test Preparation Guides**
☐ **Cliffs Complete Study Editions**
☐ **Bilingual Books**

P.O. Box 80728
Lincoln, NE 68501

NAME _____

ADDRESS _____

CITY_____ STATE _____ ZIP _____